GODS and GUERRILLAS in TIBET

George N. Patterson, F.R.G.S.

Copyright© 2005: George N Patterson
Lesmahagow, Scotland

All rights reserved. Without limiting the rights under copyright reserved above, no part of this publication may be reproduced, stored in or introduced into a retrieval system, or transmitted, in any form or by any means (electronic, mechanical, photocopying, recording or otherwise) without the prior written permission of the author and The Long Riders' Guild Press.

The Long Riders' Guild Press

www.classictravelbooks.com

ISBN: 1-59048-174-7

Cover photograph: The author is top right, with the Tibetan guerrilla commander, Tendar, on his left, with the rifle. On the left is Chris Menges, who later received two Academy Awards for his filming in the Hollywood films *The Mission*, and *Killing Fields*.

ACKNOWLEDGMENTS

My special thanks to my long-time friend and colleague, Adrian Cowell, for the photographs used in this book and taken from our project, ***Raid Into Tibet***.

Also to the tribal Khamba freedom fighters of Tibet who gave their lives in a cause worthy of dedication.

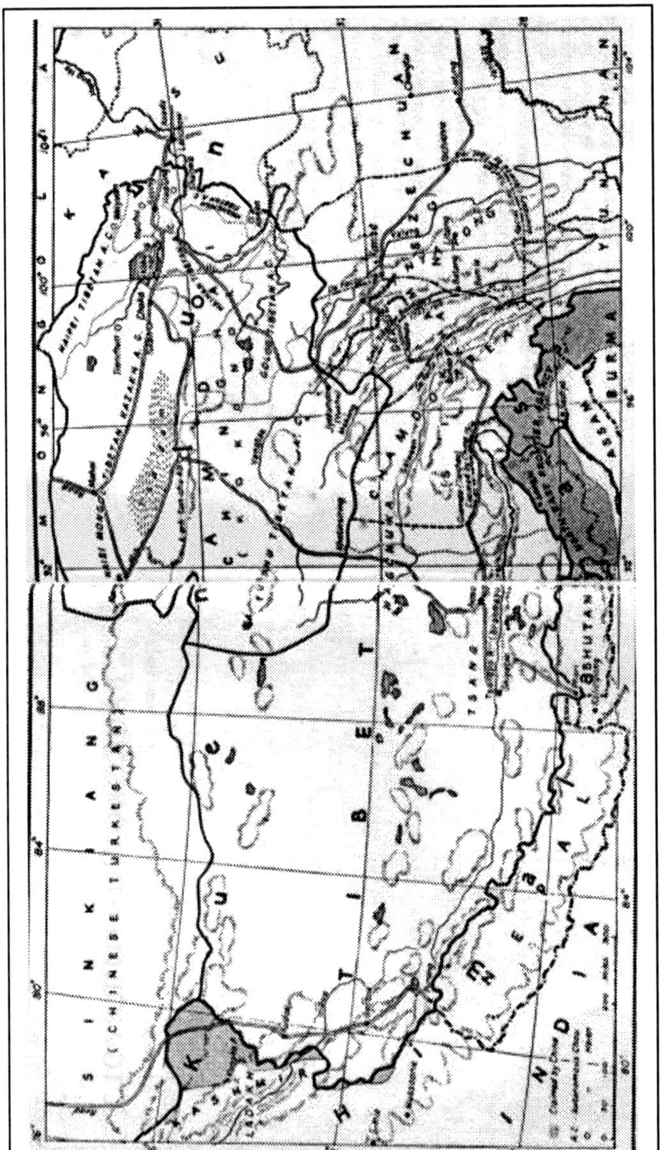
SINKIANG
(CHINESE TURKESTAN)
INDIA
BHUTAN
BURMA

INTRODUCTION

In the Easter Term of 2005 George Patterson delivered an electrifying talk at Cambridge University providing the dynamic perspective of a "history maker" to the rather more sedate world of research and analysis. His *tour de horizon*, covering over half a century of the Tibet's dramatic attempt to assert its independence from China provided the detail and authority only possible from one who was there. His life with the Kampas on the high plateaus of the Himalayas, his daring and unprecedented three month journey in the dead of winter traversing 20,000 foot passes, his uncertain arrival at the British High Commission in Calcutta where he relayed news of an impending invasion of Tibet by China's Peoples Liberation Army, offered new insight to the workings of international affairs.

George Patterson's remarkable experiences underscore the complexities of the emerging "Cold War" politics of the time. As he relates in this volume, not all turns out the way one might wish nor, in a rapidly changing environment with great power interests at stake, can one be certain that good intentions will carry the day. What one can say is that with controversy and risk as his constant companions, George Patterson's passionate belief in his mission, in the Dalai Lama and in the Tibetan people, and his broader belief that a transcendent morality can and should guide relations among peoples, remains true to this day.

George Patterson has worked tirelessly for the independence of the Tibetan people he loves and provides us, in this volume, a unique perspective on the irony, passion and great power politics that have informed the Tibetan drama – they are all a part of his vivid tableau.

Stefan Halper (D. Phil, *oxon*), (Ph.D, *cantab*)

PREFACE

I have given an abridged account of our internationally-acclaimed television film saga, **Raid Into Tibet**, in a chapter of my autobiography, **Patterson of Tibet**. One television critic enthused:

*"The new TV series, 'Rebel' got off to a smashing start last night with a fantastic documentary entitled '**Raid into Tibet**'. It was a sensational film, full of excitement, daring enterprises, superb photography, crisp commentary – glowing with the virtue of simplicity.*

*"It was the shatteringly realistic record of a raid by Tibetan Khamba rebels against a Chinese convoy across the Nepalese border in Tibet. '**Raid into Tibet**' was one of the most hair-raising half-hours ever seen on television…"*

I have been asked by so many who knew some of the circumstances, or others who wanted to know more details, to include them in another book and in response to their requests for a full account I have written this book. Another, more personal reason for writing this expanded book version, is that I wish to publicize the issue of Tibet once more at the request of my many Tibetan friends, in yet another, and possibly final, attempt to help that tragic country. For fifty years my destiny has been uniquely linked with it, and I am happy to make any contribution to them that I can.

The most baffling political problem of the twenty-first century is why, when major nations went to war several times in the previous century over large nations threatening smaller ones - Germany-Poland, Iraq-Kuwait, Yugoslavia-Bosnia - no-one even protested when China invaded Tibet and insisted without legal validation that it was *"an internal affair"*.

From 1950, one year after the Chinese Communists took over power in China, they have killed over a million Tibetans, destroyed Tibet's religion and culture, plundered Tibet's monasteries and artefacts, unilaterally annexed two-thirds of Tibet, and poured millions of Chinese Han nationals into Tibet in a ruthless genocidal program of miscegenation, without any effective action being taken by any major Power. Even when the Dalai Lama of Tibet was awarded the Nobel Peace Prize in 1989 for his principled non-violence, the Chinese Government have refused to meet with him to discuss any serious form of dialogue about Tibet, and the major countries of the United Nations - who have held special sessions to impose sanctions on Iraq and Sudan, and given approval to a pre-emptive war on Iraq by the United States and Britain on the basis of an unproven concealing of weapons of mass destruction – have ignored the greater violation of United Nations' principles by China in Tibet without even a word of rebuke.

In the nineteenth century it was agreed between the Great Powers Russia, British India and China to keep Tibet isolated and without national delineation in their so-called "Great Game" in Central Asia for strategic domination, in which Tibet figured geopolitically as "the saddle of Asia". Out of this collusion Tibet was conveniently and vaguely described in political word-games on appropriate occasions as a British "protectorate", or a Chinese "suzerainty", and Tibet's indigenous feudal and tribal autocracies were encouraged to remain in their remote mountain-encircled "Roof of the World" isolation to suit their Great Power imperial interests.

In late 1946 I arrived on the eastern border of Tibet, in the small town of Kangting. Through a series of remarkable circumstances following on my arrival I had been befriended by the key leaders of the tribal Kham rebels against the feudal nobles and monastery overlords ruling Tibet from the distant capital, Lhasa. The Pangdatshang family had emerged into prominence when the father of the three sons – Yangpel, Rapga and Topgyay – provided significant assistance to the 13th Dalai Lama during his temporary exile in India in 1911-12 when he fled there following China's 1911 revolution. The patriarch Pangdatshang was given extensive trading privileges as a consequence, which he expanded into Central Asia, China and the West.

Later his eldest son, Yangpel, was appointed Minister of Trade, an official ranking normally reserved to Tibet's hereditary aristocracy. In 1934 Topgyay, a charismatic chieftain, and Rapga, a brilliant scholar, launched a Khamba tribal rebellion against the feudal Lhasa regime, but were betrayed by monks in Chamdo en route to Lhasa, and the two brothers fled into exile in British India. There they established The Democratic Party for an independent Tibet and were expelled by the disapproving British authorities, and they went to China. The Lhasa government requested China to deport the two brothers, but instead Generalissimo Chiang Kai Shek made Topgyay an honorary Colonel of the Nationalist Army, with responsibility for safeguarding the eastern provinces of Tibet. With the increasing likelihood of the Nationalist's defeat in China, Topgyay used his military position to acquire huge supplies of weapons from the defecting Nationalist troops and began preparation for another revolt against the Lhasa regime.

When Britain left India in 1947, the newly independent Indian Government was uncertain how to handle the question of Tibet when China began threatening invasion of Tibet in 1950. The Congress Party of India was the dominant influence in Indian politics, but it was divided between left- and right-wing party political groupings.

Unfortunately for Tibet, the left-wing triumvirate of Prime Minister Nehru, Ambassador to the U.N. Krishna Menon, and Ambassador to China Sirdar Pannikar, were all very pro-China and they held the key positions of power; while the right-wing triumvirate of Sardar Patel, Acharya Kripalani and Jayaprakash Narayan, who were anti-China and pro-Tibet, although influential, had no decisive positions of power.

On April 19th, 1954, an Agreement was signed between India and China which Prime Minister Nehru claimed *"settled the question of the Tibet region of China"*. This was the first time this emotive phrase was used, later canonized by China in its claimed authority. India's Agreement with China in the question of Tibet was declared to be on the basis of the *"Five Principles of Peaceful Co-existence"*, established at the Bangkok Conference, and listed as: *(i) mutual respect for each other's territorial integrity and sovereignty; (ii) mutual non-aggression; (iii) mutual non-interference in each other's internal affairs; (iv) equality and mutual benefit; (v) peaceful co-existence.*

India's Leader of the Opposition at the time, Acharya Kripalani, was furious with the terms of the Agreement, declaring:

"I consider this (China's aggression against Tibet) as much a colonialist aggression on the part of China as any colonialist aggression indulged in by Western nations...In this age of democracy when we hold that all people should be free and equal. China's act of aggression is a deliberate act of aggression...In international politics, when a buffer state is abolished by a peaceful nation, that nation is considered to have aggressive designs against its neighbours. It is also said that in the new map of China other border territories like Nepal, Sikkim, etc figure. That gives us an idea of the aggressive designs of China...."

What complicated matters even more in Tibet's tragic isolation was that the two international "super powers" of the United States of America and the Soviet Union in their Cold War stand-off at the time mutually agreed to add a "third bloc" of a linked India and China on the basis of the Bandung "*Five Principles*". Also, with the departure of France from Indochina, the USA was increasing its interest in the region, and the Bandung Agreement suited its current policies. So the fate of Tibet was sacrificed.

There was a flurry of U.S. interest in Tibet when reports of a possible revolt in Tibet against the Chinese occupation began to circulate in 1955. For five years since the Chinese invasion, many leading Tibetan families and officials had taken up residence in the Indian-Tibetan border region of Kalimpong. And it became a notorious centre of intelligence activity by several nations as they sought information from the influential exiles living in India. Again, unfortunately, not many of the important Tibetan leaders spoke a foreign language, and the various intelligence agents had to find informed interpreters - of whom I was one.

Throughout this period and experience I discovered that there were conflicting policies emerging from the US representatives: one anxious to help Tibet in some way, and one anxious to keep talking but offering no positive help. The various government experts - political, diplomatic, intelligence - were totally unequipped to deal with the internal Tibetan situation, which conformed to no known modern national paradigm. Briefly, Tibet was believed by Tibetans to be "a country of the gods, by the gods, for the gods", and this meant that all important decisions were submitted to tantric adepts for prior approval. Because of the country's enormous geographic configuration of 15,000-feet average altitudes, vast distances, incredible climatic extremes, a central feudal-dominated province, and two eastern tribal-dominated provinces, monumental distance and dialect differences, simplistic understanding and solutions were out of the question. Most importantly, the central, feudal, inhabitants, dominated by an aristocratic and monastic autocracy, were intensely disliked by the freedom-loving Khamba tribal warriors of the two eastern Tibetan provinces who constituted two-thirds majority of Tibet's population - and who were the key factors and fighters in the armed revolt against China.

When the Khamba leaders in Kalimpong talked with the USA's intelligence agents they did not ask for American soldiers, but only for weapons to assist them in their revolt against China. They were not interested in the intricacies of subversion by other means. They wanted guns and ammunition, and they would deal with a Chinese Army who were finding it extremely difficult to cope with the high altitude problems in Tibet. Unfortunately for the Tibetans, their US State and their CIA intelligence departments were divided into two factions – one planning armed aid for the Tibetans, and one plotting advisory help only. In the United Nations only one small country supported the Tibetan appeal for a hearing, and the question of Tibet was quietly buried.

PROLOGUE

In the nearly three years I had spent living in east Tibet I had been educated by Topgyay and Rapga, and their friends, in the complex manifestations of Lamaistic Buddhism - both good and evil aspects. The scholarly Rapga was stringently critical of many of the practices of the priesthood, and was planning a major reconstruction of the monasteries in their revolution; while the sardonic Topgyay was scathingly humorous regarding the pederastic sexual habits of the majority of the priests. Both of them were bitterly sarcastic about the greed of the monasteries, and they had radical plans for getting rid of the extortionate and exploitative practices of the monks. Rapga had translated into Tibetan the **Three Principles of the People**, by China's previous president Dr Sun Yat Sen; and also Karl Marx's **Das Kapital**.

As we rode steadily at a plodding pace across the vastness of Tibet, the conversations between the members of the caravan usually included some mention of the miraculous in their daily lives. Even when the discussions were political there was always the consideration that the powers of the gods could be invoked on behalf of Tibet against the atheistic Communism of China. As I lounged in the saddle I read my Bible and reflected on the conflicting phenomena of the spiritual world. I had wanted to know God, and how He could be contacted, and I was living in the land, and among the people, whose lives were dedicated to full-time intercourse with the spirit world.

Guidance was sought through tantric oracles, mathematical divination, the drawing of lots, breathing exercises, voice control and projection, *mandalas* (a pictorial representation for approach to the gods), and trance possession. Guidance was sought for travel, trading, naming children, holding weddings, health, investments, choice of spouses. This trip we were on now had only been decided after the Pangdatshangs had "consulted the gods" through the family lamas and had been told the day to leave. They were here because their gods had told them. I was here because my God had told me. Was there a point at which such apparently opposing spiritual guidance would intersect?

Each day we travelled slowly, strung out in a long, colorful line, across the magnificent scenic panorama of mountains and plateaux, some of which were familiar to me from previous visits. On all sides stretched barren, stony stretches, giving way at intervals to equally spacious flowered grasslands rising to dark, jagged mountains crowned by snow-peaked giant ranges. The trail led through huge forests above saucer-shaped valleys, where the luxurious grass was carpeted with gentians, primulas, asters and other flowers in glorious profusion.

Occasionally there was a village, usually of two levels, the walls of each house about two feet thick, built solidly from stone and mud, the floors and flat roof being of smaller stones and mud to give a smoother finish. The roof had a low parapet, and often a built-up verandas or small room on top, giving it a battlemented look. Tall walls surrounded the houses, forming courtyards for the animals, stacks of wood, piles of drying dung, and the inevitable snarling Tibetan mastiffs. Every day scouts rode out ahead to patrol the high points, searching for roving bands of Chinese deserters, or even dangerous groups of bandits who might swoop down fast on the caravan shooting first and finding out too late who we were.

One evening, while we camped out on a high outcrop above a wide sweep of river, I counted fifty-five yak-loads of arms and ammunition being ferried over to join our caravan. Topgyay informed me later that he had thousands of these loads in various places in Kham - including monasteries.

On the sixteenth day out from Kangting we made preparations to enter Litang, one of the highest towns in the world at an altitude of 14,500 feet. It was bitterly cold when I crawled out of my sleeping-bag to take the bowl of butter tea which Loshay provided for me. Fires blazed all around the camping place, and the Pangdatshang servants and muleteers saddled or loaded animals, then returned quickly to the blaze to thaw out frozen fingers. More than one looked longingly at the towering peaks where, first the rose color, then yellow, of the sun crept slowly and tantalizingly downwards with the promise of heat for cruelly cold bodies. We had passed through one gloomy valley and were well up a second before the sun finally touched and caressed the whites, reds, and greens of clothing, the dull blue of rifles, and the silver and gold of god-boxes, glinting on the movements of the gaily saddled horses and pacing mules as they passed and re-passed each other on the way to the summit. Away ahead the flat plateau that was Litang - the "Nickel Plain" - shimmered in a heat haze.

As we rounded a bend in the trail there was a thunder of hooves, a cloud of dust, and several galloping riders swirled up in a confused mass, their horses rearing to a slithering halt. The leader was a giant of a man in a huge yak-skin gown, Gyabon Bundi, one of Topgyay's famous captains. He produced the usual ceremonial scarf and garlanded Topgyay, who returned it to him, then passed up the line of bowing, respectful riders on either side of the trail.

More and more riders were now arriving in a constant stream and, as we left the mountain trail for the flat plain, the single file of our daily riding pattern disappeared as riders known to each other bunched together talking animatedly. The horses caught the excitement of the new arrivals and pulled restlessly at the bits, and the speed of the party increased perceptibly. Some of the more high-spirited horses had to be brought round in a wide circle and back to join the main group, so restive were they to get away and gallop over the flat plain.

The riders were not averse to this restlessness, and used it to exhibit their skills as horsemen with a nonchalant and apparently effortless control. A collection of filthy, square-built mud houses, looking like a neglected archaeological site, appeared and this was pointed out as being part of the old town of Litang, which had been devastated in an earthquake the year before, claiming over a thousand lives. It never even made the media in the chaotic mess that was China being convulsed by the political earthquake of the Communist takeover.

We finally reined to a halt on the outskirts of Litang proper, beside a large, solidly built house of the usual Tibetan design. Servants were running all over the place, leading in horses or driving off the pressing, curious onlookers. The Pangdatshangs were to have the upstairs as their quarters, while I had the ground floor, where the space usually occupied by animals had been cleared to make room for stacks of tea-bales with spaces between where we could place our folding beds.

When we joined Topgyay and the others he informed us that the house was the one in which the famous Sixth Dalai Lama had been "reincarnated". He pointed out five lumps of wood, two large and three small, hanging above the outside door; these, he said, indicated that five other incarnations had been born in that house, two great and three lesser in rank and importance.

It was strange in the sunlit silence of that afternoon to listen to the quiet voice of Rapga saying that the last time he had been in that house was in 1934, when he had passed through Litang from Markham to exile in India, after their defeat at Chamdo.

And now here we were again, on the eve of another Tibetan revolution, returning along familiar trails. The three weeks of traveling had brought an impressive array of men and munitions with exciting possibilities of success. So Topgyay decided to wait for a few days in Litang, within reach of news from down country, and then begin the last stage of the journey to the mountain retreat of the Pangdatshangs in Bo-mi.

We had been invited to a feast shortly after our arrival, and with a quick wash-up and change of clothing we started for the town, followed by servants, bodyguards and a crowd of town-people. The path from the house to the town lay across a wide open space on which an incredible sight met our astonished gaze - incredible even for Tibet, and even more for Litang, one of the largest and most sacred monastery-towns in Tibet.

At intervals of every fifty yards or so there was a small camp of nomads, with a series of rough wooden frames pitched around their black tents. On these were hung the steaming carcasses of freshly slaughtered yaks. Thousands of crows were perched on the cross-pieces, picking at the carcasses, while overhead huge vultures circled on a slow wing-beat. Everywhere scavenging dogs tried to snatch at entrails, while one or two more audacious than the others tried to drag away the huge yaks' heads that were lying scattered on the ground. Nomads, stripped to the waist, were covered in blood, steaming in the cool of the afternoon; and crowds of porters, men and women, were lined up with baskets to carry the meat away into the monastery.

For it was the monastery that had ordered the slaying of the animals to supply the monks with meat for food, and also to stock against future profitable trade. Three hundred yaks were being slaughtered every day, and the butchering had already gone on for several days. Rapga and Topgyay said nothing as we walked through the carnage, but they shook their heads disapprovingly; until one sight was too much, and Rapga whipped out his camera to photograph a maroon-clad monk carrying a yak's head in one hand and a large lump of meat in the other. The monk looked up and saw Rapga pointing the camera at him and he quickly dropped the yak's head and meat and guiltily ran into a nearby tent to hide himself.

About 200-300 yards beyond the nomads' tents the path turned to the right below a slight overhang of rock, on which were a pile of "mani" stones and prayer-flags, and then rose sharply to enter the main street of the town. The street was wide, about forty feet from side to side, the northern end facing us terminating in the Chinese magistrates' *yamen*, or offices and quarters. The houses on either side of the street were all one-storied and flat-roofed, and they were built in a continuous block from the top of the street to the bottom. The doorways led straight off the street and nearly all of them had two or three steps down into the room.

Through a curved-roof gateway to the left of the government offices could be seen the market-place of the town. Here the "road" was only an alleyway some ten feet wide, with small busy stalls and shops lining each side for over a hundred yards or so. There was a surprising variety of goods for such a remote place: colored silks, carpets, saddlery, religious paraphernalia, exquisitely worked silver ornaments from the famous workshops of Dege, flour, sugar, matches, household utensils - and, of course, butchers' shops with freshly slaughtered meat. At the end of the narrow street there was another gate leading into the famous monastery, larger than the town itself.

As we passed through the gate we had to step around a dying horse, its ribs showing, its bloated belly heaving in agony, its eyes opaque with approaching death. No one would kill the horse to put it out of its pain, for the lamas said it was a sin to kill. Yet, five hundred yards away, three thousand yaks had been killed by the orders of the same lamas; and the meat was being carried into the monastery through an alley-way not five yards away from the dying horse. The ordinary Tibetan, carrying a god-box with powerful charm-relic to protect him, would carefully pick a louse from his hair and gently lay it on the ground so that its life might be spared, for it could be a human soul in a different but lower state of the reincarnation process. But he would then turn to pick up his rifle and start oiling it lovingly in preparation to fight and kill his fellow-Tibetans.

When I spoke with them about it, they saw no contradiction. Acts of spiritual power, they said, were for the tantric practitioners to exercise on request when necessary, and had to be paid for in goods and worship by the supplicant. But personal desires and ambitions had to be fought for and taken by force. All that was needed was to make sure the gods were placated so that they were on your side when the action took place.

When I persisted and asked them, for example, why they were mobilizing armed forces to withstand the atheistic Chinese Communists, and not harnessing the spiritual power they believed in so deeply in defence of their passionately held pacific Buddhism, they looked at me as if I was mad. How could spiritual belief stop the Chinese, let alone Communists, they asked? I pointed out my personal dilemma: that that was what they said they believed all over Tibet, in the practices of their tantric monks, and in the everyday action of carrying god-boxes to stop sword-cuts and bullets!

Our Litang Abbot host was an interesting character, a Chinese and not a Tibetan. Rapga informed me quietly that his name was Liu, that he had been a major-general in the Nationalist Army but reputedly had left everything to become a lama. He must have had considerable influence with the Sikang Governor, General Liu Wen-huie, or even higher, the skeptical Rapga said, for he had not only been appointed head of the prestigious Litang Monastery but also of all the monasteries in Kham. This use of influence to gain high position detracted considerably from the sincerity of his renunciation, and the Tibetans suspected him of being a spy.

He was tall and thin, with a narrow, inscrutable face, and typically Chinese in speech, manner and gesticulation although dressed in usual Tibetan lama fashion. The other guests were magistrates of Batang, Litang and Nya Chuka. There were over twenty dishes in the feast, and with an appetite sharpened by the monotony of trail diet I contributed little to the bland social conversation and concentrated on eating.

The days that followed were filled with a round of feasts and discussions as messengers came and went with reports. Jekundo, an important small town in Amdo province to the north, had fallen to the Communists, and this meant that the Khambas were cut off from some of their allies there. It came as a surprise to the Kham leaders, for they had expected the Chinese Moslem Generals in north-west China to make a committed stand against the Communists in view of their religious beliefs. But they, too, were steeped in the endemic corruption apparently afflicting all Nationalist leaders, and they were swept away by the moral judgement of Communism, and the Chinese People's Army poured through relatively unopposed to the Tibetan border in the north. Jekundo was only fifteen days' journey over the mountains, and the news was that the Chinese were calling on all local Tibetan leaders to surrender.

Topgyay weighed the situation coolly and carefully and decided to wait for a few more days in Litang. He reasoned that he could always leave for the mountains to the west beyond Litang at a moment's notice, and although there were Communist spies in Litang there were not enough supporters to stop him.

On one of the days it was decided we would visit the hot sulphur springs in the vicinity of the town. They were about an hour's horseback ride away, and a small party was formed. While waiting for the horses to be saddled Topgyay called me over to look at a horse in a nearby courtyard. It belonged to a lama, he explained, but it had the reputation of being a "killer", even "demon-possessed", and no one was prepared to ride it. It was said that he, Topgyay, was the only one capable of riding the horse, but he had declined since he had been out of that kind of skill for some time now. I gazed at the magnificent, rearing animal and its white eyes and striking hooves, and wondered idly if I could ride him. I had come a long way from my early days of classical British-style riding learned in Scotland. I recalled with amusement the doggerel:

> "I learned two things
> from an early riding teacher.
> He held a nervous filly
> in one hand and gestured
> with the other, saying, 'Listen.
> Keep one leg on one side,
> the other leg on the other side,
> and your mind in the middle.'

"He turned and mounted.
She took two steps, then left
the ground, I thought for good.
But she came down hard, humped
her back, swallowed her neck,
and threw her rider as you'd
throw a rock. He rose, brushed
his pants and caught his breath,
and said, 'See, that's the way
to do it. When you see
they're gonna throw you, get off.'

I found myself asking Topgyay if I could have a try at riding the horse. He refused at first, then with the slow, reckless smile that I had become used to, he said, "*Dri-ge-ray* (Alright)."

Everyone stood back as I approached the grey terror, which retreated as I drew nearer, its eyes rolling and ears laid back. With the halter stretched taut, and unable to retreat further, it suddenly turned and flashed out with its hooves and I had to slide aside nimbly to avoid them. The movement brought me close to the horse's neck and I remained there, circling as the horse circled, speaking quietly and soothingly. I noted out of the corner of my eye that someone was untying the halter and I reached out my hand to take it, still moving with the horse but drawing the halter tighter.

The horse's ears gradually flickered upwards and then, as I lifted my hand towards its neck, they flattened again. With my fingertips I slowly began stroking the arching neck, traveling further with each stroke until I was moving near to where the reins and halter lay. Picking them up gently I continued stroking with the other hand, and at the same time I eased my left foot off the ground into the stirrup.

The silence could almost have been cut as I tensed and swung suddenly up and across the saddle, settling myself for the battle. The grey began pitching immediately, throwing its head high in the air and then plunging downwards as it tried to hurl me from the saddle. It was like a bolt of chained lightning as it curvetted about the compound, its legs like steel springs hurling it upwards each time it touched the ground, scattering the watching crowd.

After a short time testing the horse's mouth and my seat in the saddle I took it through the gate of the courtyard on to the plain outside. There it became almost frantic in its attempts to break away, go wild, and gallop. Already the crowd had lost their initial fears for me and were shouting and whooping in encouragement, but I held the grey down to a jolting trot to give me time to establish some control.

Topgyay, Geoff and the others were now mounted and came out on to the plain near me in a fast canter, and the grey went away in a bucking spree in the excitement, its nose almost sweeping the ground in its attempts to get free. The jolting drove the hat from my head and I automatically made a grab for it with my left hand. It was my undoing.

The grey rocketed away in a thundering gallop over the undulating plain, weaving crazy patterns as it sought to throw me off. The wind sang in my ears as I exerted all my strength and skill to bring it under control, but it had a mouth of iron and I began to feel my legs grow numb. At 15,000 feet altitude I knew that such exertions could cause immediate blackouts, and it could only be a matter of minutes before I was thrown and either dragged or kicked to death. With the thought came the determination to have one last attempt at breaking the horse.

I had gone round in a wide circle and was now almost back amongst the other riders again. They had pulled their horses to a stop as they watched the exhibition of riding; both man and beast were under scrutiny by the ruthless standards of Tibet. As I swept past them in a cloud of dust and stones I went almost as savage as the horse. When the horse threw its head down I broke the movement with a jerk and wrenched it up again. When the head came up with the flailing forefeet I beat it down by bringing my whip down between its ears. When it sprung to the left I wrenched the reins and bridle to the right until its body curved in a semicircle and it had to move crab-wise; and when it swung to the right I did the same to the left.

We were like a couple of mad things, and I was covered from head to foot in a bloody froth blowing backwards from the horse's mouth. Then, miraculously, I was moving along with the others, the horse still quivering and breaking into an occasional flashing gallop, but always coming round in a wide circling again at my prompting to join the others.

We were almost at the hot springs, situated in some low foothills, and I decided to test its stamina by putting it at the steep side of one shoulder of the hill ahead. It responded like a flash of lightning and was away before the others could draw breath. I let loose a wild Tibetan "yee-hee" and the staccato beat of its gallop increased into a thunderous roll. I was almost drunk with the speed and power of the animal under me, and it was still straining in a gallop when we topped the ridge and dropped down on the far side, and I had to fight it to a standstill when we arrived at the springs.

As we lay and soaked in the hot springs the performance of the grey horse was the sole topic of conversation. I lay back with my eyes shut, aching in every bone and muscle, my body quivering with the strain and reaction, my fingers raw flesh where the reins had burned and skinned them, while Topgyay urged me to buy the horse. He knew the lama owner, he said; he knew he couldn't ride the horse and that he was afraid of it; he knew he could get a bargain price for it, so why not buy it? I would never get a chance like this again, for a Tibetan never sold a horse if it was as good as this one. The lama would only sell it now because of its widely known deadly reputation, and, if it did kill someone, he would be held responsible.

I wanted the horse, but I was sore and exhausted and knew that it would take weeks of such riding before it could be brought under proper control. The thought in my present state was almost too much for me. I finally agreed that if I could ride it back again to Litang without being unseated I would buy it at whatever price Topgyay fixed.

It was agony on the return journey. The grey knew it was on its way home and refused to stay with the other riders and I had to fight it all the way, but I stayed on. I had to be helped from the saddle when we arrived, but my reward came when Loshay, my Tibetan servant, whispered that I must buy the horse, that there was none like it, and I was its master. He had been one of the most insistent against my trying to ride it before we left for the hot springs, and he was reckoned to be one of the finest horsemen in Kham.

This was one of the few regions of Tibet in which there were regular seasons of rain; and this, with the very warm daytime temperatures, produced great crops of grain and fruit. Batang had become famous throughout Tibet, and even China, for its variety of luscious fruits. The forests which so thickly covered the lower slopes of the mountains contained several species of antelopes, bears, lynx, leopards, monkeys; and herds of wild asses and horses, wild sheep and goats, roamed the great plains. Pheasants, partridges, and other wildfowl were common, as were marmots and hares, but the Tibetans had an aversion to shooting the last-named for food.

For centuries, the ordinary life of the village passed uneventfully, except for the occasion inter-tribal quarrels and fighting, and the even rarer revolutionary uprising such as the Pangdatshangs'. The land was still worked by wooden ploughs drawn by crossbred yaks, called dzo, or by a line of men, women and children using long-handled, long-bladed spades. The crops were cut with a short reaping hook, and taken to the threshing areas around the villages on the backs of donkeys; threshing was done with wooden flails, or by driving cattle round and round over the sheaves. The grain was winnowed by the wind. Amusements were few and simple; singing, dancing, horse-riding, shooting; visits to the local temple added some color and awe to life, and there were the religious festivals and family feasts.

But the pastoral placidity of the scene was deceptive, not only because of the looming catastrophe moving towards Tibet from China but also in the daily domestic tragedies in the lives of the ordinary people.

In addition to the pressures engendered by the oppressive monasteries, with their extortionate taxes and money-lending, there were the family crises brought about by diseases, or wounds gained in fighting, which could only be treated by the superstitious applications of the monks' urine and faeces in pills and poultices. In a country where very few people washed for weeks or months, or even years - mostly, it has to be said, because of the intense cold which could split dry skin like a tomato - a cut from a knife or sword could develop rapidly into a fatal gangrene.

For me, this meant a constant demand for medical treatment wherever we travelled or were resident for any length of time. Over the three years of my stay in East Tibet, because of my association with the Pangdatshangs and my evident medical help for the family and their friends, my reputation as a "doctor" had spread widely throughout the region and people travelled considerable distances for me to treat them. Often the condition was well beyond my limited capacity; but, when I protested that I could not help the sick persons in such conditions, either they or their relatives insisted I do something, for their only alternative was a lingering and unpleasant death. Usually I tried, and had been fortunate that most had recovered and none had died. This was very satisfying, but it also meant that it brought more people with greater medical problems.

While the cycle of daily living went on in the village of Bo-mi after the initial excitement of our arrival, messengers arrived at irregular intervals bringing news from all over Tibet. In early January, 1950, a fast-riding messenger brought important news from Batang. It was the long-expected official communication from the Chinese Communists, but it was much more serious than the Pangdatshangs had anticipated.

There was the usual long Communist preamble on "democracy" and "liberation", and all the new "freedoms" the people would enjoy under the new Chinese Communist regime, and then came the important contents. The new Tenth Panchen Lama - like the new Fourteenth Dalai Lama, also from Amdo, or the Chinese-claimed Tsinghai Province - had approved the new Chinese regime's calls for "the liberation of Tibet". This public commitment had been followed by a nation-wide broadcast "confirming" the claimed agreement with the four Amdo and Kham leaders of the "East Tibetan Peoples' Revolution". With the surrender of the two Moslem war-lord Generals in north-west China, and the imminent surrender of General Liu Wen-huie in Sikang and Szechuan in the south-west, the way was now open for the Chinese Liberation Army to enter Tibet.

The Communist authorities had learned of the Pangdatshangs' plans for a revolution against the reactionary feudal government in Lhasa, and they approved of the plans and desires to further the interests of the Tibetan people. They were to go ahead with these plans and the Chinese authorities would supply them with the necessary arms, ammunition and financial help. The only difference was that it would not be a factional regional uprising as planned, but a "people's revolution" against the Tibetan Government. They were not to consider opposing the Chinese Liberation Army, for the Chinese authorities were not just viewing the Pangdatshangs as intransigent rebels to be punished and then withdraw as in the past. The Chinese Army intended to liberate the whole of Tibet as part of their long-term plans to liberate the whole of Asia. Within one year Tibet would be liberated; within three years Nepal, Sikkim and Bhutan would be liberated; in five years India would be liberated; and thus the East secured for Communism. If the Pangdatshangs did not fully co-operate they and their Khamba supporters would be swept out of existence.

The Pangdatshangs were stunned at the implications of such an ultimatum. Fundamentally, it meant that instead of being a Tibetan nationalist reform group they would now have to become traitors fighting for the Chinese against their own people. It would not help to send to Lhasa to inform the Government of what was planned and to seek their assistance, for it was already known in Lhasa that there were plans for a revolt in East Tibet and this would be interpreted as just a ruse. Further, such a mission to Lhasa would take more than four months by a sufficiently important delegation taking the normal route through

Chamdo, and by the time the matter was given appropriate consideration, and a reply sent, it would be too late to be effective. It was obvious from the Chinese communication that they expected to attack soon.

After a great deal of thought and discussion the Pangdatshangs concluded that there was only one possibility: someone would have to get through to India, on the little known trail to Sadiya in Assam in north-east India, which, by fast traveling might be completed in two months. This would mean that the news could be given to leading Indian, British and American officials in India, and a decision to offer help could be quickly communicated to the Lhasa Government, who, in turn, could inform the Pangdatshangs in Kham. The Kham and Amdo leaders could then launch a holding action against the Chinese until more effective help arrived from the outside world.

But who was to be the messenger carrying such a message? Topgyay was required to stay in Kham as the recognized military leader of the Khambas. Rapga could not go to India, for the order of expulsion against him was still in effect, and he might be arrested on arrival before he could do anything. No other Khamba leader would know how to go about visiting embassies and government departments to talk with appropriate officials.

Topgyay and Rapga halted in their description of the situation and looked meaningfully at me. What did I think about going to India on their behalf, Topgyay suggested, to alert the necessary officials in India, and also any Lhasa officials who might be there, as to what was really happening in East Tibet and see if I could get help for them?

I gaped at him in disbelief! Assuming that I could survive the journey across the unexplored area of Tibet that I would have to travel to reach India in the time at my disposal, what would I do after I had delivered my message to the appropriate authorities? Who were "the appropriate authorities" anyway? How would I contact them, and how would I get them to believe an unknown missionary, with no influential connections, from an obscure village in Scotland? More, assuming that I could make contact with someone, and was heard, after I had been shown the door what could I do? Return to Kham with fresh medical supplies but a "tainted" message, and a new vocation as a political revolutionary? Or, go back to Scotland with an unfinished spiritual odyssey?

After my first reaction of outright disbelief, then an instinctive rejection of such an overt political involvement, I asked for time to think about it. The Pangdatshangs agreed, but pointed out reasonably enough that time was in short supply in the circumstances. If I didn't go, then they had to make other life-or-death decisions regarding preparations for revolt immediately. There was no question of surrender to the Chinese.

Until that moment I had been happy to go along with each day's circumstances as they happened, satisfied that I was in the will of God in a general fashion. Now I was being asked to make a decision that would radically alter my whole way of life. Up to that point, although my activities might have been classed by others as somewhat unorthodox - especially by those who were traditionalists in their outlook or conviction - I had contended that I was completely orthodox from the Scriptural point of view, and it was the ecclesiastical insitutionalists who should be classified as unorthodox or heterodox. But if I agreed to become an emissary of the Kham revolutionary leaders I would be removing myself from even my own broad definition of what constituted a modern missionary, and placing myself unequivocally in a political environment - and a revolutionary one at that!

www.classictravelbooks.com

One of its most obvious consequences would be to put me outside the accepted fellowship of Brethren - not excommunicated, but ostracized. My earlier defection from the system of preaching and teaching, and all the usual activities, might have been forgiven and forgotten as a temporary eccentricity if I had returned from Tibet as a "successful missionary". But a deliberate move into a public participation in politics, especially on behalf of warring heathen tribesmen, would exclude me from any useful let alone significant role among Brethren - or even the wider evangelical community.

Modern Russia, with its state acceptance of godless Marxism, was interpreted by most Brethren commentators as the modern fulfillment of the Biblical "Russ", the "king of the north", that was to rise up at the End Times to fight for the Antichrist against God's people, Israel, at Armageddon. The association of China with Russia as a Communist bloc would only serve to emphasize that God was using them in His sovereign plan to punish the heathen Buddhists of Tibet, and that any attempt to frustrate them in this task would be seen as an act of opposition to the will of God.

These were only some of the considerations pouring through my mind as I sought to find out what God wanted; there was a multiplicity of others that spun off from them. Gradually the turbulent flow of possible options were winnowed out as I brought my thoughts "into the obedience of Christ". The words of the Apostle Paul came into my mind and calmed me: "The weapons of our warfare are not carnal but mighty in God for pulling down strongholds, casting down arguments and every high thing that exalts itself against God, bringing every thought into the obedience of Christ".

"Pulling down strongholds" - "casting down arguments" - "every high thing that exalts itself against God" - the phrases repeated themselves into a rolling, thundering chorus in my mind. God had provided me with the secret - or some of them - of these "weapons", and I was now equipped as never before to use them; whether it was against Brethren or other traditionalists, or against the unknown political antagonists lying in wait for me - or even against the known dark powers of the kingdom of Satan.

I felt a slow excitement building up in me as I contemplated the new frontiers ahead of me: the physical challenges of crossing unexplored Tibet; the political obstacles after arrival in India; the combatting entrenched shibboleths among evangelicals, especially Brethren; the confronting of Satan.

As I agonized over the decision it suddenly became clear to me that my moment of destiny had arrived: This was my rendezvous with God! Everything that had happened in China, and England, and Scotland, had been leading up to this encounter. I could see the thread of circumstances leading right back to those days and nights lying in my pain-racked bed in Laurieston as I grappled with the problem of God's purpose for me. All my doubts about societies, and politics, and revolutions, and churches; and all my questions about changing individuals and conditions, had been met by God.

I had been brought to China, and at first hand had passed through the tortured political revolution taking place there. Also, I had watched the collapse of imperialistic missionary practices, the end of two hundred years of ecclesiastical Christianity; and the emergence of a dynamic Scriptural movement in the "Little Flock", which would surpass and survive the Marxism of China as the first century Church had that of the Roman empire.

I had been brought to the Tibetan border when the Khamba tribal revolution against feudal Lhasa was being born, and had been brought right into the family and plans of the leader of that revolution. Now that China was secretly planning a war against Tibet, unknown to the world's superpowers, I was right there in the councils of those who were key figures in the decisions being made.

Two ways to India lay before me as alternatives to the unacceptably long route via Lhasa: one was sharply south-west across the Yangtze River, down into Yunan, and across Burma; the other was to start in that direction, then angle in across Tibet obliquely to the Mishmi tribal areas into Upper Assam. The former route, while presenting many difficulties from bandits and warring tribesmen, had been travelled by a Lieutenant-Colonel Baillie some years before; but the latter route had never been travelled at all by any foreigner.

Topgyay said that very few Tibetans either had ever done the complete journey through Zayul and Rima to Sadiya in Assam. He and Rapga had considered taking it in 1935 but had ruled it out because of this uncertainty about getting through. However, he did have a soldier who had done it five years before, traveling on foot, and he now sent for him. Meanwhile, we discussed other possibilities, but ended up preferring the Zayul route. When the soldier, Tsering Dorje, arrived he was questioned by all of us in great detail.

He had come from India by that way, he said, because he and some friends had done some trading in India but had no horses or money to hire them to carry the goods across the usual Lhasa route. It was cheaper to hire local porters to carry the loads from village to village along this shorter route from Sadiya to Batang. It had been a long, arduous and dangerous experience, and he would not like to do it again. Topgyay informed him sardonically that he would be surprised to hear that he was about to do so - with *Khamba Gyau*, "the Bearded Khamba", his nickname for me. He added that it would be better this time, he would have a horse. He was being appointed as my official escort to see that I got there safely.

With that settled, Rapga helped draft a request for official permission from the Lhasa Government for me to travel by this route, without mentioning my purpose, of course. This was sent by fast-riding messenger to Dege Sey, or "Prince of Dege", who was the Lhasa Commander of Tibetan forces in Markham Gartok on the other side of the Yangtze River, and a good friend of the Pangdatshangs. He would transmit it to Chamdo, from where it would be radioed to Lhasa. With these arrangements completed I would have to wait until we had a reply from Lhasa.

When we had exhausted the topic of the possible implications of my proposed journey to India Topgyay called for a meal to be served, and the conversation became general.

CHAPTER ONE

An "Impossible" Assignment

TIBET - known as "Roof of the World"; also, because of the strategic Central Asian location between Russia, China and India, as "the saddle of Asia", or "the world's third pole; the highest and, until fifty years ago, the most remote country in the world. Three-quarters-of-a-million square miles in area, an average altitude of fifteen thousand feet above sea level, situated between three of the world's greatest mountain ranges over twenty-thousand feet: the Himalayas, the Karakoram, and the Amne Machin. The origin of its people and spoken language mysterious; the origin of its written religious language, Indian Sanskrit; the origin of its religious system, Mahayana Buddhism from Nepal and China, mixed with Hindu tantricism and Mongolian shamanism; the origin of its great fighting Khamba tribes in East Tibet, from the occupation by Genghis Khan warriors in the twelfth century.

Tibet's capital is called "*Lha-sa*"" meaning "god-on-earth". The Tibetans call Mount Everest *Chomolungma*, meaning "goddess mother of the world." The mountains in Tibet were considered sacred to the gods, and no mining of their wealth of gold. silver and oil was permitted. On the top of every mountain pass, where Tibetans crossed, there were heaps of stones, and rows of multi-colored prayer-flags, many of them carved or inscribed with the mystic prayer-mantra, *Om mani padme hum*, meaning "The jewel in the heart of the lotus", or "the precious sum of all spiritual truth" Almost every Tibetan man and woman carried a 108-bead rosary, or prayer-wheel, or both; and, when they weren't talking, they were muttering the prayer-mantra in low tones. Every household and nomad tent had its altar with gold, silver, bronze, or paper gods.

In every village, encampment, town and city there was a *chod-gyay*, a tantric adept, who was consulted on every matter of family, community, or national life: the naming of a child, the date for a wedding, the selling of an animal, the time to travel or sow crops, to bring rain, to provide amulets to stop wounds from swords or bullets, to heal sicknesses, to make official decisions. The *chod-gyas* did this by going into "trance-possession", or, as they called it, *lha-babs,* "calling down the gods."

I had known nothing about Tibet when I first decided to go there as part of a spiritual experience. I hadn't even thought about Tibet at all, until it was thrust on me while I was reading a mountaineering book, **Blank on the Map**, written by one of the great mountain-climbers, Eric Shipton. While absorbed in his experiences of mountain-climbing in the Himalayas I became conscious of a voice prompting me to *"Go to Tibet."* How that vague stimulus became a spiritual odyssey is recounted in my autobiography, **Patterson of Tibet.**

During the late-1940s I had lived for three years in Tibet, with the great warrior-tribes in the eastern Kham-Amdo provinces, and had become friendly with their chieftains. When the Chinese Communists threatened to invade Tibet the chieftains asked me to become their emissary to the outside world and seek help in their planned resistance against the invading Chinese. The usual trans-Tibet route went from Kangting on China's eastern border, and then over a thousand miles of precipitous mountain ranges and road-less valleys through Chamdo and Lhasa, to Kalimpong on the India-Tibet border, and it took the trading caravans about six months to make the journey. A direct south-east route from Kangting and Batang to Sadiya in

India was considered preferable in the context of imminent invasion by the Chinese Communist Liberation Army, but was only a feasible direct possibility as no-one had ever done it before. It would mean crossing the savage and impenetrable region of the eastern Himalayas, known to wartime airmen operating in south-east Asia as the notorious "Hump", and the unknown upper reaches of four of the world's greatest rivers - the Yangtze, the Salween, the Mekong, and the Brahmaputra - in the worst possible winter season.

It was a memorable journey to India. I made it in just over fifty days of horrendous traveling difficulties involving blizzards and landslides, roaring river crossings and swaying fiber bridges, glacial ice-fields and hidden snow-crevasses, and over a hundred degrees in difference between mid-day and midnight temperatures. On several occasions my small caravan of animals and Tibetan muleteers were caught in especially severe blizzards in a tangle of high mountains and plunging valleys with heavily forested slopes. During the nights it was so cold that even in my sleeping-bag, wearing all my clothes, I was too cold to sleep except in snatched fitful dozes. Above the steady roar of the wind I could hear the sound of trees splitting and rocks shattering in the sub-zero temperatures. In the morning it was agony to get up and saddle and pack the animals, the cold freezing not only the fingers and ears but also the beard and breath as well. It would have been better to walk than to ride, except for the freezing numbness of body and the difficulty of breathing at altitudes of over 17,000-feet through roaring winds and heavy snows.

As we moved out of the tree-lines on to the exposed ridges of snow-shrouded valleys between towering mountains. the full force of the blizzards drove into our faces, shutting out all visibility. The point man of the caravan had to battle wind and snow as he forced a path for the others to follow, each tied with a length of rope to the man behind so we would not get lost in the blinding vastness.

We passed from treacherous trackless snows into hazardous trackless ice-fields, and we had to dismount to help our animals forward through jagged ice and blanket snow nightmares. The blizzards were a constant muted roar among the mountain peaks and valleys, and a shrieking horror on the vast plateaux; and always the snow a thick drifting curtain, adding to the ghostly terror. Time after time, we lost all sight and sound of our caravans in the blanketing snow and ice wilderness.

When I arrived in Calcutta in India fifty days after I started my journey, my report regarding the imminent invasion of Tibet by the Chinese Army was not believed and, before I could return to Tibet, the Chinese army invaded and occupied the country. I remained on the Indian-Tibetan border for the next eleven years; and, as a journalist, reported the subsequent invasion, occupation, atrocities and, later, the inevitable Tibetan revolt.

The fanatically independent Kham-Amdo tribal warriors, unlike the suppressed serfs of feudal-governed Central Tibet, comprised about eighty percent of Tibet's estimated five million people, divided among some sixty-six tribes; and their dislike of their own Lhasa Government was exceeded only by their traditional hatred of their Chinese neighbors. When the Lhasa Government accepted the Chinese occupation of Tibet in 1950 the Kham-Amdo tribes began preparing for a long and bitter war with the hated invader. From 1952 onwards, they fought on an ever-increasing scale against Chinese soldiers, who were unaccustomed to the problems presented by the high altitude and Siberian-like climate.

www.classictravelbooks.com

My journalistic reports in national and international media annoyed India's Prime Minister Nehru, and he threatened to expel me from the country if I did not desist from what he called "publishing bazaar rumors as fact." From my Tibetan friends inside Tibet I knew they were planning a nation-wide revolt, and also to remove the Dalai Lama from Chinese-occupied Lhasa, to India, which would not only embarrass Prime Minister Nehru but would also precipitate conflict between hitherto friendly China and India, and perhaps even war. Prime Minister Nehru rejecting my journalist reports in the Indian Parliament, declared, "There is no violence in Tibet. What is taking place there is a clash of wills and not of arms", and ordered my expulsion from India. On the day this order was to be officially explained and ratified in India's Parliament, Prime Minister Nehru instead was forced to announce he had received word that the Indian Consulate in Lhasa had been bombed in fighting there, and the Dalai Lama had escaped and was on his way to India.

I returned to Britain - voluntarily, not expelled! - when the Dalai Lama accepted the Indian Government's official ultimatum to refrain from Tibetan propaganda and politics while living as a refugee in India, because I concluded that Prime Minister Nehru's policy was to sacrifice Tibet in the interests of India. He had told me personally, in a private interview before I left India: "The future which I dream is inextricably woven with close friendship and something almost approaching union with China." There was no way he was going to permit anti-Chinese activities from Indian soil.

When the inevitable war broke out between China and India, as I had foretold, I returned to write a series of articles for the British weekly, *Observer*, from Kashmir in the north-east to Nagaland in the south-east, along the

Himalayan border countries. While doing this I renewed my acquaintanceship with many of my previous Tibetan friends, most of whom had become increasingly disillusioned with the lack of positive leadership from the young a-political Dalai Lama and his inner circle of self-interested advisers.

Two of the key people in the Tibetan revolt were close friends of mine: one, Yangpel, was the eldest brother of the famous Central Asian trading family of Pangdatshang, with whom I lived during my time inside Tibet, and on whose behalf I had traveled as emissary to India; and the other was Surkhang, Chief Minister in the Lhasa Cabinet and key figure in the revolt. The official *New China News Agency*, at the height of the revolt, had declared furiously:

"In the summer of 1955, Surkhang Wongching-Galei...and other rebel elements for Tibet, after following the Dalai Lama to attend the national Peoples' Congress in Peking, passed through the Szechuan Province on their way to Tibet. Surkhang Wangching-Galei...went by separate routes to the northern and southern parts of the Kantse Autonomous Chou to instigate and direct rebellion along the way. Data now at hand proves that Surkhang Wangching-Galei directed the reactionaries in the area..."

I had known Surkhang Shapay (his Cabinet title, "Minister") for some years while living in India, and had become close friends with him and his family. His brother was a General, and the Surkhangs were closely related to another powerful aristocratic family, Yuthok. They, with the most powerful family in Tibet, the Tsarongs, were part of a loosely organized group who were opposed to the second-rank and second-rate group of Tibetan nobility and monks advising the Dalai Lama. They wanted the Dalai Lama to leave India to be free to take whatever effective action was necessary against the Chinese occupying Tibet.

According to the powerful Tibetan revolutionary leaders such as Surkhang and Yuthok and Tsarong, the Dalai Lama had been brought out of Tibet to India in order to make known the predicament of the country to the world, by going to the United Nations, if necessary. But he had been advised against this by his brother, Gyalu Thondup, and Thondup's commercial partner, Shakapba, whose financial interests were in India, Hong Kong and Taiwan. Thondup had hardly ever resided in Tibet, going to China as a schoolboy and accompanying the Nationalists when they retreated to Taiwan after defeat by the Communists. He arrived in India in 1952, went to Tibet for five months, then remained on the Indian-Tibetan border in Darjeeling, doing a little trade and dabbling in Tibetan politics. He had worked himself into control of the Dalai Lama's treasure when it was brought out of Tibet and kept in Sikkim. There were varying estimates of the treasure, with Thondup saying it was only "six or seven million US dollars"; others claimed it was eleven million, and one trustee told me it was thirty million dollars.

What was known was that it was Gyalu Thondup who, with the Maharajkumar of Sikkim, the Prime Minister of Bhutan, Jigme Dorji, and Indian business associates in Kalimpong and Calcutta, who appropriated and invested huge sums of the treasure in dubious business ventures which never materialized, or which collapsed through lack of sufficient funding or expertise. The Khambas in India, who were supposed to have benefitted, were furious and protested vociferously to the Dalai Lama. Eventually the Dalai Lama was forced to disassociate Thondup from the treasure, but only after considerable damage had been done.

For this, and other, reasons Surkhang and his colleagues had resigned their official positions in Tibet's government and, with the Kham and Amdo tribal leaders, were planning another rescue operation for their almost doomed country. They wrote to me in London asking if I would help Tibet once again and, if I could not come to India, could I arrange for them to visit England to discuss what might be done..

One of the major problems in the Tibetan situation, however, was the antagonism between the independent Kham-Amdo tribes and the sycophantic and disputing feudal aristocrats and monks of Central Tibet. The numerous and martial Kham-Amdo tribes hated Gyalu Thondup and Shakapba both before and after the revolt to the point of swearing to kill them, and it was a suicidal policy for India and their Western government counterparts to expect that these two individuals would ever be accepted as representatives of the majority of Tibetans. Yet this was what the former colonial "advisers" to the British Government, who were now retired but anxious to offer their "expert" services to the naive Gyalu Thondup and Shakapba, recommended. Their advice was unwanted in British official circles, useless in American official circles and ridiculed in United Nations official circles.

Meanwhile, India had already lost about fifty thousand square miles of Himalayan territory to China in a Sino-Indian border dispute and minor war, and had suffered the humiliating defeat of her best regiments in the North East Frontier Agency of North-East India.

That was when Surkhang and Yangpel approached me to request that I make one more attempt to publish Tibet's genocidal circumstances still being perpetrated by China's occupation army in Tibet. It meant, among many other things, getting the impoverished, out-of-favor Surkhang and the rich scheming Yangpel away from the isolation and oblivion of a small back room in an obscure Himalayan border town in North Bengal to responsible media, academic and government circles in Britain and America. It meant doing this without the cooperation of India, Britain and the United States, who were desperately trying to maintain the facade of the Asian bloc's internationally-acclaimed Bangkok Agreement of "Five Principles of Peaceful Coexistence" while ignoring the destruction of Tibet. It meant convincing a cynical world that the issue of Tibet was not dead beyond recall; that there was still a sufficient nucleus of resistance inside Tibet to make Tibet more than just a fantasy humanitarian project. It meant trying to persuade a skeptical world that the Chinese Communist Government was an unscrupulous and genocidal pariah unfit to associate with civilized people as well as rule over their own.

It meant, in short, putting together a television team to attempt the herculean assignment of breaching the Indian Himalayan Border Defence Region, misleading the government, diplomatic, and intelligence officials of five countries represented in Nepal - Nepal itself, India, China, Britain and the United States; and, most challenging of all, overcoming the monumental physical challenge of secretly crossing the 20-30,000-feet Himalayan mountains with a company of Khamba guerrillas to film their attack on a Chinese military convoy on the strategic Chinese-built main highway inside Tibet in order to demonstrate China's destruction of all things Tibetan and their own vulnerability to Tibetans determined to get rid of them..

My wife, Meg, and I had only just emerged from a traumatic spiritual crisis involving our continuing participation in a life of primary commitment to God. My personal involvement with Tibet had begun with a spiritual crisis during World War II when I had taken the radical step of finding out if God still communicated with His creatures and events in the twentieth century as it was claimed He did in the past. To my astonishment God told me, "Go to

Tibet", without further explanation, and so began my spiritual odyssey of exploration into God in the twentieth century, and my involvement with Tibet's destiny. But then I had been a bachelor in my mid-twenties; now I was in my early forties, married with two children and a third on the way, with many answers but also many more questions. I felt I had paid my dues as a young Christian, and now would live a more "normal" life - whatever that was.

I had no special ambition to be a journalist, despite the skills I had acquired and the possibilities; I had no ambition to be a scholar specializing in Asian affairs, as that was how I was designated as a broadcaster; I had no ambition to be an author although I was having books published regularly. To be truthful, what I wanted to do was continue to be a servant of God - but on my terms instead of God's. So, we left London for Scotland, where my brother Bill had a small estate with two farms, in a remote part of the Highlands, to resolve our situation.

The experience was similar to Jonah's trying to flee from God and ending up in the sea. We didn't end up in a whale but it rained all the time we were in the wilds of Scotland, until we were forced by weather and circumstances to face God and the consequences. We surrendered to God - and Tibet - once again, and returned to London.

There is a popular Chinese proverb: "A thousand mile journey begins with one step." So, first of all, I arranged for some wealthy and generous friends of mine, with a strong humanitarian interest in Tibet, to bring Surkhang's two children to England to be educated; and then, shortly afterwards, to sponsor and finance a visit to them in England by Surkhang, his wife and General brother. I also arranged for Yangpel Pangdatshang, the leading Khamba representative in the Lhasa government, a Minister of Trade, to come to Britain "for medical treatment." When they arrived, I arranged for Surkhang to lecture at the prestigious foreign affairs center, St. Antony's College, Oxford; and the Royal Institute for International Affairs in London. That provided a solid academic foundation for an assessment of Tibet's parlous situation that was considerably different from the official Indian and British approach.

In an interview with the British *Daily Telegraph*, Surkhang stated:

"Certainly there is hope (for Tibet). If we had not run out of arms and ammunition we could have defeated the Chinese Army in Tibet. You must remember that our country is very mountainous, at an average altitude of 15,000 feet, and the few roads are really only mountain trails. We cut the roads, destroyed the Chinese convoys, and put the Chinese troops on their feet in the high altitude where they cannot manoeuver against our fast-moving fighters. But we need large supplies of arms to exploit these natural advantages to defeat the Chinese...

"There are at least about 100,000 Tibetan guerrillas still inside Tibet, and about 20,000 in India, who are anxious to take up where they left off in 1959, and if all of them are given supplies of modern arms they are certain they can make it impossible for the 300,000 Chinese troops in Tibet to pose a major threat to India..."

From Surkhang and Yangpel I obtained the information that there were an estimated five thousand Khamba guerrillas located somewhere in the high Himalayas who were conducting raids into Tibet against Chinese military convoys on the north-south highway the Chinese authorities had built parallel to the Nepal border inside Tibet. But there were some eight hundred miles of the highest and most difficult mountain terrain in the world delineating Nepal's border with Tibet, with only a few negotiable mountain passes at certain times of the year. The topography of Nepal encompassed the northern border of twenty-thirty thousand-feet mountains dropping in savage snow-covered ranges to fifteen thousand-feet; the mid-level of the country fell from fifteen thousand-feet to five thousand-feet in a tangle of ridges and valleys and forests; and from there to the plains of India there were the cultivated and terraced fields of the bulk of Nepal's population.

The natural physical problems of making contact with any elusive group of Tibetan guerrillas - who did not want to be found by anyone - in these towering mountainous and officially inhospitable regions was made even more difficult by the political and military considerations. Following on India's defeat in her border war with China, the Indian government was extremely sensitive about allowing anyone near any part of the Himalayan borders - especially myself - and they had explicitly forbidden access to these territories controlled by them.

To the south-west of Nepal, Bhutan was a closed country, jealously guarded by India from any outside influence except through India. I knew the prime minister of Bhutan, Jigme Dorji, as a good friend, and thought I might be able to influence him to give permission to visit - but I would have to come up with a good reason for any visit. He knew me too well to accept any superficial fabrication. Sikkim, between Nepal and Bhutan, was out of the question, because it was too open and inhabited, with too many suspicious Indian and Sikkimese officials conspiring to annex and incorporate Sikkim within India - just as the Chinese were annexing and incorporating Tibet within China.

While discussing possible physical and political approaches to Tibet, I also had to find a television team willing to accept the apparently impossible assignment. For the normal mountaineering expedition in the Himalayas there were usually many months of preparation. These preparations involved physical and proficiency tests, information briefings, personnel screenings, mental aptitudes, prior knowledge of the region and so on. None of these were possible in this top secret television film assignment, yet it required the highest level of physical toughness, professional expertise, personal character and unique courage. Even if the proposed television team could cross over the Himalayas and reach Tibet, and successfully film the battle, it could all be lost unless the film was brought back safely to London and shown to the world.

Among my other activities in London at the time, was to help set up, and become director of, a non-governmental organization, a commission for minorities, called "The International Committee for the Study of Group Rights" (later to become "Minority Rights Group"). Their aims were to take up the grievances of small nations oppressed by others and who had no representation at the United Nations. There were several issues under consideration by sub-committees at that time - Kurds, South Sudan, Nagas - and we were approached by a noted television producer who had produced some remarkable films about the exploitation of tribal Indians in South America, Adrian Cowell.

Adrian had just completed a remarkable television film about the Xingu Indians of Brazil, their exploitation and that of their rain-forest environment. He came to the International Committee for the Study of Group Rights to see if we could do anything on their behalf. Adrian had been born in China and he was very interested in hearing about the Tibetans and Nagas and, as he was between assignments at the time, when I suggested a film about them, he eagerly agreed and proposed a series on "Revolutions in Asia", to include them and Shans of Burma, and Nationalists raiding mainland China. He brought in Chris Menges, who had done some excellent camera work for the commercial ITV network program in Britain, "World in Action", and whom Adrian considered one of the three best documentary film makers in Britain at the time, and we were a team ready to go.

Unfortunately, we could find no one to finance the project. All media stated flatly that it was an impossible project, until Granada regional TV agreed to advance £10,000 (or US$15,000) for first call on the film if it ever came off. We had to find the extra money needed out of our own resources, which my wife and I did by selling off our Tibetan objets d'art given to us by friends or grateful patients.

Our domestic situation had just survived a crisis as my wife and I had tried to grapple with living with two Tibetan revolutionaries and their wives and families, and two Naga revolutionaries, all in one small house. We had three children - two boys, Lorne and Sean, of four and two, and a baby girl, Myrrh (named after the rare and costly bittersweet perfume offered to Jesus at his birth and death) of six weeks. Adrian was married with two children, Chris was unmarried. We anticipated being away on the assignment for about eighteen months: several months on the Tibet project, several months getting behind the Indian Army lines and into forbidden Nagaland, several months to get into the remote Shan States of Burma where the Shans were in revolt against their Central Government, and then some months on the China mainland project.

Then there were the technical problems faced by Adrian and Chris in trying to anticipate filming at 15-20,000-feet altitudes, in extremes of climate and temperature and environment and circumstances. To the normal calculations of adequate film stock there were added the problems of weight, unknown effects of exposure, what uncertain time delays would mean for processing in either black or white, and whether special cameras were essential. And even when all of these problems were solved, there was the most important problem of all: how to get the completed film material safely out of Tibet and Nepal to London

But eventually we were ready for the great adventure.

CHAPTER TWO

The Intricacies Of Professional Duplicity In India

The wing of the giant jet tipped up and the indescribably beautiful, hazy, pastel-colored Indian dusk fell away on one side and the multi-colored checkerboard of lights that was New Delhi appeared on the other.

No matter how often I visited this capital of India, and I had done it times without number in the previous thirteen years, it never failed to excite me. The soft red-brick majesty of Lutyen's imperial buildings and impressive carriageways; the crowded, colorful, stimulating city streets of Chandi Chowk, in old Delhi; the history-permeated forts and gates and temples; the challenging and successful designs of India's architects in the modern new suburbs. It lay harshly exposed in the brilliant mid-day sun, but in the evening it took on a new eye-caressing softness of outline. I loved Delhi and India, where so many of my best years had been spent, so many friends made, so many experiences shared.

Yet the thought which had never been far from the surface of my mind during the plane flight now pushed itself to the forefront - would I be permitted to land?

Just before leaving England I had heard from my publishers, Faber & Faber, that my latest book, Peking Versus Delhi, had been favorably reviewed in a lead article in the Times Literary Supplement. But it had been banned by the Indian government, and it was being rumored that I would not be allowed to return to India. Certainly, what was no rumor was the action of the Indian government in stating that my much-admired surgeon-wife, Meg, who had built up an impressive hospital in the Darjeeling region and reputation in India and Britain, receiving an award from the Queen for her "outstanding medical work in India", would be welcome anytime in India "but not Mr Patterson."

There were many reasons for this, so I was neither surprised nor offended. After I had been dramatically exonerated from threatened expulsion from India by Prime Minister Nehru because of my journalistic reports regarding the revolt in Tibet and the arrival of the Dalai Lama in India seeking sanctuary, all Indian Government officials without exception had refused to help with my request for an interview with Nehru. The Minister of External Affairs, Jaghat Mehta, a good friend, in refusing my request, had said wryly: "George, a Government might forgive you for being wrong, it won't forgive you for being right." Even another good friend, the British High Commissioner, Malcolm Macdonald, turned down my plea for his help in obtaining an interview, saying, "The Prime Minister has just returned from a busy visit to the UN, and is not even seeing me at present. You have no chance."

So I typed out a personal request for an interview, hand-carried it to the Prime Minister's residence, and handed it to the guard with a generous tip and asked him to have it delivered to the household. Next morning, I had a reply from the Prime Minister to say that he would be happy to grant me a short interview at eleven o'clock that morning. Despite our very public confrontations in the past, he was his usual very courteous self, and - despite the earlier protests of his office secretaries that no recordings were permitted without prior permission - he smilingly agreed to have me record our interview.

We had what is euphemistically called "a frank interchange of views", which ended with his statement: "For my part I am almost always more concerned with the future than the past. It satisfies one's conceit to imagine that one might mould it...the future which I dream is inextricable interwoven with close friendship and something almost approaching union with China."

And here was I about to enter India with secret plans to investigate, film and expose a situation in Tibet that would infuriate him and China and Britain and the United States and the United Nations.

Since my arrival in India from Tibet in 1950, and the Chinese Communist occupation of Tibet, I had made no secret of my spiritual conviction that my personal destiny was interwoven with Tibet, of my liking for Tibetans and championship of their cause, and my equal disapproval of the pusillanimous policies vis-a-vis Tibet of India, Britain and the United States. This had not only involved me in public clashes with Indian officialdom but also in many cloak-and-dagger escapades, necessitating the outwitting of a growing number of Indian police and security personnel, which had not made me popular with them over the years.

My highly publicized clash with Prime Minister Nehru, at the peak of his world-wide popularity, when he accused me of being "alarmist and irresponsible" for my reports of the fighting in Tibet, and I had accused him of "endangering the security of India" in ignoring what China was doing in Tibet, had provided every petty official with just the excuse he or she needed to be as obstructive and difficult as possible. Sometimes the battle was amusing, but more often than not it was exhausting and irritating. I would present my passport on entering the country, and there would be the usual bored scrutiny, and referral to a large well-thumbed book beside the official.

Then there would be a sudden change as the name was noted to correspond to one in the book. I would be told to "Please wait for a minute, sir", and the official would signal for a colleague to come and see what he had discovered. The colleague would look at me with a mixture of suspicion and triumph and go off to bring a superior official. This superior official would ask me politely to accompany him to his office, where I would be offered tea or coffee as a prelude to pleasant or unpleasant discussion regarding my purpose in visiting India. I would say "Business" and evade every specific detail, while the superior official would ask increasingly probing questions. When the superior official had delayed me long enough to allow a special interrogator to arrive, I would be taken to a fairly bare room and given the third degree process of no-holds-barred questioning by a trained Indian spook who knew every detail of my record. I had quite often been delayed from an hour to three or four hours before being released, when either of us tired of the game and began using effective threats of media or official reprisals. I had known there to be not one but two or three cars following me as I left the airport for my hotel. If I felt annoyed by the delays and treatment I would tell my taxi driver to circle the road roundabouts several times to trick the following cars into pursuit, until I either identified them, or they caught on and slipped out of the roundabout hoping to pick me up as I drove away into one of the other exits.

Now my book had been banned and, although favorably reviewed by London-based Indian newspaper correspondents and critics, the publicity following the banning was certain to inflame an already explosive situation. And, in the midst of all this, I had to attempt to bring off my biggest journalistic coup yet.

What happened was something of an anticlimax. There were only a few passengers disembarking at New Delhi, of whom I was the first to alight. Never on any previous occasion in India, and seldom in another country, had I been treated with such consideration and politeness. I was completely through all formalities, including customs, in less than five unusually pleasant minutes.

Chris had already arrived in New Delhi, and Adrian arrived the next morning, both with minimum fuss and bother at the airport, and we spent the rest of the morning discussing plans. By afternoon we had worked out the broad outlines of our approach and decided that our first move was to pay the usual formal courtesy call of all media personnel to the Press Relation Division of the Ministry of External Affairs.

In previous years, after a short wait, I had always been shown to the office of the chief press officer, Obadiah Rahman, who had chatted pleasantly over a cup of tea while we discussed my assignments in broad terms. On this occasion I noticed Obadiah had been promoted and, although he saw us arrive, he did not come to greet us, sending instead an assistant to meet us and take us to a side room. I guessed the reason for his change of attitude may have been based on a stormy interview which I had had with the Indian acting high commissioner in London, T.N.Kaul, at which Rahman was present, over the question of my newspaper articles regarding India's relations with the Nagas, with whom India was in dispute over the issue of Naga independence. So Rahman may well have been incensed and determined to "put me in my place." On the other hand, he might have been instructed not to meet me but pass me on to someone else, who, to my suspicious mind, would be from Security and not just a routine Information Department official.

This was a Mr. Mahajan, who introduced himself unsmilingly. His whole attitude was edgy and unnecessarily aggressive. I began the interview mildly and pleasantly, explaining that this was a courtesy call to let the Indian government know our tentative program and requests.

Adrian would deal with the TV aspects, but my contribution was (i) to assist in the making of a TV film about Tibetan refugees (which was true, at least to some extent, as we were going to be filming exiled guerrillas!); (ii) discuss with the Dalai Lama the possibility of a future feature film about Tibet and his possible appearance in it; and (iii) discuss with the leading officials in India, Tibet, Nepal, Bhutan and Sikkim the feasibility or otherwise of a Confederation of Himalayan States as a possible solution for the Sino-Indian border conflict.

My decision regarding option (iii) was very risky as it had been a considerable cause of controversy during my reporting years in India. I had pursued it in various forms among the officials of all the Himalayan border countries to the suspicion and annoyance of Indian officialdom because it was opposed to India's own self-interested political agenda of border politics. But, paradoxically, I concluded it was the most likely of the three possible options to be believed by India and, therefore, would be the best cover for our real plans to enter and film secretly in Tibet.

I had scarcely finished talking when Mahajan bluntly demanded to know what sort of film the TV unit wanted to make, who were my publishers, when was the film commissioned and by whom and on whose initiative, where was it intended to shoot this film, and what were our credentials?

I felt the familiar stirring of amusement and mental stimulation which these officious types always produced in me; in which the desire to provoke them into incoherence was stronger than the caution in not making another official enemy. But most of these lower-level Indian bureaucrats took themselves too seriously. They usually viewed the man across the desk from them as a supplicant rather than an applicant, and in their petty tyrannies and pomposities they were too many times encouraged by the poor Indian newspaper reporter dependent on them for their official favors.

However, I decided with a twinge of regret that there was too much at stake this time to needle Mahajan and I remained mildly polite, simply pointing out that we had valid contracts, that we had answered the requisite questions, that it was not incumbent on us to produce every detail at this stage, and that all other details could be discussed with the proper people at the proper time.

He didn't like it, but he saw he had pushed his luck too far, and he backed off, consenting grudgingly that we could film in India under certain conditions, which he produced in writing for us. But, he maintained, we would have to submit a synopsis of our proposed filming program, then a detailed script and, afterwards, if this were approved by the government department concerned - say, in one or two months - we would be able to proceed.

We thanked him, saying that we would discuss the proposed film with the Tibetans and then return with an approved script at a later date. I was confident that the sequence of events which would follow this interview were reasonably predictable in the bureaucratic warren that was Indian procedures and, whatever our future activities, the interview would serve as an adequate smokescreen in the present as we headed toward our main objective in Tibet.

An unexpected development occurred to help obscure our real intentions. In my previous visits to India, among other assignments I had written articles about the Nagas' nine-year war with India over independence, taking the Nagas' part. Now, within two days of our arrival, several Indian newspapers carried large-headline reports of armed battles between Nagas and the Indian army in East Pakistan. There were also reports of tension in Sikkim regarding confrontations between Indian and Sikkimese government officials over Sikkim's status. These events coincided with my arrival in India and created an official and media suspicion that they, and not Tibetan refugees, were the real reason for my presence in the country.

Then three Opposition leaders launched a violent attack on the official pro-China policy of Prime Minister Nehru. The respected veteran Socialist leader, Acharya Kripalani, declared:

"The government should stick to the resolve to get every inch of territory vacated by China and not talk in terms of the Colombo proposals. The 'illusion' created by repeated support to the proposals that they were something good, should be done away with. There should be no talk with China unless she vacates the entire land forcibly occupied by her."

When it was known through the media grapevine that I had arrived in India, I was approached by colleagues I had known in the past for comments on the Sino-Indian border situation, and these subsequently appeared in the newspapers and journals. Then, while we were still in New Delhi, the Bhutanese Prime Minister, Jigme Dorji, arrived with a Bhutanese delegation to discuss the growing Himalayan border crisis. Bhutan, like Nepal and Sikkim, were very suspicious of India's paternalist policies in their Himalayan countries. Nepal was fairly strong in its insistence on independence from India, but Bhutan was having problems as India claimed representative rights over Bhutan's defence and external affairs, and Sikkim was the weakest of the three and facing likely absorption into India. I had discussed this with Jigme Dorji when I was writing my book, *Peking Versus Delhi*, and knew that he intended removing Indian influence from Bhutan. In London I had planned to meet up with him in India to discuss the possibility of a visit to Bhutan, as an alternative to Nepal, so his arrival in New Delhi was extremely providential. I made an appointment to meet with him at his hotel in New Delhi.

I also called on the "Bureau of His Holiness the Dalai Lama" to renew my acquaintance with the representative in New Delhi, T.C.Tethong. He was a younger member of a leading Tibetan aristocratic family, with whom I had been friendly for years. He had been to Germany for political studies under the internationally known German scholar, Klaus Mehnert, and spoke fluent English and German. I arranged to call on him the next day, with Adrian, to make a formal application to the Dalai Lama for an audience. While there was hope of an audience there was not much hope of having him appear in a film, as the Indian government was adamant in controlling all of Tibetan activities on Indian soil; but it was an essential part of the "cover" for our main objective.

When we met with T.C. the following day, Adrian made formal request to make a film, explaining how the film made by a pro-Chinese journalist had portrayed a completely false set of circumstances in Tibet, which we wished to refute in our film. T.C. agreed to send our requests, plus copies of our contracts, by special messenger to the Dalai Lama in his refugee retreat in Dharamsalla to the north-east of New Delhi, but it would be a week before we could expect a reply.

When I went to meet with Jigme Dorji I was alone, as I reckoned Jigme would say things to me he would not be prepared to say in front of a stranger. He was his usual friendly self, jokingly familiar. He was a striking, Yul Brynner-like figure, his head completely shaven, and dressed in colorful, loose Bhutanese gown, hitched up to his knees, like a kilt, by a wide scarf tied around the waist. The Indian "adviser" was with him, and still hovering after I arrived, but Jigme informed him that this was a visit between friends and he withdrew reluctantly. Jigme's sister, Princess Tashi, was present, and Jigme said that part of their discussions with the Indian government in New Delhi would involve his proposal that she become Bhutan's "Minister of External Affairs". I cynically wished them both good luck and they smiled understandingly.

After an exchange of family news over cups of sweet tea Jigme replied to the possibility of a visit to Bhutan in his own typical, drily humorous fashion: "You can tell Meg from me, Patla (my "English" nickname among Tibetans; my Tibetan name was *Khamba-Gyau*, "Bearded Khamba"), that if she wants to come to Bhutan she is welcome anytime, but you - keep out! You are trouble. You went to Tibet, and they were invaded. You came to India, and they were invaded. Your big mistake was to turn from missionary work and football to politics."

"And yours," I retorted, "could be said to turn from horse-racing and football to politics." We had both played together in the same Himalayan soccer team.

"Seriously, Patla," Jigme continued, "how about giving us another year before you visit us? You know we are having problems just now; but give us a year to get some of our projects off the ground then come and film all you want."

"Jigs," I said, equally seriously, "I tell you, I don't think you will have another year - neither personally nor nationally." I smiled to take the edge off the remark, for Jigme knew that although I liked him personally I strongly disapproved of some of his autocratic policies.

"Why must you always be such a bloody Jeremiah?" he demanded irritably. "Which reminds me, you owe me ten pounds. When we last met you bet me that the Chinese would be in Bhutan within a year and that was, what, eighteen months ago."

"You bet the ten pounds," I replied drily. "And let me remind you that I was the only writer on Asian affairs that came anywhere near the mark. In any event, inside three months the Chinese attacked in the North East Frontier Agency only a few miles from Bhutan; and, although you and the Indian government both denied it at the time, we both know that the Chinese troops did enter Bhutan. So, I could claim the ten pounds from you."

"I'll pay you the ten pounds and more if you tell me the sources of your information," he suggested gloomily. "You could be right, but I can tell you that the possibility of invasion worries India more than it worries me."

We went on to discuss Bhutan's relations with India, including the worrying influx of thousands of Tibetan refugees entering Bhutan from Tibet which China could use as an excuse to interfere in Bhutan. I broached the subject of a Confederation of Himalayan States and he threw up his hands in protest. "Hell, you aren't still riding that old horse?" he protested. "I told you before that I wouldn't touch it because we'd be overrun by these Nepali bastards. India wouldn't look at it anyway, and - don't quote me! - we're doing too well from India to consider it."

But when I began explaining my new approach to him he sat back and looked at me thoughtfully.

The idea of a Confederation of Himalayan States originated in China, and not with me, although I had written most about it. While it had been one of the most intriguing of China's many activities on the Sino-Indian frontiers in recent years it had a much longer history than that.

The position of the Himalayan border states, before the confusion created by a succession of British administrators and British and Chinese military expeditions in the nineteenth and early twentieth century, had been stated clearly in a British official document: "Nepal is tributary to China, Tibet is tributary to China, and Sikkim and Bhutan are tributary to Tibet." The British authority on Tibet and the Himalayan region, Sir Charles Bell, had also said, "Britain has the right to intervene only in the case of disputes. If Bhutan agreed to Chinese intervention we could do nothing."

At the turn of the twentieth century China proposed to Nepal, "...a blending of five colors representing Tibet, Nepal, Bhutan and Sikkim" as part of a program to assert China's claims in the region. Mao Tzetung had stated categorically, "In defeating China in war the imperialist states have taken away many Chinese dependent states and a part of her territories...England seized Burma, Bhutan, Nepal..." Then, in 1960-61, the Chinese delegates to the Sino-Indian Boundary Commission discussing frontier questions refused to include Bhutan and Sikkim in the discussions because they claimed they came into a different category.

When, in late 1960, King Mahendra of Nepal took over "direct rule" several disapproving statements were made by Prime Minister Nehru and other Indian leaders. The King-controlled Nepali media reacted violently, and four leading newspapers warned the neighboring countries of Bhutan and Sikkim of Indian intentions, called on them to free themselves from "Indian interference", and proposed a confederation of Nepal, Bhutan and Sikkim, with Nepal taking the lead.

Whatever outside observers thought of the proposals - and there were many who scoffingly dismissed them as fantasy - the peoples concerned in the region were all convinced that they wanted less "Indian interference", more "self-determination and separate identity" and such a proposal was exceedingly attractive to them.

After seventeen years of independence, India had only a precarious foothold of influence in a sensitive Nepal, a tenuous influence in Bhutan through an uncooperative prime minister and a weak king, and a hated military-imposed occupation of Nagaland. China had shrewdly and successfully exploited the antagonisms at every level and in every situation to India's disadvantage.

My proposal to an obviously fascinated Jigme was to steal the Confederation of Himalayan States from China by suggesting that Tibet, Kashmir, and the tribes of North-East Indian Frontier such as the Nagas, be included, based on several reasonable assumptions. First of all, there would have to be some advantages for India as well as for China, and some disadvantages for China instead of an apparent free gift.

The next essential, therefore, would be the withdrawal of Chinese military forces in Tibet in return for the withdrawal of Indian forces from Bhutan and Sikkim. Despite the Chinese claims that the Tibetan people were living in peaceful friendship with the Chinese occupation force, they were highly vulnerable and knew it. That was what we intended to demonstrate with our film. Making the Himalayan States a buffer zone between India and China was a reasonable working proposition.

Another part of my proposal was that the Dalai Lama would return to Tibet on condition that the Chinese military forces were withdrawn. I knew that this was a possible consideration at the time in China because Prime Minister Nehru had sought to persuade the Dalai Lama to return to Tibet on this basis on assurances given to him by the Chinese.

Jigme heard me in silence until I had finished then asked, "What makes you think you'll be able to persuade that crowd around the Dalai Lama to agree? Surkhang, Yuthok and the others can plot as much as they like, even with you helping them, but I can tell you they haven't a chance. India wants the Tibet issue kept quiet and you know that Gyalu Thondup and Shakapba have too much to lose to do anything to annoy India."

"But, Jigs," I argued, "let's assume that Gyalu and Shakapba can be isolated, or better still, that their self-serving interests could be demonstrated to be advanced along with India and the Confederation - what then?"

"If you can get the Tibetan leaders to agree and accept this," he said slowly, "then I'm with you. Bhutan, Sikkim and Tibet - plus the others you mentioned - is a more likely proposition than just Bhutan and Sikkim. Nepal couldn't dominate such a group. But I suspect it hasn't a prayer. India and China won't touch it. You're mad, Patla. I always said it, now I know it for sure. Some bloody scriptwriter; Britain's secret weapon is more likely. Give my love to Meg and tell her to come and visit me sometime - preferably without you."

"Give my love to your wife, Tess," I grinned. "She has my sympathy as always in having you for a husband. We shall meet at Philippi."

"God - yours and mine - forbid," he riposted.

Now that I had started the ball rolling, the next step was to get something into the media so I went to see two Indian journalists I had known in the past, Pran Chopra of the Statesman, and Shan Lan of the Times of India, and had long discussions with them. They were naturally skeptical, but I saw they were intrigued enough to write up something about it.

Finally, I arranged to meet with the leader of one of India's Opposition parties, Minoo Masani of the Swatantra Party, who had protested in India's Parliament against the banning of my book. Before I went to meet him I called in on a whim to the leading bookshop in New Delhi's Connaught Square to ask if they had a copy of Peking Versus Delhi by George Patterson that I could present to Mr. Masani. The assistant didn't seem to know about it being banned and said he would find out if they had a copy. He came back with a colleague who took me aside for a private conversation, and he said, low-voiced, "We don't have that book but we have Fanny Hill"! For those who don't know about Fanny Hill, it was a major pornographic book before others became more sexually explicit.

I took a taxi to where Masani lived at Lodi Estate and asked the security guard at the reception desk for Mr. Masani. The man looked at me blankly and said, "There is no Mr. Masani living here."

He called out to an Indian gentleman who was hurrying past, "Sahib-ji, do you know a Mr. Masani?"

The man stopped and began to reply, then looked closely at me, his eyes lighting up with recognition. "Patterson Sahib," he declared delightedly.

I looked at the stocky, striking individual, with piercing black eyes and magnificently parted and curled Rajput-style beard and moustache, and dressed flamboyantly in an unusual embroidered tribal jacket. "Not Chahvan!" I said, with a mixture of pleasure and consternation.

"Yes, Chahvan," he said cheerfully. "What are you doing here in Delhi?"

"What are you doing here is more like it?" I asked him pointedly, then added hastily, "No, don't tell me. I have an important appointment and I'm running late."

"Who do you wish to see?" Chahvan asked curiously.

"Masani, the M.P." I replied.

"Masani?" he queried with rising inflexion. "What do you - ?" He stopped with a grin. "Masani doesn't live here."

"Lodi Estate," I said. "He gave me his address."

"Ah!" Chahvan exclaimed. "This is Lodi House. Lodi Estate is different. Come on, let's find a taxi and I'll give the driver directions."

"When am I going to see you?" he asked as I got into the taxi, and he had given the driver directions.

"I've only just got here," I said cautiously, "and I have a lot to do."

"You say the time," urged Chahvan in his lilting, Welsh-like accent, "and I'll come to - " he stopped suddenly as an idea seemed to strike him. "How long are you going to be with Masani?"

"Oh, an hour or so I would imagine," I replied, adding hastily, "but I must get back to the hotel for discussions with my colleagues. I am with a television film team."

"Then you must come straight back here," Chahvan said firmly," after you've seen Masani. Only for a little while. I tell you, you will be very interested. I have Mrs Chettri - you remember Maya Devi? - the M.P. from Darjeeling - coming to see me and you will want to be there. I know."

I laughed aloud. He was so typically the Chahvan I had known on scores of previous occasions - the "fixer", the "wheeler-dealer" par excellence. Nothing was too big for him to attempt, nothing too small for him to arrange. Did you want a bottle of whisky in a prohibition State? Chahvan would get you a case - Haigs or Grants? A copy of some secret official document? He would get a copy of the original. To meet a Minister? Chahvan would fix a time "at your convenience, sir". To arrange a party or a national revolution? "I have a certain plan right here, sahib." Occasionally, but only rarely, he would mess it up, but then he would bounce back again with an even more outrageous proposition. He was always good company, but I was in a hurry and late and didn't need anything fixed. I had a sudden thought. Perhaps I did.

"OK," I told him, laughing. "If I have time I'll come and see you later. If not, I promise I'll give you a ring soon."

"Where are you staying?" he persisted, and I grinned at him. He knew a brush-off when he saw it.

"Maiden's Hotel," I said.

"Right, sahib," he stood away from the taxi and gave a smart salute. "I'll expect you anytime up to midnight. Remember: Mrs Chettri, M.P., Darjeeling. Very useful to you."

I waved to him as we drove away, and found myself wondering what story Chahvan would be telling the mysterious Mrs Chettri about me. On the other hand, he must know something that would interest me. I would probably go.

Minoo Masani was very polite and understanding about my late arrival. Apparently, he had just written a letter to me in London seeking to discuss my book as he wanted to bring up the matter of its banning again in a formal protest in the Indian Parliament. He was an extremely able political leader of a party that had only a small but vocal influence. He wished to inform me that the question of my book was to be raised in Parliament shortly; and also, he had received a reply from the Home Minister saying that he hoped to be able to read my book before the official debate.

We discussed my proposal for a Confederation of Himalayan States, and he was dubious about the possibilities. He agreed that it had considerable value but he very much doubted whether either of the two major countries involved would consider it. But, meanwhile, he would discuss it with the veteran and respected Socialist leader, Jayaprakash Narayan.

I was on my way back to the hotel when I recalled Chahvan's invitation, and I told the taxi driver to take me there. I had scarcely settled into my chair, after the introductions, when Chahvan began sending out feelers regarding my real purposes in the Himalayas, tempting me with items of secret information in exchange. I smiled refusal, and he regarded me calculatingly, nodding his head slowly.

"I have it," he said suddenly. "Yak-breeding."

I looked at him curiously. "Yak-breeding?"

"Yes," he leaned forward in his chair, his piercing eyes alight with the excitement of a new idea. "What does yak-breeding suggest to you?"

"Tibetan butter tea," I suggested, humoring him. "Wool for carpets or Santa Claus beards?"

"Tibetan refugees," he said triumphantly. "You are going to do a film about Tibetan refugees, and there are lots of them in Nepal."

"But I said nothing about going to Nepal," I pointed out to him quickly (but was it too quickly? I thought, as I saw his shrewd eyes weighing my response), "And in any case Tibetan refugees don't breed yaks, and the Nepal government wouldn't allow a film to be made about Tibetan refugees in Nepal - or, at least, in the mountains where we would want to go."

Chahvan looked at me in undisguised triumph; ideas were boiling up his fertile mind, he felt he was on the right track, and he was looking for the right remark that would open the door to him for his next venture - at my expense.

"I don't know if the Tibetan refugees in Nepal breed yaks or not," he said smilingly, "but this or something like it would be your story for the Nepal government. Once there, with official permission, you could film, say, the Khamba rebellion or the new Chinese military road to Kodari. You could leave all the arrangements to me. I can fix it. You just employ me as your assistant and I can get you anything you want."

He was an impossible rogue. His impregnable assurance was breath-taking. And yet... He had brought off the most seemingly impossible feats for me in the past. And now he had me hooked again, as I sat pondering several ideas of my own; and he knew it as he sat back, stroking his luxurious moustache contentedly, his eyes gleaming with secret amusement.

"When I was in Nepal two years ago," I said tentatively, "cooperation from the Nepal government was not very evident."

"That was then; this is now," he said with unassailable confidence. "What do you want? To meet the Nepalese Ambassador here in Delhi? I can fix it. How about tomorrow morning? I'll even have him ready to give you permission before you arrive," he added with outrageous nonchalance.

"Let's keep away from fantasies," I warned him. "You have failed before, as I know only too well. I can make my own appointments with ambassadors."

"Sometimes," he waved away his past failures with a wave of his hand. "But take my advice. The Nepalese ambassador knows me, and he also knows that my cousin is chief of protocol in Kathmandu. So, he knows that if I go with you to Kathmandu I can get you anything you want - and any favor for himself that he chooses to ask me in exchange for his cooperation."

I was about to ask how the chief of protocol of the Nepal government came to be a cousin of his, when I suddenly recalled other occasions when I had challenged his claims.

One, more sweeping than some of the others, had been that his brother-in-law was a General in the Indian Army, at that time in command of a strategic area of interest to me, who, according to Chahvan, "was likely to be Commander-in-Chief". When I had this checked out, I found it to be true. And General Chaudhari was now chief of staff of the Indian Army. You could never tell with Chahvan.

"Right," I said, getting to my feet. "You win once again. We'll meet tomorrow morning at Gaylords in Connaught Circus for coffee, at, say, ten o'clock? I will bring Adrian Cowell, the producer, If you can convince him, you've got yourself a job."

He smiled happily, enthusiasm and excitement making him an even more bizarre and striking figure. "Leave it to me. From now on you have no more worries."

"From tomorrow," I corrected him, "I may have the greatest worry I have ever had. Good-night."

I left him and Maya Devi to carry on their discussion of Himalayan intrigues.

CHAPTER THREE

The Incorrigible Chahvan In Colorful Kathmandu

Next day, Adrian and I went to meet Chahvan. I had given a hilarious account to Adrian and Chris of my meeting and previous experiences with Chahvan, and they agreed that it might be a good idea to take him along on the project - especially since it looked as if we would be going through Nepal rather than Bhutan. We could try Chahvan in New Delhi to see how he fared with challenges there and, if he were useful, I would leave quietly for Kathmandu with him, while Adrian and Chris remained, ostensibly waiting for a reply from the Dalai Lama, but chiefly as decoys to cover my exploratory activities in Nepal.

Chahvan turned out to be in top form. When we met him he said he had already been making several enquiries at the Nepalese Embassy, and had found out that we would be very welcome to film in Nepal. But, he continued, the ambassador was about to leave that afternoon for a tour of Southeast Asia, and if we wanted to meet him, he, Chahvan, would have to get busy right away to arrange an appointment.

I was skeptical and expressed my doubts that this was possible. I thought it was a typical Chahvan flourish in gilding the lily.

"Ah, Mr. Patterson," he declared in affected pained surprise, "how can you say such a thing? Just give me permission and I will telephone the ambassador right away for an appointment, and you will see."

Adrian looked at me to see if Chahvan was serious, and I grinned back at him. I always enjoyed Chahvan's sorties, even when they were outrageous or failed. "Chahvan," I said gravely, "you have our permission."

"Right, sahib," he said promptly, and stepped purposefully towards the telephone behind our chairs. I turned in my chair to watch and listen, because I knew he was quite likely to put on a performance for our benefit without making an actual call. He dialed a number and said something in Nepali, then asked for the First Secretary. I only had a little knowledge of Nepalese phrases, but I understood enough to follow that, after a few words with him, obviously trying to persuade a reluctant official, he asked impatiently in English to be put through directly to the ambassador. I raised my eyebrows interrogatively at the amused Adrian and Chris.

Chahvan winked across at us in delight, then his face sobered and his voice became respectful and less demanding. He gave a glowing description of the well-known TV film team that had just arrived in New Delhi, with a distinguished author-journalist friend of his, Mr. George N. Patterson, as a member. He, Chahvan, was trying to persuade them to make a film in Nepal, with his assistance, and we had finally agreed to do so on condition that we were given every official cooperation. He was sure the ambassador appreciated the importance of such a film for Nepal, and would he agree to meet Mr. Cowell and Mr. Patterson to discuss the possibility? Before the ambassador had time for a polite refusal, Chahvan went on quickly and smoothly to anticipate any objection by adding that he was aware that the ambassador must be very busy, but, if he would agree to give us fifteen or twenty minutes of his valuable time, it could have great significance for the future of Nepal.

It was one of Chahvan's better performances, and I mimicked applause silently. Chahvan winked at me, a triumphant gleam in his eye as he listened to the ambassador, then held up his thumb in a gesture of success.

"Thank you, sir," he said politely. "Twelve o'clock. We will be there, and we promise not to delay you." He replaced the telephone and turned towards us with upturned hands and an expressive shrug of his shoulders. "There you are, gentlemen," he declared. "Is there anything else you would like? An appointment with the king?"

"I'll have a redhead with green eyes," I said sardonically.

"Right, sahib," he said confidently, "which nationality? Give me a few hours and you shall have her."

With less than two hours before meeting the ambassador we had to draw up yet another satisfactory and airtight supplementary mythical project. We had prepared two or three contingency plans and what we decided now was to outline a film project that was as close as possible to our true assignment while providing nothing that would raise official suspicions. We proposed, therefore, a film on "The Changing Face of Buddhism" which gave us wide latitude; it sounded religious enough not to raise suspicion, it was something that could interest someone with my "religious" reputation, and yet it was true that the Chinese military occupation of Tibet was changing the face of Buddhism. Also, Buddha's birthplace was in Nepal, as were several temples and places of pilgrimage, and this would justify our traveling outside the capital, Kathmandu. The one weakness of the mythical project was that it was restricted to the southern regions of Nepal and our goal was in the northern high Himalayas. But that problem could be solved later.

When we met the ambassador we spent a pleasant fifteen minutes over drinks discussing a brief outline of the proposed film, and he volunteered that he thought permission was possible and he would recommend it. But would we discuss the details with the First Secretary as, unfortunately, he had to rush off to catch a plane?

The next few days were filled with hectic preparations to get ready to move at a moment's notice. We planned that, if the Dalai Lama gave a definite date for an audience, I would have to return from Nepal to join Adrian and Chris on the trip to Dharamsalla to meet with him. If, on the other hand, the Dalai Lama delayed a reply or an appointment, as I expected, then Adrian would write to say that we had been called away urgently from New Delhi to Nepal and would write again on our return.

Chahvan was supremely confident that all our plans would be accomplished, not only because of his usual unassailable assurance but because, he insisted, it was God who had brought us together so remarkably in that unexpected encounter. I remarked caustically that it was more likely to be Satan, as far as he was concerned, with his Mephistophelian appearance and Machiavellian intrigues.

"'There is nothing so bad, but thinking maketh it so,'" Chahvan quoted piously, his eyes creasing mockingly.

"Where is that taken from?" Adrian asked him challengingly.

"Shakespeare," Chahvan replied promptly, "Much Ado About Nothing."

Adrian gazed at him with mock admiration. "Which Folio?" he asked, not really expecting an answer.

"I'm not sure," Chahvan said, with simulated modesty. "The fourth? I'm forgetting the classics these days. With my kind of life, one isn't always able to keep in educated company. That is why I appreciate being with Patterson Sahib and his journalist colleagues." He grinned across at me, conspiratorially recollecting with enjoyable rapport some of the incidents experienced together in what he had euphemistically termed "my kind of life."

We completed the usual formalities - visas, passports, photographs, money changed - in a mad rush over the next few days. Chahvan insisted, "Leave that to me, I can get seven rupees to the dollar instead of four." Chahvan and I were then ready to leave for Kathmandu while Adrian and Chris waited in New Delhi for word from the Dalai Lama or me.

Chahvan took over the plane to Kathmandu. He kept it waiting for five minutes at Safdarjung Airport in New Delhi while he made a sudden and probably mythical "important telephone call" just to enhance his importance He greeted the pretty Nepali air hostess with elaborate courtesy, detained her in earnest conversation as the plane took off, then, to my increasing embarrassment, requested as a priority that coffee should be given quickly to Mr. Patterson while she was distributing breakfasts. He helped her with the preparations, chatting cheerfully with the passengers, brought me papers and magazines, and only after I had finished breakfast did he settle down - beside the air hostess - to eat his own. I wondered what, beside his amorous intentions, he was up to.

After a long and serious conversation with the air hostess, he began to move about the plane, stopping to chat with the various passengers, in the course of which I heard snippets of conversation - "distinguished author-journalist", "international authority on Asia", "going to Nepal for talks with the Nepal government", "making television films for international distribution." I was annoyed, then amused, then intrigued as I considered what confused and bewildering stories would circulate in Kathmandu when we got there. If I could keep our real intentions from Chahvan I could safely leave all smoke screens and red herrings to him.

One of our greatest problems would be to get the films of Khamba guerrilla attacks on the Chinese safely out of the country, after we had successfully planned and accomplished the project. With Chahvan around we would not be short of ideas, but I would have a few of my own in reserve of which, hopefully, he would know nothing. From past experience I knew it could be done; it was very, very difficult! You not only had to be up early in the morning to outwit Chahvan, you had to be unsleeping. I had already considered the not unlikely possibility that Indian security had "planted" him on me, and rejected it in view of the circumstances of our meeting; but, if the price were high enough, Chahvan would agree with alacrity - and an engaging smile and convincing story.

Outside the plane windows, beyond the low-lying heat-haze that always lay over the plains of India, the Himalayan mountain range was distantly outlined against the deep blue of the sky. Brown patchwork fields slid away into the greeny-blue foothills as the ancient Dakota droned its monotonous way across India's plains towards the mountains of Nepal. There was some turbulence from the rising air currents and rearing mountains as we entered the foothills forming the gateway into Nepal.

Modern Nepal, according to modern geographers, was used to describe all the territory lying within the present Gurkha Kingdom; but, to the Gurkhas and the many other tribes, until the eighteenth century Nepal meant only the Nepal valley including Kathmandu, Bhatgaon and Patan - and no more. From that time the Kingdom had been expanded by warlike chiefs and petty kings to include the wide regions acknowledged in the present day, 520 miles in length, 100 miles in depth, and from the Sarda river, tributary of the Ganges, to the eastern border country of Sikkim.

Four large rivers, and the towering jutting mountain ranges covering the two northern levels of the country, split the country into almost impenetrable regions. Travel in the savage terrain was further complicated by a series of four "terraces", or four natural steps running the whole length of the country from north to east, from the plains to the peaks. First, there was the flat plain adjoining India; then the "Terai" with its heavy jungles and occasional clearings; then the "trans-Himalaya", the great central trough of valleys; and, finally, the "inner Himalaya", with peaks varying between 17,000 and 29,000-feet. In addition to the 51 peaks between 23,000 and 29,000 feet, there were an estimated further 38 unclimbed and unnamed peaks from 22,000 feet and upwards. It was so awesome that it was no wonder that the mountains were not just considered "habitations of the gods", but where the mountains themselves were often worshipped as gods.

There, in that savage and icy wilderness slowly being brought closer as the plane droned on into Kathmandu, lay our objective: to meet the Khamba guerrillas somewhere among the inaccessible tangle of mountains, cross, in a short and strictly limited period of time, some of the highest and most challenging peaks that mountaineering expeditions took months and even years to plan and accomplish, go behind the lines of what was considered the most ruthless army in the world, film what we assumed would be their defeat in an armed encounter, and then come back with the film successfully across the same mountains and jungles - without it being discovered or our being arrested or killed.

Kathmandu, the capital, lay just over the outer ring of mountains in the foothills. At one time it was said to have been a huge lake, about 242 square miles at an altitude of 4,500 feet above sea level. It was surrounded by dark-green tree-covered mountains, except where the millions of small terraced rice-fields rose like a giant's light-green step-ladder to the mid-level summits, with the eternally snow-covered backbone of the world's highest mountains behind.

The geographical isolation of Nepal from the plains of India not only produced a proud independence of character among the mountain tribes, it also bred a contempt for the "weaklings" of the plains. Consequently, they developed their own distinctive customs and forms of Hinduism. But while external politics and religions beyond their boundaries passed them by, internally the rise of the tribe and state of Gurkha transformed the country and its policies. The Gurkha kings and nobility were recognized and courted by the British, and the Gurkha warriors became a prized part of the British imperial system.

When Nepal was opened up to the outside world in 1951 the Kathmandu Valley had about a half-million inhabitants, but it was expanding phenomenally and space was being eaten up voraciously by the newcomers. The first automobiles for the new elite had been brought over the foothill mountains into Kathmandu on litters - and carried back to India for trade-in. The first road to India was built a few years later and, now, the modern bugbear of a heavy pall of smog hung over the valley from the exhaust fumes of the heavy traffic.

Our Dakota was flying between the steeply terraced sides of the mountains into the cupped jewel that was Kathmandu. Beyond the wing-tips the fantastically patterned green mountains were criss-crossed with pencil-like paths, and brown-thatched villages scattered among them. Beneath the airplane, an eye-caressing, patchwork counterpane of variegated greens and yellows were split by the glinting blue, green, grey and brown streams and rivers. The immensely rich soil of the Valley yielded three harvests every year and was almost self-sufficient in food grains.

Every arable square foot of land as far as the eye could see was cultivated, even reaching into the gardens of the city. In the center of the Valley, where rivers met and parted and met again lay the great golden-roofed temples and small red-brown houses of Kathmandu.

The temples were the most important part of Nepali life and the lives of the people were woven around worship in a variety of forms of Hinduism and Buddhism. As I recalled, it was almost time for the annual celebration of "Siva's Night" in Kathmandu's religious calendar. Nepal's paramount deity was Pashupati, one of the infinite number of avatars of the Hindu god, Siva, which could attract at least a hundred thousand worshippers to the erotically-ornamented temple shrine. A walk down the streets would show worshippers bathing in the Bagmati river amid incense and burning corpses, and, all around, scrambling and chattering rhesus monkeys splashing off the cremation ghats into the waters. Kathmandu's main tourist attraction was in the famed Durbar Square, along an avenue called Freak Street, where the world's hippie "flower-children" were gathered to indulge their hashish and marijuana drug habits, and to introduce a growing market in heroin and other modern designer drugs of abuse.

The Dakota touched down and taxied up in front of the long, single-storied, cream-colored airport offices. There were some scattered groups of spectators, several embarking passengers of various nationalities with friends come to see them off, all standing around chatting, relaxed and smiling in the warm sunshine.

And there was Boris. He saw me at the same time as I saw him.

"George!" he exclaimed in pleased surprise.

"Hello, Boris," I greeted him. "I gather from your surprise you didn't get my telegram?"

"When did you send it?" he asked.

"Yesterday," I replied.

"Then it will come tomorrow or the day after - or sometime," he said, laughing.

"Have you accommodation at the Royal?" I asked him anxiously.

"We'll find something," he answered. "Here, you go with my man to the hotel and he'll fix you up. I have to wait here to meet Doris Duke. Do you know her - the tobacco heiress? I'll see you later."

Boris was - well - Boris was Boris. It was difficult to describe Boris in anything less than a whole book: dancer with Diaghelev, gunrunner, chef, revolutionary, owner of nightclubs for top people, friend of Maharajahs, confidant of criminals, escort of some of the world's loveliest women, Boris was now owner of the leading hotel in Kathmandu, the Royal. Friend of the great, his generosity towards the poor and disadvantaged was legendary. We had been close friends for years and an important informant when I required some definite confirmation of a report.

After lunch Chahvan went off on his own, "to see a few people, arrange a few things" he said mysteriously. In the double room which we had to share, he was a strutting effervescent dynamo. Three different suits he hung in the wardrobe - Nepali, Indian, Western - plus several styles of loose shirts - handloom, khadi, bush, and fold-over blouse. He ordered a stream of bearers around, altered the setting of the furniture in the room to a more acceptable arrangement, gave instructions regarding our laundry, ordered the sweeper to do a better job of cleaning our bathroom, called for more papers, lights, a small table, another chair. When he finally departed - "to arrange your final program" - the room, the hotel, and even life itself, seemed to have acquired an empty space.

Knowing something of Nepali officialdom from previous experience, I did not accept Chahvan's optimistic forecast that he would be back in about two hours. Also, I knew something of Chahvan's capacity for picking up unexpected situations, and from them to conjure new opportunities of interest and profit. So I called for a taxi and went to pay a courtesy call at the British Embassy, whose First Secretary, Peter Wild, I had met during previous visits. While chatting with Peter, the new British ambassador to Nepal, Mr. (now Sir) Anthony Duff, came in and was introduced by Peter, with a thumb-nail sketch of my activities. The ambassador invited me to dine with him the following night.

When I returned to the hotel Chahvan had still not come back so I set out to gather what information I could on the present political situation in the country, especially who were the movers and shakers in the key circles of power. Until fifteen years before, Nepal had been a closed country to all foreigners, its feudal "Rana regime" an archaic anachronism introduced by a former power-hungry prime minister, who passed a law making the office of prime minister hereditary in the family without abolishing the institution of the monarchy. The second senior-most among the brothers held the office of commander-in-chief, and so on over all senior positions of rank. He also persuaded the king to issue a decree giving him power of life and death in the whole of Nepal, to nominate or dismiss all government officials, and to declare war or make peace with other countries.

But the promiscuity practiced by the leading families in Nepal, and the proliferation of children inside and outside of wedlock, necessitated a modification of the agnate system introduced, and so they created three categories of "Rana" administration. Those who were born in wedlock were

"Class A" entitled to the highest offices; those born out of wedlock but legitimatized afterwards were Class B who, together with "Class C" born out of wedlock, were not entitled to high office. Naturally, there was a great deal of intriguing for wealth, status and power.

The Indian freedom movement inevitably influenced the situation in Nepal. An underground "democratic" party had been formed along the same lines as the Indian Congress Party, who gave them financial and other support. In 1950 the Nepali Congress took to armed rebellion and, after successfully removing the king from the ruling Ranas, an agreement was signed to form a coalition government.

When the Chinese Communists invaded Tibet in 1950, this, with the increasing internal crisis in Nepal, compounded the confusion. A popular Nationalist led a successful revolt, then had to flee to China when it collapsed. The introduction of an Indian Military Mission gave rise to the belief that India was controlling the Army; and, when India offered financial assistance to build an 80-mile road from India to Kathmandu, this was bitterly denounced as an attempt to bring Nepal within India's influence.

Internally, corruption and nepotism grew to a magnitude never known before in the history of Nepal, even under the notorious Ranas. Venality in one form or another was openly practiced by everyone in authority. On December, 1960, the king had taken over "direct rule" and put the prime minister and other officials in jail.

Shortly after the king took over, the Chinese government announced that they approved his action "in the circumstances" and that they were extending further support to Nepal. A boundary agreement was signed, diplomatic relations were begun for the first time, and China offered to build a road from Tibet to Kathmandu - an offer which the king promptly accepted, and which infuriated an anxious India.

Now, inside Nepal, the king was still in full control; some political leaders who had agreed to work with his regime had been released from prison, other leaders I had known in the past were still being detained, and the chairman of the present council of Ministers - "a puppet body" I was told - was a Dr. Tulsi Giri, a Nepali politician I had never met.

Chahvan returned at six o'clock that evening, with bulging briefcase, purposeful stride, and a Nepali friend, whom he introduced as Mr. Josse. Mr. Josse, it appeared, was one of a family of merchants who had the largest business interests in Nepal. I had known his uncle, a member of the influential Gurkha League, some years before. Mr. Josse had come, said Chahvan, to invite me to the wedding of this uncle's son, to be held tomorrow. Chahvan leaned forward, his eyes moving from left to right conspiratorially:

"The elite of Nepal will be there," he said, *sotto voce*, as if there was a bugging device in the room, "including Dr. Tulsi Giri, the king's right-hand man. We will meet them all there socially, then - wham!" He struck his hands together with a loud smack. "Everything's fixed."

Mr. Josse smiled indulgently. Obviously he had known Chahvan for some time and was aware of his extravagances, so I had no need to soften my remarks. "It will be very useful for you to come," he agreed quietly, "but we would also like you to come just for the enjoyment of our wedding customs."

I expressed my appreciation for his thoughtfulness and courtesy and, after some polite conversation, Mr. Josse went off.

Just to keep Chahvan in a proper frame of mind - that is, in humble recognition of my superior intelligence - I gave him a bawling-out for being away so long on the important first day. He spread his hands expressively, expostulated that he was deeply engrossed in furthering my interests. In addition to the wedding invitation - he picked up his briefcase, opened it, took out a newspaper and pointed to an article as he handed it to me:

BREACH OF PROTOCOL BY CHINA
Direct Communication to Maharaja of Sikkim

"The Government of India has taken exception to the 'improper' procedure followed by China in sending a condolence message direct to the Maharaja of Sikkim on the death of his father last year.

"The Minister in the External Affairs Ministry, Mr. Lakshmi Menon, said that since India was responsible for Sikkim's external relations, China's action constituted a breach of protocol and disregarded India's treaty relationship with that Himalayan state.

"She said that so far as the Government was aware this was the first direct communication China had addressed to Sikkim. The Sikkim Government sent a reply to China directly."

"Ah-ha!" said Chahvan triumphantly. "You see - the Sikkim Government sent a reply to China directly. Our old friend, the Maharaja's son, wants to be free of India, as we have said all along. What about confederation now?"

I looked at him sharply. What did he know about my ideas on Confederation? Was it that he had just read some of my earlier articles, or had he found something out in his own inimitable fashion? But, if so, how? I decided to show no interest, except the casual remark that the Maharaja was probably just being provocative. But, inwardly, I added this latest news item, with considerable satisfaction, to the accumulating favorable circumstances I was weaving around our project.

CHAPTER FOUR

Chahvan Complications and Personal Plot Successes

The following morning we had a visit from Chahvan's cousin, Prakash Thakur, the chief of protocol. He was quite different from Chahvan in both appearance and manner - taller, stouter, more cherubic, suave, charming, and even more evasive. I got the impression that he was a man of many faces, and many loyalties - or, rather, many alignments.

I gave no hint of this, however, listening politely to his lengthy reminiscences of his early days with the militant Gurkha League, what he said as a member of a Gurkha Delegation to Prime Minister Nehru in favor of a Gurkha State - I wondered if he, too, had heard about my Confederation proposal from Chahvan or wherever? - and his complaints about General Tuker's conclusions in his book, The Gorkhas.

Eventually, he got around to our visit and its purpose, and he was fulsome about promises to help but vague about specific appointments or commitments. I resolved that this was one contact of Chahvan's on whom I would place little reliance, at least until I had made sufficient headway of my own through other channels. Once he saw which way the higher officials were likely to receive me he would no doubt decide then to do likewise, but until that time all I could expect from him would be flowery words.

My next appointment, arranged by myself, was with the king's press attaché, Renu Lal, who, I had been given to understand, had considerable experience with the king about what could or could not be written - or, in our case, filmed. I spent some time in polishing the details of my approach because, after the press attaché, I would have to work within the outlines specified and not "off-the-cuff" as I had been doing until then.

When I went to the palace offices I met the saturnine Renu Lal, who was dressed in black Western jacket and tight white jodhpur trousers of the official class, and leaning back casually in his chair. I also sat easily in my chair to give the same appearance of confidence - and lack of guile - and said: "I have three matters which I would like to discuss with you, Mr. Lal. The first is that we are a television unit under contract to produce several films on Asian affairs, and our first subject is that of Tibetan refugees. We have asked for an audience with the Dalai Lama to discuss and film this, and my colleague, Adrian Cowell, is still in New Delhi waiting for a reply. Since Nepal has a considerable number of Tibetan refugees it comes directly within our sphere of interest. However, there is not sufficient reason to attract us to Nepal to film refugees unless we are permitted to travel outside the Kathmandu Valley in order to film them in their natural environment in the mountains.

"I may say at this point," - and I sat up to emphasize my frankness and importance of communication - "that we have no wish just to go about filming unfortunate Tibetans in camps. We are interested in the subject from the political angle." I noted his heightened interest. "That is, the Dalai Lama has persuaded several countries to receive and train Tibetan refugees in various skills, and he must now decide what is to be the future of these trained refugees."

I spread my hands, and sat forward in my chair, and he shifted to follow me, his interest fully caught. "Is it the Dalai Lama's intention to have 'Little Tibets' in each country? In India, Nepal, Sikkim, Bhutan - even in

Switzerland, Denmark or England?" I asked, rhetorically. "Many Tibetans are either finishing technical training in these countries, or are thinking in terms of marriage or settling down. Whatever their problem, they also face this decision which only the Tibetan leaders can resolve - has Tibet itself any realistic future? The Dalai Lama is not only their spiritual leader but also their temporal leader, and as such he is responsible for political decisions. If he evades or abdicates this responsibility then his senior officials must take the decision for him."

I swung the subject around while his interest was still focused.

"You, in Nepal, come in here with between ten and twenty thousand Tibetan refugees in a very strategic part of your northern territory on the borders of Tibet. With your government's permission we would like to film some of them in this setting."

Then, before he had time to let his mind dwell on this and begin to suspect something, I moved smoothly on. "We are also contemplating doing another film, or maybe working the theme into the same film, of 'The Changing Face of Buddhism'. You must have noted the near-elimination of Lamaistic Buddhism in Outer Mongolia, the destruction of the religious infrastructure in Tibet, and the growing political character of Buddhism in countries like Burma, Ceylon, South Vietnam and Japan?" He nodded, and I thought with satisfaction that he was hooked, and continued: "This is what we want to portray and analyze, together with the usual important aspects of Nepal as Buddha's birthplace, its early Buddhist temples and places of pilgrimages, and any other useful background material."

"Finally," I slowed down, put my fingers together thoughtfully in a triangle under my chin and, after a significant pause, looked straight at him meaningfully, "I would like to discuss with your leading officials the possibility of a Confederation of Himalayan States."

It came as a shock to him and he sat upright in his chair. A shutter seemed to drop behind his eyes, and he sat very still for a few moments waiting for me to continue. But I sat back to let him absorb it as if I had said everything I had to say.

"What - " he began, and as the word emerged throatily he coughed and began again. "What do you mean by a Confederation of Himalayan States?"

"Well," I said, judiciously, "it's a big subject, much too big and time-consuming to discuss now. But briefly, I know from previous visits and conversations in Nepal that Nepalese leaders have for some time been interested in a federation or call-it-what-you-will of Himalayan territories, such as Nepal, Bhutan, Sikkim and other Nepali-inhabited areas. In my opinion this never had a chance of materializing. But due to recent developments I can see how there might be proposed and formed a Confederation of Himalayan States that would include Nepal, Bhutan, Sikkim and Tibet. This I would like to discuss with your leaders, both for writing and filming, with their approval."

There it was. For good or ill the chips were all on the table, to win or lose it all. From now on, in various ways and with different emphases, these three subjects would be passed upwards in Nepalese circles and outward in Kathmandu's diplomatic gatherings. Hopefully, in all the talks, what we really wanted to film inside Tibet would be missed, and as I was passed from official to official, and diplomat to diplomat, the two subjects of Tibetan refugees and political Buddhism would coalesce into what everyone would suspect was my true "scoop" interest, the Confederation of Himalayan States.

www.classictravelbooks.com

Chahvan and I went straight from the interview with the press attaché to the Josse wedding. The father was chairman of the Chamber of Commerce, a privy councillor and a director of the Royal Nepal Airways Corporation. The cream of Kathmandu royal, government and social circles were present. The wedding festivities were to be spread over a period of several days, but today was the first and most important occasion. A huge marquee had been erected in the forecourt of the two-storied nondescript house and lesser dignitaries were gathering there when we arrived.

On the other side of the marquee a twelve-man band, in gaudy uniforms with black facings and white epaulets and gloves, was blaring forth a selection of Nepali and Western popular tunes. Outside the house were the leaders of Nepal, including Chahvan's "friend", General Shamser, whom I recognized now as one of the people on the plane with us.

But, as might have been expected, it was Chahvan who stole the show. When the chairman of ministers arrived and was being introduced deferentially to the waiting and respectful groups of guests, inevitably he came to Chahvan beside me - gleaming eyes, upswept pomaded moustache and curling beard triumphing over what was for him the restraint of a modest Nepali handloom outfit which he had worn for our palace appointment.

"This is Chahvan, Dr. Giri," said the host's son politely. Dr. Giri smiled pleasantly. "Chahvan? I've heard of you. Where are you from?"

"Nowhere," Chahvan said conversationally. "Everywhere," he added, his eyes gleaming with amusement at the shocked expressions around him. "I am, sir, a professional exile," he concluded with an infectious laugh. There was a hesitant and slightly uneasy murmur of laughter and comment from others.

Dr. Giri looked amused. "Where was your last exile?" he asked.

"Delhi - Dehra Dun - Darjeeling." Chahvan dismissed them all with an airy wave of his hand.

The father of the bridegroom smilingly interjected: "Chahvan is the man who organized our Gurkha League activities in Assam and Darjeeling, sir. He is a kind of frontier rebel."

Dr. Giri and the others looked at Chahvan with renewed interest. "And what are you organizing here?" Dr. Giri asked jokingly.

I saw it coming, but could do nothing to stop it. "Confederation, sir," Chahvan said with calculated devastation. There was complete silence for a moment and then Dr. Giri moved on.

I gazed at Chahvan with a mixture of awe, fury, disgust and sheer admiration. With cold logical planning I had laid a foundation on which to build a platform of discussion of an extremely delicate and dangerous implication. Chahvan, with instinctive political acumen and consummate sense of showmanship knew that the subject would now be discussed in every leading household for weeks to come - with himself as the center of interest. "What did Chahvan mean by Confederation"? "Was Chahvan serious or joking?" "Is Chahvan really organizing something about Confederation?" "What are Chahvan and Patterson doing about this Confederation?"

I emitted a snarl at Chahvan, who merely grinned delightedly, but as I reflected on the possibilities my annoyance with him diminished and my excitement grew. It would all help to further my own purposes. This was my own field of expertise, acquired through years of experience among practiced Oriental political manipulators. I had never played chess, I was uninterested in bridge or other cards games, but in the intricate game of Oriental politics I played instinctively, sifting, weighing, calculating, analyzing, bluffing, tantalizing, forcing and persuading people and events. And now here, with a challenging "impossible" assignment involving the two armies of India and China threatening war, five countries suspicious of each other and watching every move and statement, my own gambit to come out ahead was being jeopardized by a one-word joke from the mouth of an outrageous Oriental poseur.

I would have to start a few more hares, drag a few more red herrings, toss a few more stones into the pool, and add some home-truths - to mix a few metaphors - if the subject of Confederation were to become a serious talking point and not a joke. Chahvan could be expected to complicate the situation time and again, because it was his nature to be provocative and amusing. We were united together like the proverbial frog and scorpion. The fable was that the scorpion wanted to cross a river but the frog was unwilling to agree to take him on its back because of the scorpion's dangerous reputation. But eventually the scorpion persuaded the frog by pointing out that the frog would be safe because the scorpion needed him to take him across to the far side of the river. However, while they were in the middle of the river the scorpion stung the frog fatally and, as it was dying, the frog asked him why he had done that when he was about to drown as a consequence; "Because it's just my nature," the scorpion replied, and drowned.

I had to admit, as I usually ended up doing with Chahvan, that he provided a piquancy and challenge that gave me more pleasure than exasperation. Nevertheless, at some point I was going to have to decide whether I would risk having him "on my back".

I left Chahvan at the wedding boisterously enjoying himself while I went to dinner with the British ambassador.

He had just arrived in Nepal a few days before and his wife and family were still on their way there. Also invited to dinner were the military attaché, a Colonel Charles Wylie, a well-known Himalayan mountaineer; and a Mickey Weatherall, a construction engineer, and his wife, Kay. Both of the men had had years of experience in Nepal, especially Wylie through his association with the British Gurkhas, so I gradually eased the subject of Confederation into the talk. But on this occasion I was strictly factual, in the context of briefing the ambassador regarding the politics of Nepal and her neighbors: the Chinese military build-up in Tibet, the logistical problems in vast mountain terrain, the vulnerability of lines of supply, the difficult Indian military position in Sikkim and indefensible Bhutan, the uncertain military disposition in Assam with the anti-Indian Nagas. It was a very pleasant and useful evening, and I felt I had a friend in the new ambassador - but I wondered what was likely to happen if we were successful in our secret assignment.

I had allowed myself two days in Kathmandu to get organized; or, to be more exact, I had decided to give the impression in that time of being in Kathmandu only for a short visit of two days for preliminary discussions. I knew how difficult it was to get any quick decisions in the East. As Rudyard Kipling had written sardonically about the individual who tried it in ***The Naulahka***:

> "The end of the fight is a tombstone white
> with the name of the late deceased,
> And the epitaph drear: 'A Fool lies here
> who tried to hustle the East.'"

I knew with even greater certainty that quick decisions in what passed for "normal" times in Nepal were next to impossible. But my "cover" story had to be watertight to allay the suspicions of many shrewd officials, who were aware of my reputation. I was helped unexpectedly by the news that the king was somewhere up-country, so I requested urgent permission "to film the king among his people" to help the world-wide image of Nepal. I had heard that there was a deadline for the return of the king to Kathmandu shortly, and I used this to impress on government officials the need for a quick decision.

Meanwhile, I made contact with some leading Tibetan refugees in Kathmandu and, after establishing my bona fides with them, I cautiously approached the subject of the Khamba guerrilla groups in the high Himalayas. Because my main dialect in speaking Tibetan was the Khamba version, which I used with the greatest facility, I learned from the Khambas among the Kathmandu refugees that there were two groups operating independently of each other in the region of Mustang, to the north-east of Kathmandu. It was obvious from their reluctance to discuss this that the Kathmandu refugees were both in awe and fear of these armed groups; awe, because of their fighting ability and daring; and fear, because they did not wish any snooping Nepali officials to know that they had any information about the Khamba activities. It was safer to deny all knowledge of what was going on in such remote areas.

What I did learn from the refugees was that the two groups of Khamba guerrillas in the mountains did not approve of each other. Gradually I learned that the group in the Mustang region was being secretly helped with arms and ammunition - possibly from America or Taiwan, but with the collusion of India and channeled through Gyalu Thondup, the Dalai Lama's brother. The second group, operating to the east of Mustang, in a remote region known as Dzum, did not approve of Gyalu Thondup's self-serving politics and activities, and so they were not being supplied by him, and were having to find arms and ammunition from their successful raids against the Chinese military convoys inside Tibet.

I did not take Chahvan with me when I visited the Tibetans, considering that the further away he was kept from any association with our real objective the safer our project would be. I did not distrust his loyalty, but his penchant for the flamboyant and mysterious made him unreliable in such sensitive matters - it was his "nature", like the scorpion's, that I distrusted in a crisis. He did not seem to mind as he followed up his own inclinations and interpretations of the "Confederation" speculations, and his activities served to distract the Nepali officials as they considered him my "front man" as he claimed so vociferously.

I was typing up my notes, writing letters to various officials, and making telephone calls, while Chahvan used the telephone when I wasn't using it to try to fix an appointment with the private secretary of the chairman of ministers, Dr. Tulsi Giri. He was visibly impatient with the prevarication he was experiencing, and he said irritably to me, "Juddhabir Lama is the son of Santabir Lama, who you must be knowing."

"From Darjeeling?" I asked with quickened interest. "Or, rather, Sukhiapokri, near Darjeeling?"

"That's the one," Chahvan confirmed. "His two sons, Juddhabir and Amir are now working for the Nepal government, holding good positions, and it is said that Juddhabir is influential with the king and Dr.Giri."

"Well, well, well," I said reflectively.

Chavan gave me an alert look, sensing something of interest. "What is it?"

"I have met Juddhabir Lama," I told him, "a few years ago in Darjeeling. In fact, his brother, Amir, owes his life to my wife and me."

Chahvan gazed at me with a mixture of incredulity and respect, giving way to delight as the possibilities raced through his agile mind.

"Amir Lama was brought into my wife's hospital nearly dead," I went on. "My wife held out very little hope for him, told his family that she must operate immediately but that there was little chance of the operation being successful at this late stage. To complicate matters more, he would require blood transfusions on a large scale. There was no blood bank available in Darjeeling, so my wife sent for me to come and have my blood tested so that I could donate blood. It was a match, and I was placed on a surgical table next to Amir and my blood transferred to him. Miraculously, he did recover, although his pulse actually stopped during the operation, and the family was deeply grateful to us for what had been done. Some time afterwards we visited their home during a holiday in East Nepal, and it was then we met the other members of the family, including Juddhabir."

Chahvan was excited at the account and began extrapolating several possibilities arising from this intriguing connection and how it could be used to our advantage. I held up my hand to stem the flow.

"No, no, no," I shook my head at him in mild rebuke. "This has to be played cool - and subtle, above all, subtle. We don't go asking for a return of favors; we don't even mention a straight request. Just leave it to me - and watch a maestro at work."

Chahvan grinned. "Yes, sahib," he said with mock deference. "You are the boss."

I found Juddhabir's name and number was registered under Dr. Giri's official residence, and I decided to just drop in on him in an unannounced visit. When Chahvan and I entered his office he took one look at me and exclaimed immediately, "Mr. Patterson! I didn't know you were here. Is Dr. Patterson with you?"

"No," I replied, "she is in London with the children. I am out here on a special assignment on my own - with some colleagues, of course, to do a film."

"Sit down and tell me about it," Juddhabir waved to some chairs. "This is a pleasant surprise."

"Tell me," I added, "before we talk business. How is Amir?"

"Very well," Juddhabir replied. "He has only recently returned from a visit to China and is out of Kathmandu at our family home, but his wife and son will want to meet you, I'm sure. His son has,- what do you call it? A hare-lip? - and they would love to have an expert surgeon like your wife to advise about it."

"I would like to see them," I acknowledged. "Also, my wife will be interested in news about his wife and son. She was talking about him recently when she had a patient in London with a condition like his experience in Darjeeling."

"We must get together for a meal," Juddhabir said firmly. "Amir may be going to England soon, and on to the United States, and he will want to talk it over with your wife. Now, what can I do to help you?"

I outlined the same proposal to Juddhabir that I had given to the king's press attaché, but added that I would like to meet with Dr. Giri to talk about Confederation; if possible, before I left Kathmandu to return to New Delhi for a possible appointment with the Dalai Lama.

"That I will arrange," he assured me confidently. "I'm sure you will be given permission to film in Nepal, because it is our government's position that we should publicize our present policies."

"You realize," I said seriously, "that we don't want to just film government-approved development projects? We want an interesting angle to reflect Nepal's increasing importance in international as well as regional affairs. Keep in mind that we represent not only an audience of some eight million viewers in Britain, but at least a hundred million across the world when the film is distributed."

"I'm certain that will interest the government," Juddhabir said slowly and thoughtfully. "I will arrange for Dr. Giri to meet with you." I noted the construction of the sentence with interest; normally he would have said "for you to meet Dr. Giri". "Unfortunately, tomorrow is a holiday. If you talk with me the day after I will have more definite word then."

We chatted socially about mutual friends in the Darjeeling area for a while and then we left.

Chahvan was ecstatic. "After Dr. Giri, the king," he exclaimed, punching the air. "The sky's the limit - and even that is not impossible because the king is also a god here."

Chahvan's public declaration about Confederation had created the talking point I had anticipated, and my own more calculated and informative discussions had provided more interest and impetus. With every position I varied the emphasis, depending on the individual's status, or official position, or political nous. I delayed my departure to New Delhi for discussions with Adrian and Chris with the prospect of a quick meeting with Dr. Giri. He was the most powerful man in the country after the king, and I knew that Juddhabir would inform him of my professional background in considerable detail.

When I next spoke with Juddhabir it was obvious that he had been informed of the extent of my discussions regarding Confederation, because he raised some shrewd possible objections. But I noted that none of them were from Nepal's point of view; they were all what China might think or do in such a possible development.

"What about India?" he argued. "In the event of China withdrawing from Tibet wouldn't India take advantage of that to move into the vacuum?"

"Not if India's withdrawal from Bhutan and Sikkim - and the Military Mission in Nepal - were part of the quid pro quo agreement," I replied. "A few years ago I discussed this very possibility with leading Indian military commanders, and they agreed that Bhutan and Sikkim were not defendable anyway against any determined Chinese attacks."

"And what about Bhutan and Sikkim?" he asked. "You have contacts there, haven't you?"

I smiled at him. "Wait to hear this. Only last week in New Delhi I spoke to Jigme Dorji about the possibility, and he said if the Dalai Lama, for example, made such a proposal, and it was accepted, then Bhutan would definitely be interested in such a confederation - but on condition that the Tibetan government was progressive and not the old feudal one ruled by discredited nobles and monks."

"Why don't you do this while I'm waiting for Dr. Giri to respond about your appointment. See General Khatry, the foreign secretary, and talk to him about your film project, but keep off Confederation until you have spoken with Dr. Giri. If he raises the subject say you will be happy to talk it over with him later. I will also set up a meeting for you with the director of publicity, Mr. Banskota, as you will also require his official permission to film."

I thanked him for his help and arranged a meeting with General Khatry, the foreign secretary. At our meeting I outlined the proposals for the TV film on Nepal along the lines I had described officially with the press attaché. The foreign secretary was polite, intelligent, taciturn, but not obviously suspicious as he listened, then he said he thought it was too late to join the king's tour now but that he would send a radio message to His Majesty to find out. He also said he would like to talk about Confederation at a later date, and I said I would be happy to do so at his convenience.

When I returned to the hotel Juddhabir telephoned to say that he had fixed an appointment to meet with Dr. Giri two days later. Dr. Giri had been very interested in the Confederation idea and looked forward to discussing it with me. He also indicated that there should be no objections to the film project.

Juddhabir escorted me into Dr. Giri's office and introduced me as "the well-known journalist, Mr George Patterson." After chatting about my highly publicized confrontation with India's Prime Minister Nehru over the issue of Tibet, he said that we could proceed with arrangements for making the film we had requested. When I had thanked him, he went straight into the subject of Confederation.

I proceeded cautiously, conscious that this was no longer a game but a serious political matter. I passed quickly over what might have been told him by others, and was only elaboration of the central idea, to the reasons why I thought it was a feasible proposition, if Nepal and Tibet agreed. He sat listening quietly, only occasionally asking a question, until I had finished. Then he gave his reasons why he thought it was not possible - but, I noted with rising excitement, none were based on Nepalese objections.

I sat forward and said intently, "But, Dr. Giri, I agree that neither China or India would want such a Confederation. My contention is based on the premise that they do not want it but can be persuaded to accept it. China will be in a position to ignore regional or international attitudes, so it is imperative that any possible action should be taken immediately. China is seeking United Nations' representation, and from reports emerging from China she is prepared to accept the Dalai Lama's return under certain conditions. The Dalai Lama, therefore, could offer to return on condition of China's withdrawal - for three reasons:

"One, because the basis of the United States' objection to China entering the U.N. is China's invasion of Tibet, and withdrawal would eliminate that objection. Two, because the counter-proposal that Indian military withdrawal from Bhutan and Sikkim should be a part of the condition would satisfy 'face-saving', and also reduce the possibility of a Sino-Indian border war. Three, because it would not tie China down to the presently unacceptable Colombo proposals with the restrictions on China, and would enhance China's 'peace' image in Asia and the world."

Dr. Giri was now obviously interested. "And India?"

"India," I replied, "naturally would be very reluctant to part with her influence in Bhutan and Sikkim. But, from my talks with Indian military leaders, there would only be token objections to withdrawal from Bhutan and Sikkim, especially if the countries were to be neutralized. Remember, India's greatest military commitment is only in Sikkim, with about fifty thousand troops and equipment dependent on a single narrow road from the Tibet mountains to the Indian plains."

"Bhutan?" Dr. Giri was definitely intrigued.

"I spoke with Jigme Dorji a week ago, and he said, if Tibet came into the Confederation, Bhutan would come in."

"How do you see such a Confederation being proposed?" Dr. Giri enquired. "Neither Bhutan nor Sikkim has authority to do it because of their association with India, and the Dalai Lama is not permitted political activities in India."

I smiled as beguilingly as I could. "My proposal is that the Dalai Lama make a non-political proposal for peace in Asia in his spiritual capacity, and offer his return to Tibet as his contribution to peace in Asia. Of course, in the interests of peace China would withdraw, and so would India. Only Nepal, of the Himalayan countries, has the diplomatic status and established machinery to carry forward the proposals in the United Nations. This, in turn, would increase Nepal's international image."

"So," Dr. Giri sat back in his chair, and said slowly, "the key to success of your proposal lies in the Dalai Lama's willingness to make his offer to return; and then, in Nepal taking up the proposal and acting as honest broker between India and China?"

"Yes," I nodded agreement. "Another thought to be considered. If there is initial interest in the four countries of Nepal, Bhutan, Sikkim and Tibet, then it might be extended to include Kashmir, the North-East Frontier Agency and Nagaland, making a two-thousand-mile Himalayan buffer between China and India."

Picking up a pencil Dr. Giri scribbled a few notes in silence, and then said crisply, "If the Dalai Lama will make such a statement then Nepal will cooperate fully. But he must make the first move, and then there must be detailed cooperation between Tibet and Nepal regarding the next steps."

"That is more than I considered possible," I told him sincerely, but wondering what I was going to do with this developing political bombshell I held in my hand. I had only meant it as a conversational decoy and smokescreen, and now it looked as if I was launching a serious diplomatic initiative. "I still don't know how the Dalai Lama will respond. I am still waiting to have an audience with him."

"What about Britain and the United States?" he asked interestedly.

I smiled at him ruefully. "To tell the truth, I don't know, but I guess they would not be too pleased to hear about it."

Dr. Giri smiled and rose to his feet, holding out his hand. "It has been very interesting, Mr. Patterson. I look forward to hearing more."

I thanked him for receiving and hearing me and left, satisfied with my progress to date.

When I returned to the hotel, the usual daily newspapers from India had arrived, and I was interested to see the prominent news of a speech by the Dalai Lama on the anniversary of the Tibetan revolt. According to the Indian daily newspaper, The Statesman, he said:

"The Dalai Lama has appealed to freedom-loving countries 'not to be misled by the propaganda of the Communist Government of China but to continue to help the unfortunate people of Tibet...'

"Recalling the Tibetan struggle against the Chinese, the Dalai Lama says thousands of Tibetans have been massacred, thousands have been rendered homeless, and thousands of others have escaped to neighboring states.

"But the barbarous atrocities, even to the extent of exterminating the race and religious belief of the Tibetans, still continue, and the struggle of the people still goes on..."

It was very significant, coming as it did at this very time of our project to help publicize the ongoing Tibetan revolt against the Chinese, that the Indian government was either relaxing its strict control of the Dalai Lama's "political" statements or the Dalai Lama was becoming more insistent on being heard despite Indian opposition.

The next day the Dalai Lama's brother made another public statement, which was widely publicized in Nepal, that the Dalai Lama was considering visiting some neighboring Buddhist countries. The thought leaped to my mind, that it probably meant Nepal, because Nepal was where Buddha had been born. I wondered if it was likely to happen in the near future when we could film the occasion and include it in our film - or as another possible film on the subject of Confederation!

I had the Prime Minister's verbal permission to make our proposed film, and I had a respectable cover under which to operate while making arrangements. But now, with the permission, it was necessary to move from the conspicuous Royal Hotel, where all our contacts were easily seen, to less exposed quarters. In making our film arrangements we would be meeting with some very suspicious-looking individuals who would draw attention in a popular leading hotel. Accordingly, I made arrangements for our television team to stay in the Imperial Hotel, whose Chinese owner I knew when she lived in Darjeeling.

From the time I had returned from my successful interview with Dr. Giri, Chahvan had been typing furiously, presumably setting up more deals with his contacts. When I told him about our move to the Imperial Hotel he argued against it, claiming that it would "damage our reputation." I told him our reputation was already damaged having him as our associate, but he wasn't in a mood for repartee. He said to go ahead and he would move the next day as he had several important letters to complete, and I agreed. He was welcome to his commercial and other enterprises so long as they didn't interfere with our plans.

However, when he did not turn up on the following day, I went looking for him and found him still ensconced in the Royal Hotel, still typing furiously, and with no signs of leaving. I asked him what games he was playing at our expense, and he gave a long, complicated explanation about having to watch mysterious strangers living in the Royal

Hotel. I told him, if he was too busy to join us, to pay the bills himself. He said grandly that he worked for no man, only for Chahvan, and Chahvan's interests, and I replied, "Fair enough; consider yourself fired." I paid our bill at the hotel, and told them that Chahvan was now their responsibility and left. I was sure that I had not heard the last of Chahvan, but it wasn't the first time he had disappeared on some project of his own. My only concern was that his machinations might rebound to our disadvantage. I guessed it would add interest to the growing drama in which we were now inextricably involved.

CHAPTER FIVE

National, Regional, International and Family Problems

In Delhi, Adrian and Chris still had not heard from the Dalai Lama, but we decided by telephone that, having Prime Minister Giri's permission to film in Nepal, we should go ahead with arrangements there. I went to the Kathmandu Gauchar Airport to meet their plane's arrival at ten o'clock in the morning.

Every time I had arrived at, or departed from, the Kathmandu airport it had looked like a social event. There seemed always to have been arriving or departing notables of some kind, or scores of tourists being met or seen off, and the place a riot of color and babble of voices. I had even seen servants handing round drinks and trays of appetizers like a cocktail party in the departure section. It was all very relaxed, informal and pleasant.

That day was no exception. Red-robed Tibetan monks, and tall powerful Tibetan traders leaving for some up-country destination; Indians in spotless white shirts and *dhotis,* the loose baggy trousers; with their wives and daughters in brilliantly colored and graceful saris; Nepali merchants and officials in smartly cut jackets and trim light jodhpurs, with their khol-eyed and rouged wives and daughters. The British were usually represented by the traditional sober dark suits, complete with old-school striped ties, moving with proper protocol from group to group. Americans were easily identified, too, with their lightweight seersucker suits or open-necked tunic shirts, wives or girl-friends in designer dresses or, at the other extreme, tight shorts, dark glasses and shoulder-bags. The rise and fall of conversation was broken by the occasional shouts of airport officials and scurrying porters, loudspeaker announcements and the staccato coughs and roars of arriving and departing aircraft.

Adrian and Chris stepped off the plane, with several other passengers, among whom I was surprised and delighted to see was T.C.Tethong, the Dalai Lama's representative in New Delhi. His visit to Kathmandu could not have come at a better time had I been in the position to cable and ask him. As we waited for baggage to be unloaded and checked through Customs, I chatted with T.C. and discovered that he had made no prior arrangements for transport and lodgings in Kathmandu. I had a word with the owner of the Imperial Hotel, Mung Hsueh, and fixed him up as a guest at the hotel - which meant we would have plenty of opportunities to talk unobserved.

It was time to push ahead rapidly with our plans now that we were all together as a team. Every day our movements and contacts would be scrutinized by a variety of individuals for their own purposes. We not only had to plan and execute the making of the film successfully, we had to get it out of the country on our return, with the best brains of five countries determined to stop us. So, from the time of our arrival we laid our plans. In Customs, we meticulously reported every canister of film we had with us so that there would be no likelihood of bureaucratic obstruction when it came to leave. I knew from bitter experience how the best laid schemes could go wildly wrong at the last minutes in Customs because of an ambitious or avaricious official. Like all good detective stories, our plot had to be conceived from the anticipated conclusion at the end backwards to the beginning.

We began a round of telephone calls to make appointments for Adrian, as producer-director of the team, to meet the various officials I had met as well as others, particularly the director of publicity, Mr. Banskota. After some discussion it was agreed that Adrian and Chris would visit him on their own, as I had already talked with him the day previously regarding the film and appointment.

When Adrian and Chris arrived at his office in the government secretariat, there was no sign of Mr. Banskota. The secretary did not know at what time he would come. Adrian asked the secretary for another appointment, and the secretary said noon of that same day. Adrian returned at noon, and there was still no sign or news of the elusive Banskota. Adrian asked for another appointment and was told two p.m. At two p.m. Banskota was there, but without explanation or apology, and very formal and coldly official. What could he do, he asked, as if he had never heard of the film or the television team. Adrian asked for an official permit to film as verbally approved by the Prime Minister, and Banskota said he would be in touch. Adrian said to me that he feared the worst. Banskota was the quintessential bureaucratic obstructionist.

Meanwhile I had met up with Amir Lama. While Adrian and Chris were wandering around the labyrinthine eighteen-hundred-room government secretariat looking for the offices of the various officials, I had an unexpected but very welcome visit from Amir Lama, brother of Juddhabir, whose life had been so dramatically saved by my wife. Both he and his brother were good-looking and intelligent, with Amir the more intense and charismatic of the two. After exchanging family news we got down to our present activities. He listened with interest as I outlined our "official" program - as opposed to our clandestine one, which we were keeping strictly to ourselves - especially the subject of Confederation. Then I asked about his political career since we met.

He laughed. "Did you hear that after you left Darjeeling and India I joined you in the doubtful distinction of being one of the few people to be expelled from India?"

"No," I exclaimed, surprised, "I didn't even know you were involved politically in anything likely to be subversive,"

"I was even more unique than you," he laughed delightedly at the memory, "because I was the only Indian citizen, although a Nepali by birth, to be expelled from my own country."

"How did you manage that?" I asked, fascinated, because I had never heard it of him or any other.

"Political activities," he smiled provocatively. "In support of His Majesty, King Mahendra of Nepal. For expressing approval of his action in taking over direct control in Nepal to the disapproval of the Indian government, I was expelled from Darjeeling District, as you were, with wife and family. I came here to Kathmandu, was offered a good position in His Majesty's government, and took up residence here. I am one of His Majesty's nominees to the National Panchayat, a useful platform for future interests."

"Congratulations," I said. "Do I get to hear what these future interests are likely to be?"

"Well, I'll tell you what has been happening. Shortly after I came to Kathmandu the king also appointed me President of the Buddhist Society, and as such I was invited to China as leader of a delegation of Buddhists. When the Indians heard of this invitation, and my acceptance, there was an outcry in their media and I was attacked for this as a subversive manoeuver, everybody claiming that I was not only a Nepali undercover agent but a pro-Communist as well!"

As Amir talked, my mind was leaping away on another new and exciting possibility. If Amir was President of the Nepalese Buddhist Society, then he would be a key figure in any link between Nepal and Tibet. Just how, at the moment, eluded me, but I could feel it shuttling around tantalizingly at the back of my mind. Amir was talking of his visit to China, and the favorable impression it had left on him.

"I asked Prime Minister Chou En-Lai straight out," he said, "how he reconciled atheistic Marxism with encouraging Buddhist delegations such as ours, and Chou said that, while he and many other Chinese were certainly atheists, they respected the beliefs of those who felt they had to have religion until the public could be educated out of such superstitions. He was very frank. I was encouraged by this to ask him if we held a Buddhist convention in Nepal would China send a delegation? He said yes. When I asked outright how China would feel if we invited the Dalai Lama, or a top Tibetan religious delegation, Chou said that he would have no objection."

There it was! The link I had been trying to resurrect in my mind - an appropriate mechanism to link Tibet and Nepal - and it was being presented to me *gratis* by a close friend! If the Dalai Lama came to Nepal with some of his ministers as part of a high-level religious delegation, India could not object at it being "political activities" - especially if it was being attended by approving Chinese representatives. The Dalai Lama could combine it with his proposed visit to Buddha's birthplace in Nepal. It was a winner.

I took the first opportunity to speak to T.C.Tethong, the Dalai Lama's representative in New Delhi. First, for my own interest, I asked him, "T.C., who went to the Indian Ministry of External Affairs to discuss the Dalai Lama's proposed visit to Buddhist countries?"

"I went," T.C. replied, looking curious. "With Mr. Gyalu Thondup, the Dalai Lama's brother."

I smiled at him enigmatically, and before he could ask his question, I said, "How did you find the Indians - obstructive or cooperative?"

"Well, to tell the truth," T.C. said frankly, "we were surprised at how cooperative they were. We were expecting some opposition, as in the past, but they were very sympathetic and approved of our proposal."

My smile broadened into delight. Events were meshing with an encouraging smoothness. To pursue the automobile metaphor, all I had to do now was to find a suitable gear lever to coordinate the political machinery of Nepal and Tibet - and in Amir I might have that gear lever.

We talked well into the night, and after T.C. went off to bed I went outside to think over what was happening. High above the jumbled city dwellings of the Kathmandu valley rode a brilliant three-quarter moon, glinting from the white buildings and golden roofs of temples, and reflecting serenely from the still pools of water. It was difficult to believe that away to the north and south, beyond the now dark and jagged rim of the encircling mountains, the best brains of the two greatest countries in Asia were pondering the moves that would bring this romantic but confused and exploited people of Tibet within either of their spheres of influence - to put it at its kindest.

I hadn't had time to read the newspapers for a day or two but next morning when I opened a copy of the *Times of India* there on the front page was the prominent headline:

600 NAGAS RETURNING FROM PAKISTAN
Indian Troops Ready To Meet Situation

"Indian security forces are on the alert to deal with a column of about 600 hostile Nagas armed with Pakistani

rifles, light machine-guns, explosives, mines and ammunition, reportedly moving from East Pakistan towards Indian territory through Burma,

"This was disclosed in the Lok Sabha (Parliament) today by the Minister of State for External Affairs, Mrs Lakshmi Menon, in response to a calling attention order.

"The Minister said there were two reports in regard to the hostiles' whereabouts. The first was that they were on the move through Burma..."

The second report was that the hostiles, who had escaped to Pakistan the previous December, had reached Burma on the return journey, that their strength was confirmed as six hundred and, that apart from weapons, they had also been furnished with sufficient Burmese and Indian money.

I was shattered - not at the news, because I had been expecting this, but that it had been prematurely discovered. The importance of the incident was that I was deeply involved, and some of the leaders in the group were probably the Generals and politicians who had been living with us in London. Our next assignment, after Tibet, was to go to Burma to meet up with a contingent of Naga troops, arranged by these same Generals, who would escort us behind the Indian Army lines to do a film about the Naga revolt against India.

It had begun a couple of years before when the editor of the Observer had asked me to meet and debrief the Naga revolutionary leader, A.Z.Phizo, with a view to writing about their claims of Indian atrocities in Nagaland.

After several months' investigation of Phizo I concluded that he might be a professing Christian, as he claimed, but, in my opinion, he was an unreliable informant. If any serious publicity was to be done on behalf of the Nagas the information they provided would have to be as solidly substantiated as it had been in my experience with the Tibetan revolutionaries.

I told this to Phizo bluntly, and said that if he wanted support he would have to bring other prominent Naga leaders to the West, and I conveyed this to Guy Wint, my friend and leader-writer, and David Astor the editor, of the *Observer*. They approved, and a reluctant Phizo was persuaded to get someone like the charismatic and very effective Naga, General Kaito, to come to the West and support Phizo's claims of Indian mendacity, intimidation and genocide.

Frankly, I thought Phizo was only pretending to be co-operative and I expected nothing from his assurances. I was totally shattered, therefore, when reports began to appear in Indian, and then international, media that a group of armed Nagas were conducting a series of hit-and-run engagements with the Indian Army in the hills and jungles between Assam and Burma, heading for East Pakistan as it was then called, now Bangladesh.

I was even more surprised when David Astor told me he had had an urgent telephone call from Field Marshal Ayub Khan, President of Pakistan, demanding an explanation why 153 Naga soldiers, including two Naga Generals and two Naga politicians, had arrived in East Pakistan, after shooting their way through the Indian Army, seeking "George Patterson of the *Observer*."

David Astor sent me to Pakistan to deal with the situation, and Prime Minister Nehru sent his popular and formidable relative-ambassador, Madame Pandit, to Pakistan, to discuss the situation with the Pakistan authorities and me. The issue was highly volatile, as India claimed the Nagas were Indian subjects and could only travel abroad with Indian documents and Indian permission. Madame Pandit declared that India would take a grave view of any contemplated Pakistan permission for the Nagas to travel without Indian authority.

I was on my own, between two powerful Asian Governments, but at least I had the advantage of having just spent the best part of a year in research at St. Antony's College, Oxford, for my book, Peking Versus Delhi, which provided me with the historical background necessary to more than hold my own with the Asian diplomats involved.

Also, before I left England, David Astor had retained a former Minister of Commonwealth Affairs, Sir John Foster, and a noted lawyer - and co-founder of Amnesty International - and (now Lord) Louis Blom-Cooper, to advise us on the Naga situation. So, in Pakistan, I argued the Naga position that the Indian Government had no official status in Naga affairs, which was still in dispute; that as citizens of a former British Commonwealth territory they had the right to travel to Britain to make their case known.

In Pakistan, I won the right for the two Naga Generals and two politicians to travel to Britain. The British Government threatened to take legal action against any airline bringing the Nagas into Britain, and refused them permission to land. I threatened to sue the airlines if they refused to fly them according to their stated documentation. The British Home Secretary, Sir Henry Brooke, ordered the Nagas to be detained at Heathrow Airport in London, and returned to Pakistan within twenty-four hours. While I held a packed Press Conference at the airport, David Astor, Sir John Foster and Louis Blom-Cooper took the British Government to law - and won the right for the Nagas to be allowed to remain and make their case in Britain.

The British official and military establishment, which had been so opposed to the unreliable Phizo, now responded rapturously to the charismatic Naga hero, General Kaito. The four Naga leaders were invited to meet Lord

Mountbatten, uncle of the Queen and former Commander-in-Chief of British Forces in South-East Asia, Field Marshal Slim, and other British Generals; and they were invited as special guests of the Burma veterans' organization, Burma Star, to attend the annual Remembrance Day parade in Whitehall.

When we were discussing the television team's extended assignments of "***Revolutions in Asia***", we had planned to meet up with the Naga military leaders in East Pakistan or Burma and travel back to Nagaland with them to make our second film. Now, it appeared from these newspaper reports that our "escort" had been discovered on the move and our proposed plans were in some disarray - not to mention my own seriously involved situation with them.

According to the reports further on in the article, Prime Minister Nehru said that Phizo had turned down an invitation to come to India for discussions because the conditions laid down were not acceptable to him. The failure of the proposed discussions would probably mean a new escalation of military attacks in Nagaland, and increasing danger for ourselves, so it meant that we should get into Tibet, and out again quickly, before the trip into Nagaland became impossible - or more impossible than it was already.

Adrian and Chris were finding Banskota continuing to play his infuriating game of "hard-to-get". When Adrian did manage to get him on the phone to ask about issuing our official permit to film, he curtly replied that he would get in touch with him when it was available. He was also supposed to make arrangements for Adrian to meet with General Khatry, the Foreign Secretary, but he stalled on this as well. I began a slow boil on the subject of Banskota. It did not help any to be told that this was standard operating procedure for Banskota. Some of the U.S., and other "Aid"

Gods and Guerrillas

Missions, had projects piling up just waiting for Banskota's signature. Other Nepali officials referred scathingly to his reputation for delays, and his heavy public drinking in the city's hotels. But no-one seemed to be prepared to take any official action against him because of his influential family conections..

I began my own standard operating procedure when I was being stalled; that is, I requested, pleaded, bribed and hectored my contacts to find out Banskota's weaknesses. It didn't surprise me unduly when I discovered through them that our friend Chahvan, with his cousin, the Chief-of-Protocol, had been plotting with Banskota to obstruct us for obscure reasons of his own.

Then I had a fortunate break. The manager of the Imperial Hotel, Mark, had offered to get routine stamps on our visas, which he did for any guests who required the procedure. He reported to me that, while he was waiting for the final initialing by the chief officer, Chahvan had come into the office with his cousin, saw Mark and the chief officer, and asked what was happening. Chahvan then warned the chief officer that he had better check with the Department of Publicity before he signed anything for us. When the official did this, he returned to tell Mark that he could not release the documents.

I had to take action immediately, because the news that Chahvan and his contacts could play games successfully with us would ruin my reputation and our assignment. But if word of summary action and punishment got around it would produce the proper respect and response. It was all a matter of who knew what to do to whom most effectively.

Meanwhile Amir Lama had arranged for us to film at the Buddhist monastery of Swayanbunath, and as we drove there together we talked about the many Tibetan refugees around. I asked Amir about the Tibetan refugees said to be in the high Himalayas and he said that there reported to be some ten thousand of them, many of them supposed to be carrying arms. He said that the government wasn't publicizing this because they didn't want it to be known in case the Chinese declared it a serious threat and took action against them without Nepal's knowledge or approval. The government officials and military were keeping a close watch on the situation.

This was not very good news for us, because it meant more problems for us in approaching the area without alerting officials. But I took the opportunity to suggest to Amir that it might be a better policy to have some government official in charge of the region who could estimate what was happening and who could recommend measures to counteract it. What I had in mind was to get an appointee to travel with us who would be well disposed towards us in order to help his own career prospects.

When Amir showed interest I suggested he might consider taking up the suggestion himself, if not the appointment, by meeting with T.C.Tethong for a discussion about Tibetan refugees in Nepal.

"Can you fix a dinner at my place tomorrow night, if he's free?" Amir asked abruptly. "Just him, you and me."

The Buddhist temple, *Swayanbunath*, was one of the oldest if not the oldest of the two to three thousand temples of Kathmandu, with their tens of thousands of gods and goddesses. Its origin was lost in myth which claimed that a disciple of Buddha threw a lotus into the original lake of Kathmandu, and from the flower there appeared *Swayanbu*, "the Eternally Existing", in the shape of a flame which was claimed to still flicker in the shrine of Swayanbunath. The temple was built on a solitary hill which rose sharply out of the plain. Its gilded roofs reflected sunlight from whichever part of the valley it was viewed. The legend was that the

Gods and Guerrillas

gods drained the early Kathmandu Lake by earthquakes, then, from a burning lotus from the waters, they created the hill called *Swayanbu*.

At dawn, as the sun rises behind the distant ring of snow-covered Himalayas, the light strikes the dome of hammered gold and it begins to glow with an unearthly aura, as if the mythical lotus still flamed; and, as the light intensifies, the priests blow on their long silver trumpets while pilgrims circle the shrine with prostrations - an endless human-chain prayer-wheel of worship of the gods. Inside the dim temple hundreds, if not thousands, of butter lamps flickered in worship of the "fire-god".

Outside the temple over three hundred steps led upwards, past giant Buddha statues, through avenues of stone gods and mythological beasts to the main temple courtyard. Here the stupa, or central cupola, was a gigantic affair, surmounted by a square tower from the four sides of which blue-painted, penetrating eyes of Buddha representatively watched over Kathmandu and the world. Above the eyes were thirteen gilded, pagoda-shaped, roofs, each smaller than the one beneath, and crowned by an umbrella-shaped device, the symbol of majesty, or rule.

It was the idols in Kathmandu which inspired the poet, J. Milton Hayes. In his poem, **The Green Eye of the Yellow God**, when he wrote:

"There's a one-eyed yellow idol to the north of Kathmandu,
There's a little marble cross below the town;
There's a broken-hearted woman tends the grave of Mad Carew,
And the Yellow God forever gazes down..."

The poem goes on to tell of the dare-devil Mad Carew stealing the green eye of the yellow god in order to win the heart of the Colonel's daughter. When her birthday celebration ball was at its height she was summoned to Mad Carew's room, and she found him with the green eye of the yellow god which he had risked his life to get for her:

"...His door was open wide, with silver moonlight shining through,
The place was wet and slipp'ry where she trod;
An ugly knife lay buried in the heart of Mad Carew,
'Twas the 'Vengeance of the Little Yellow God.'"

There was still an air of mystery in the enigmatic countenance of the yellow Buddhist idol to the north of Kathmandu. At one time or another, every Tibetan trader or official who visited Kathmandu came to Swayanbunath, and the refugees we met were no exception. It was a place of rendezvous - religious, social or clandestine - and there were hundreds of tourists, scores of movie cameras, several film units from different countries - and the Tibetans we wished to recruit for our secret journey to Tibet.

The usual practice of mountaineering expeditions climbing in the Himalayas was to hire the famous mountain people, the Sherpas, whose region was in the north-east of Nepal. I knew Tenzing and Gompu, the great Sherpa mountaineers who had climbed Everest, but the very special character of our project ruled out the use of the excellent Sherpa porters and guides. What we required were Tibetans, and very special Tibetans at that.

In the first place they had to be Tibetans who were strong enough to carry heavy loads, not an easy matter among thousands of refugees who had been starving for several years. They had to be from an area right up on the northern Himalayan border so that they could take us from

Kathmandu through all the village officials and military border check-posts. They also had to be from an area near to where the Khamba guerrillas were operating, again not an easy matter, for the Khambas were clannish and feared, living in remote, inaccessible places. Above all, they had to be trustworthy, so that they would not betray our intentions to the Nepalese authorities, either going or returning, or to the Chinese while we were near or in Tibet. Finally, when we had successfully completed the project, we would have to be so sure of them on our return to Kathmandu that they would say nothing, however excited they might be; and would even help us in the complex and near-impossible task of getting the completed film out of Nepal without the authorities knowing anything about it.

After filming at *Swayanbunath*, we went to a nearby Tibetan refugee center at Jowlikell, near the ancient city of Patan. Basically, it was an encampment, with the Tibetans living mostly in pitched black tents, and it brought back a sudden wave of nostalgia of my years of travel among nomad encampments in the high grasslands of Tibet.

When we walked over to the tents, a striking-looking elderly Tibetan in the maroon robes of a lama, emerged and greeted us courteously with the natural dignity and friendliness of the Tibetan people. Since he was not shaven like the majority of lamas, but had long grey hair wound into a top-knot, I asked him his religious persuasion, and he said that he was a Kagyupa, one of the minor sects in Tibet. He was called Gorschen Rabden, was aged fifty-nine, and the spiritual leader of the Tibetans scattered in the tents and outhouses. He launched into their history:

"We began with two thousand people and many yaks and sheep in the year when the revolt broke out in Lhasa (1959), and His Holiness left Tibet for India. The Chinese captured our leader, then tried to stop us leaving for India, and we lost many hundreds in the fighting. When we crossed the border into Nepal we were only two hundred people with no herds of animals, and facing great hardship. Five months ago we decided to go to India to join His Holiness and place ourselves under his care, and we are now reduced to forty-three. It is very hard."

"How do you manage to live?" I asked him gently, as the old man, bronzed face ravaged into a simple but impressive nobility, wiped away a tear slowly rolling down his wrinkled cheek without self-consciousness.

"We do what we can wherever we are camped," he replied. "Sometimes we carry water to earn a little money; sometimes the women tease wool and roll it into balls for others who can make clothes or carpets or tents; sometimes we dig, or carry wood, or plow in the fields."

A bystander broke in: "And all the time the *Rimpoche* (honorific for senior lama) goes out every day begging on our behalf, and brings back what he gets to share with us. We only do a little, but he does much. We would have died many times but for him and his care for us. He has a great reputation for goodness, and everywhere people respect him".

"These are my people," the *Rimpoche* said simply, "and I am their priest."

I looked around at the circle of faces, wondering again as I had done so often in the past, whether it was just their Mongolian features that made them into so striking-looking a race even when they were simple peasants and herdsmen like these here; or whether I had romanticized them in some way so that my association with them projected them as a race of heroes with more than the normal virtues of the human family.

I don't know. I only know that, as I moved among the forty-three men, women, and children - dirty, smelly, the

Gods and Guerrillas

children with thick snot on their noses - I felt a fierce pride in knowing these people, at having given the best twenty years of my life to helping them, at the way in which they asked for help without being abject, at the steady courage unflinchingly staring out of their slanted eyes as their whole world disappeared around them. I went into the surrounding outhouses as Adrian and Chris filmed, and found people jammed together with only pieces of rag curtains separating them, and more often than not with nothing at all, and I was proud of the simple cleanliness and order in the midst of such appalling squalor and vast poverty. With only a little to eat every three days from the occasional work they were able to find, whose children lay listlessly on the bunks or mud floors in pot-bellied starvation and dysentery-wracked lethargy, and they still showed no signs of despair. Only bewilderment and confusion at why they could not find permits to go to India to join their Dalai Lama who would look after them.

I wept for the listless children, and their simple parents, and I raged inwardly at the heartlessness and selfishness of the governments of Nepal and India and China and the West with their policies which produced this set of circumstances. But, most of all, I raged at the Dalai Lama and his circle of inept and selfish advisers whose lack of commitment to challenge the major governments consigned these people and millions more to suffering, starvation and destruction. So Tibet as a nation must die, and the Tibetans as a people must die. Five million wonderful people, who individually warmed the hearts of all who met them, would have to disappear because of the necessities of delicately balanced power politics.

When we returned to the Imperial Hotel I met T.C. who agreed to meet with Amir, and I briefed him about Amir and his importance before he received Amir's invitation, and a possible line of proposals to get Amir's interest.

Then I heard from Boris that Chahvan was now becoming an intolerable nuisance. He must have been bad, because Boris was famously tolerant with all kinds of obstreperous individuals. It seemed that Chahvan was still living at the hotel, and had just had a flaming row with a young French couple over something, and they had complained to Boris to get rid of him. Boris thought he had left, but it seemed he had got himself a key and, either bribing or threatening the servants, he had returned to his room at night without Boris knowing. Boris had changed the lock on his room door, and Chahvan's belongings were inside where he could not get at them.

Chahvan had sent a rude letter of protest to Boris, with copies to the Ministry of External Affairs and the Indian Embassy. Adrian and Chris were very concerned, and, while I was furious with Chahvan, I was also pleased that his activities would now obscure our own plans so much that no-one would believe anything they heard him say regarding us.

At Amir's for dinner that night he and T.C. quickly established a close rapport within ten or fifteen minutes as they recalled people and events from their youth at schools in Darjeeling. Then T.C. asked him abruptly, "Have you ever thought of coming to Dharamsalla to meet the Dalai Lama?"

Amir was somewhat taken aback at the bluntness of it, but replied, "Yes, I have been considering it. but I need His Majesty's permission before I could do it. Do you think it would be useful?"

"I think it would be of great benefit to both Nepal and Tibet," T.C. replied. "Even if your visit is not official, I can arrange a personal visit for you."

I only prompted them on two occasions: once, to suggest the expansion of the Nepali Buddhist Society to include an official link with the Tibetan refugees; and, secondly, to suggest that Amir might propose to the king that Nepal be the first country for the Dalai Lama to visit. Apart from this Amir and T.C. found enough mutually interesting material to keep talking until late that night. Both Amir and T.C., for personal and professional reasons, would push their thoughts on Confederation in the top circles of their respective governments, where it would develop its own impetus without any further pushing from me.

Meanwhile, the extensive Press corps in Kathmandu was being driven crazy trying to follow up on the many "leads" on Confederation they were getting from their respective contacts, all claiming to emanate from "authoritative sources." At diplomatic and socialite dinners and cocktail parties the talk invariably returned to Confederation in some form, and these inevitably generated their own spate of "informed sources."

"I hear Patterson saw the Secretary today..."

"I hear Confederation is a no-no because..."

"George, are you really pursuing a story on Confederation, or is this one of your ploys?"

"If Patterson is interested in Confederation there must be something in it."

Some exasperated hostesses were said to be imposing a fine of ten rupees for every mention of the word "Confederation", because it was usurping their salon prerogatives. The gossip grapevine was also highly amusing: Chahvan was seen dining at the Indian Embassy; Chahvan had filed a lawsuit against the redoubtable Boris; Chahvan was under detention by the Nepal authorities; Chahvan was claiming that he had the contacts to have Boris expelled from the country; Chahvan was negotiating a large wool deal with the New Zealand U.N. representative; Chahvan was desperately using damaging information against high Nepali officials to head off arrest.

As Adrian, Chris and I pursued our search for the necessary official permit among the top echelon of Nepali officials I was finding that there was a distinct division of influence between the "Palace" officials, and the "Ministry" officials, with a difficult-to-determine bridge where their essential interests merged in running the country. It was becoming so frustrating that I considered taking off without waiting for an official permit, but this I quickly dismissed from my mind when I thought of all the village checkposts we would have to pass before getting anywhere near to our goal in the high Himalayas. Also, if we had no official permit in our hands when we returned to Kathmandu after accomplishing our project, we would be in serious danger of spending a long time in prison ordered by an incensed government. We had to get that official permit by some means.

Since the king had taken over direct rule some three years before, he had only superficially reorganized the government administration and put in his own supporters into key positions. At the same time he had established an elite of "Palace" appointees who had direct access to him, and through whom he was able to keep an eye on the sprawling, disorganized formal machinery of government. This was still largely manned by the corrupt, sycophantic and time-wasting officials of the earlier regimes - of whom Banskota was one. The "Palace elite" had the greater power, and were the only ones who knew the king's mind well enough to take any effective action; the other "king's men" in the "Ministries" had to wait for formal approval, either from the king himself or through his "Palace elite".

I wasn't certain how much power the king delegated to Dr. Giri, but I suspected from my past experience of autocratic rulers and leaders that it would not be much. I decided, therefore, that I would have to make a direct approach to the king myself in some fashion. It was obvious that the granting of our permit was no longer the simple matter of a stamped document, but had become an inextricable part of the increasing tangle of political issues and Chahvan's mischievous manipulations.

While we were going through the difficult, laborious, but essential chore of finding suitable Tibetan porters from among the Tibetan refugees, I was approached by a former friend and professional colleague of my wife. Dr. Anderson of the United Mission Christian Hospital in Kathmandu, to ask if my wife would possibly consider coming out to Kathmandu to help out at the hospital. My wife had been head of surgery at Ludhiana Christian Medical College in Punjab Province in India for five years, and then, after our marriage, she had built up the Darjeeling and Dooars Planters' Hospital as Superintendent to such an extent that she had been given an award by the Queen for her *"outstanding medical work in India"* only the previous year. Now, apparently, the United Mission Hospital was desperately short of medical and surgical staff, with no possibility of immediate replacements available, and they were in urgent need of a general surgeon like my wife who could operate on all kinds of conditions. Unfortunately, Dr Anderson said ruefully, they could not pay traveling expenses and could only pay a "missionary" salary.

I was shaking my head in reluctant refusal when I suddenly paused, the glimmerings of an idea flickering at the back of my mind. Our television team's return with the completed film was going to be the most difficult part of the whole operation to accomplish. That return would have to be completely "natural", as innocent - or even more so, in view of all my recent suspect activities - as any mountaineering or botanical expedition. What better "cover", then, than that my wife should arrive, with three young children under four years of age, to do the very needed medical work in a respected hospital? It was the sort of committed action that was expected of her, and would imply innocence on the part of myself by reflection - as well as a planned long stay. Surely, the authorities would reason, I could not be up to any mischief in such respectable circumstances.

I sent a cable to my wife right away to inform her of Dr. Anderson's request. I received one in return to say that she could not possibly consider it because she was suffering from a pneumonia virus and our two-year-old son had dislocated his neck. Well, that was that. It had been a good idea while it lasted. I would just have to think up something else.

Meanwhile, we had our hands full with organizing our expedition. We had picked up information of a group of Tibetan refugees some distance from Kathmandu, at a place called Trisuli, who seemed to meet most of our requirements. We went hunting them and, when we met with them, they said, cautiously, that some Khambas had been operating recently in their border home region in the high Himalayas.

We singled out one of the most intelligent, a Tibetan called Tsewang, and brought him to Kathmandu to be available for ongoing travel arrangements. With his help we were able to work out an itinerary that would, hopefully, keep the Nepalese authorities unsuspicious regarding our intentions while taking us nearer to where the Khamba guerrillas were operating.

CHAPTER SIX
Of Meetings and Departures and Consequences

A few evenings later T.C. told me that he would be leaving Kathmandu next morning because he had just heard from the Nepal government that he was not to be permitted to visit Pokhara or Daulpatan, two upcountry places where there were large groups of Tibetan refugees. This, naturally, annoyed T.C. as it was one of those mysterious decisions which made no sense, and which seemed to arise out of the Nepal government's fear of the sensitive Tibetans-in-Nepal question in the context of Nepal's current pro-China policies. It was also an indication of how difficult our own search for an official permit would be to go further into the mountains.

Later that evening T.C. received a call from the Tibetan Bureau in New Delhi asking him to go to Janakpur where there had been "an outbreak of serious trouble" between some Tibetans and the local people. T.C. canceled his flight to New Delhi and arranged to fly to Janakpur in the morning. When he reached the airport it was to find Chahvan's cousin, Thakur, the chief of protocol, who forbad him to leave for Janakpur without an explanation. T.C. was justifiably bewildered and annoyed, and he arranged to fly to New Delhi on the next plane.

Before he left I had a last talk with him regarding possibilities. I urged him to (i) inform Gyalu Thondup and the Dalai Lama about the interest in Kathmandu in Confederation; (ii) to inform Gyalu that I was prepared to meet him amicably for discussions, although I had opposed his policies for Tibet in the past; (iii) to request a quick reply from the Dalai Lama regarding an audience for us;

(iv) to arrange for a quick visit of the Dalai Lama to Nepal. T.C. smilingly took note of all my suggestions and said he would see what he could do.

He had just left when that day's issue of the Kathmandu newspaper, The Motherland, carried on its front page the news of the possible visit to Nepal by the Dalai Lama. What was so remarkable about the timing of this report - in addition to its fractured English! - was that it should be printed at all. The newspapers in Nepal were all strictly controlled by the government and this news item would never have been printed without the consent of some official at very high level.

I stopped by the Royal Hotel to see Boris and get an update from him on his latest news and, as we chatted, two guests walked past. Boris called them over to introduce them and they were a French couple, Michel and Marie-Claire Peissel. Peissel was a sort of free-lance "explorer" who had used a previous vacation visit to the Himalayas to persuade the London School of Oriental Studies to lend their name to his proposed "study of the culture and people of the small principality of Mustang, in Nepal's north-east region".

I didn't say anything to Peissel, but Mustang was where the Gyalu Thondup-sponsored group of Khamba guerrillas were said to be located, and it was a very sensitive region of Nepal. I had no interest in going there because of Thondup's dubiously opportunistic connections with Taiwan, Communist China and the CIA. Peissel had told Boris that he spoke "fluent Tibetan", but when I heard him address a few remarks to a Tibetan servant at the hotel it was very garbled and simple. It was like his description of his "expedition" which comprised himself, his wife and a Tibetan who was to recruit his porters for the journey. Peissel said that he had been assured of permits to visit

Mustang by the Nepal government and I wished them luck. He added casually that he and his wife had arrived on the same plane as a friend of mine, Gyalu Thondup.

I evinced no particular interest, because I suspected that Peissel was something of a "scoop-hunter" rather than a serious "explorer" - probably hunting for the "abominable snowman" - but my mind jumped into top gear with his information. If Gyalu had come to Kathmandu so quickly after T.C.'s return it must mean that, either he was here to discuss Confederation or he was on some important agenda of his own relating to the Tibetans in Mustang. A third possibility, of course, was that he was there because he had heard that I was there asking about Tibetan refugees, and he was anxious to know what I was doing.

We had played tennis together regularly in Kalimpong and Darjeeling, and socialised together ten years before; but as the revolt inside Tibet increased, and he became involved in his personal ambitions and intrigues with the exiles around the Dalai Lama and I attacked his and their self-interested policies, we drifted apart. But now Gyalu was here in Kathmandu, and in Tibet's interest I felt I ought to meet him quickly to discuss what we could do to help further this course. I pulled out my typewriter and began typing a letter to him.

It was ten-thirty p.m. when I finished typing, and I walked through the darkened and deserted streets to deliver the letter to him at the Royal Hotel. There was no-one at the reception desk and, I was about to drop the letter into the pigeon-hole opposite Gyalu's name, when a thought struck me. I called to the night-guard who was standing in the doorway and, giving him a couple of rupees, I asked him to push the letter under the door of Room 17, and waited. In a few minutes he returned - with Gyalu, as I had hoped. It was if the intervening years and disputes had never happened.

He was pleasant and friendly, and so was I. We asked about each other's families and health. Finally, he held up my letter.

"Thank you for your letter," he said. "We must meet sometime soon. I don't know how long I will be here, but we will meet and talk. If not, we must meet in Delhi."

"I would very much like that," I told him. "In fact, I think it is essential because I have some very important information we should discuss."

After a few minutes chat we parted.

The following morning I was told that the king's brother, Prince Basundhara, would agree to my request to speak to me and he would call on me later at the hotel. When we met I found him quiet and sincere, easy to talk to, and I quickly laid out the problems we were having after we had been assured that we would be given official permission to film. Without making it sound like a threat I said that, unless we received an official permit to film soon, we would have to drop the whole project, which would be a great disappointment for Nepal.

We spent two hours in discussion, including a long period on the question of Confederation, and eventually said he would discuss it with the king and Dr. Giri, and find out what was the problem. He would also phone General Mullah, the Principal Military Secretary to His Majesty. and ask about permission to film him. When I phoned Juddhabir to let him know of my talk with Prince Basundhara, I said to expect a phone call from him regarding our official permit. Juddhabir confessed himself puzzled at the inexplicable delay, but I guessed Juddhabir was clever enough to appear genuinely puzzled anyway. He also said that he had arranged another meeting for us that afternoon with the Foreign Secretary, General Khatry, who had suggested the interview.

Right away, General Khatry said to us that the formal permit had been granted and we could collect it from the Director of Publicity, Banskota. But we must not film any refugee camps nor my idea of a Confederation of Himalayan States, because Nepal supported the "one China" and not the "two Chinas" theory. It seemed something of a non sequitor to me, but I didn't say anything. Adrian asked if there would be any objection to filming Tibetans outside the camps, and the foreign secretary said no, and we breathed a sigh of relief. We were not interested in filming Tibetans in camps.

Next day I was called to the phone to talk with Amir, and he said that some new and exciting developments had taken place. He would come and see us about lunchtime to discuss them. When he arrived he said he had had several discussions with Dr. Giri and the king, and they were very impressed by my ideas for the Confederation of Himalayan States, and that he had been asked by Dr. Giri to keep in touch with me. Also, although at this stage the Nepalese government could not make any open overture to the Dalai Lama, he had been asked to explore the possibility of an unofficial meeting with the Dalai Lama. Could I arrange this with Gyalu Thondup? If possible, could I arrange for the three of us to have dinner this evening at his house without divulging too much to Gyalu Thondup? I said I would do this and phone him later to confirm it.

When he had gone I went to the Royal Hotel - and found that Gyalu Thondup had gone! He had only stayed overnight and left early the next morning for New Delhi. It was infuriating. The only possible conclusion was that he had been scared off by the possibilities we had discussed and, rather than face them in discussion, he had decided to slip away. I was disgusted at this further display of pusillanimity and self-interest at the expense of his desperate country.

Amir shrugged at the news. He had lived in Darjeeling and knew Gyalu and his activities, so he wasn't too surprised. He said that if it could be arranged by T.C. or whoever that he would visit the Dalai Lama unofficially, not as Nepal government representative, but as president of the Nepal Buddhist Society and, as such, invite him to come to Nepal on his Buddhist pilgrimage.

The following morning we had an appointment to meet Banskota to collect our official permit and "to discuss our program." When we met at Banskota's office, the Director of Publicity was uneasy and frowning as he fiddled with the papers on his desk. There was no difficulty about the places we wanted to film in the south of Nepal, he said, but our request to film the Chinese road in the north, and travel near the Chinese border, was a cause of considerable concern.

I noted the labored phraseology with interest. I concluded that Banskota was playing his own game; that, if he had been given official refusal, he would have phrased it with more authority. He said he would have to get higher permission for this; and, again, I had the feeling he was stalling for his own reasons – possibly looking for a bribe. I said, mildly, I hoped it would not take too long. He suggested that we go to see the Chief of Protocol for the permitted places to be listed in our visas, and he would make further enquiries. I decided it would be counter-productive to push things at that time, and agreed,

It was my first meeting with Thakur, the Chief of Protocol, Chavan's cousin, since the time we had met with Chahvan soon after our arrival. He was smoothly pleasant and sat chatting about Chahvan and his escapades for some time. Thakur said Chahvan was not a close relation, but a close neighbor and colleague in some official enterprises, and confessed that he had been a cause of some recent difficulties. I had the impression he was fishing for some form of condemnatory and incriminating response from us that would boomerang on our project, so I just listened and smiled and shrugged neutrally.

Then we got down to the question of the permit, and Thakur said that there had been some confusion caused by claims and statements made by Chahvan regarding our intentions, but these had now been cleared. When it came to the question of our requests for the north, he was very apologetic and said it had not been possible to grant these.

I was very understanding about his reluctance, but also very firm regarding our intention. "Mr. Thakur," I told him, "I'm sorry, but you must understand that, unless we get permission to go to the north, we will not make any film at all. Mr. Cowell will support me in that."

Adrian did, unequivocally, and Thakur was obviously disconcerted. He tried to explain, with smooth explanations and polished reluctance how disappointed he was on our behalf, but I wasn't buying it. I remembered his back-stabbing activities with Chahvan when our visas were being stamped earlier. We refused to consider any of his alternative proposals, and said we would be leaving as soon as we could make plane reservations and he could make our explanations to the authorities. He suggested we take time out for lunch and return two hours later, and he would see what he could do.

When we met then he said he had been successful in getting permission for us to film the Chinese road to the north, and also three places near the northern border; and he had informed Banskota to this effect. We went straight to Banskota's office, where he had already prepared our permits - and also the name of an official "liaison officer", who was standing beside him. I didn't catch his name, but as we left the office, I asked him his name and he said, "Banskota" - true to form, Banskota had managed to slip his younger brother on to us to monitor our activities!

This was a shattering development, for it meant that whatever we did it would be reported back to the Nepalese authorities, with Banskota putting the worst possible spin on the reports; also, if he was with us, it would hinder us from making enquiries regarding the location of the Khamba guerrillas in the high Himalayas. Even if we were successful in evading his scrutiny in some way, his presence would result in our film being confiscated when we returned to Kathmandu. We would just have to deal with this during the journey. It was possible, because the desk-bound Nepalese were not equipped to travel let alone suffer in the high altitudes and savage conditions of the high Himalayas, and so there was always the possibility of being able to "lose" him or render him harmless in some way..

Next morning, as I was fiddling with the radio, I had a shock. I hadn't bothered listening to the English news on Indian radio relays to Nepal because I was listening to the BBC every evening. Now, as I casually moved the tuner on the Indian station the announcer said, "The Prime Minister of Bhutan, Mr. Jigme Dorji, has been assassinated. He was shot last night and died after two hours. The assassin has not been captured."

I was stunned. Jigme murdered! I had expected all sorts of possibilities in this unpredictable region, even including Jigme's overthrow as I had hinted to him when I said he might not be around next year, but I had not anticipated his death, and certainly not his assassination. It was not that he had no enemies. He had many - Bhutanese, Nepalese, Indian, Tibetan and Chinese - despite his easy-going character, because of his tough policies. What did his death mean for my proposals on Confederation? Who had pulled the trigger? Or, more significantly, who was behind the assassination and for what reason? Whoever it was, his death would have far-reaching political consequences in the Sino-Indian border region.

If China-inspired, then it meant that China had already planned an imminent showdown in Bhutan. The intention, as I read it, would be to trap India into a series of similar colonizing moves in Bhutan as she had done in Sikkim *"to control unstable conditions in a strategic Indian border State."* If Bhutan-inspired - that is, if by a member of the outlawed Nepali-influenced Bhutan State Congress - then India would blame Nepal for interference in Bhutan's internal affairs, create bitterness and tension between the two countries - and all possibilities of Confederation would disappear. If Indian-inspired - that is, if someone in India, pro-Communist or anti-Jigme - it could expand the Sino-Indian war in the North East Frontier Agency into Bhutan. Even if Bhutan-inspired, it would provoke serious political repercussions.

The Chinese newspapers arrived in the evening with the bold headlines:

CHINESE HAND IN MURDER OF BHUTAN PREMIER

"...The assassin has been captured and had served in the Indian Army in the North East Frontier Agency during the Sino-Indian conflict in 1962. He had been taken prisoner by the Chinese, removed to Tibet, then sent back to Bhutan in mid-1963. In his confession, the assassin said that he and four others had been hired by a group of Bhutanese army officers, headed by the deputy commander-in-chief, to kill Jigme Dorji, and his two brothers. Some of these army officers are known to have had contacts with the Chinese Communists across the Bhutan border..."

A less prominent report in the newspapers said the Indian minister, Lal Bahadur Shastri, had stated that "*the Indian government would provide facilities to the Dalai Lama should he wish to go to Buddhist countries. So far no such request had been made by him nor by his brother. The government could not act on his own.*" So, it looked as if Gyalu Thondup was still obstructing any possible hope for Tibet in his own inimitable fashion of furthering his own interests at the expense of Tibet.

The Chinese government riposted, in a diplomatic note, accusing India of "*shielding and supporting the traitorous activities of the Dalai Lama.*"; who was accused of "*attempting another rebellion in Tibet.*" China accused the Indian government of "*openly directing the Dalai Lama to sow discord in China's friendly relations with South East Asian countries*", by agreeing to assist him in his proposed tour.

Speaking of publicity, I suddenly had my own share of it in bold headlines in the Indian newspapers. It appeared that there had been a comparatively mild protest when Minoo Masani began reading some extracts from my book, Peking Versus Delhi, in the Indian Parliament regarding Chinese activities and Indian policies on the Sino-Indian border; but this had blown up into an uproar over a decision by the Deputy Speaker, which the other members took to be a violation of their parliamentary rights. The Statesman account read:

MASANI QUOTES FROM BANNED BOOK
Row Over Proscribed Book in Lok Sabha
Masani Raises Controversy

"*....Mr. Masani read extracts as proof of his claim that the Government had banned the book because of critical* references to it and not because it had contained anything objectionable.

"When he did so, a member rose on a point of order to ask whether Mr. Masani could read from a proscribed book, and demanded that the parts be expunged from the proceedings.

"The Deputy Speaker agreed that this was not permissible and duly expunged the offending parts of Mr. Masani's speech. This found Mr. H.V.Kamath. a jealous guardian of members' rights, getting up, the book of rules already in hand, to quote the relevant rule and challenge the deputy speaker's authority to expunge the remarks. He was joined by Mr. N.R.Ranga...

"The Deputy Speaker agreed to study the matter and, in response to a request by Mr. Kamath, said his ruling was 'temporarily rescinded'..."

The debate had continued even more passionately after this, while Masani pointed out that that the book had been favorably reviewed "in such an august organ as the front page of the **Times Literary Supplement**, and even by responsible Indian correspondents in London and New Delhi. "Who are these semi-literates (in Government)," he demanded, "to tell us which books to read?"

The **Times of India** responded in a leading editorial in less thunderous tones, but still expressing concern with the government's action:

"...Mr. Masani's determined attempt, however unsuccessful, to extract an official explanation of why **Peking Versus Delhi** has been banned in India certainly deserves to be applauded. It is by no means clear that the prohibition can justifiably be described as 'shameful' and 'an outrage on the Constitution,' but Mr. Masani is presumably a better judge of this point since he has read

Mr. Patterson's book, and is in possession of a copy. The point here surely is that, Mr. Masani's opinion apart, there is no assurance that the Government's decision to prohibit the book is based on a broad or enlightened interpretation of the national interest. Admittedly, the executive, during an emergency, is under no obligation to justify or explain prohibitions of this kind. Yet it must be asked whether the Government should invariably take the fullest advantage of this lack of obligation and refuse to indicate, even in the most general terms, the grounds on which a particular book or publication is withheld from readers in this country. All that the Minister of State for Home Affairs had to say to the Lok Sabha in answer to Mr. Masani's points was that Mr. Patterson's book had been proscribed 'after careful consideration.' This is not very intuitive or reasonable at a time when it is very necessary to convince public opinion that the executive's arbitrary powers are being used with the utmost discretion..."

There was more of the same - all good knockabout politics, no doubt, in the democratic media game. I was interested to note, however, that almost all of the comments in the subsequent debates deplored the short-sighted and narrow-minded policy of the government in banning what was essentially a reasonably argued book. But the most important aspect of the controversy at this particular time was what effect it was likely to have on my presence and activities in Nepal. All resident media journalists and stringers knew of my presence in Kathmandu, and would soon be chasing me for a response, and it would not take long for the Indian media to follow suit – but with potentially disastrous consequences for our "secret mission".

Our plans regarding Tibet were now as fully advanced as we could carry them, and we rapidly filmed the final

Gods and Guerrillas

episodes we required in Kathmandu so that we could leave the country immediately after our return from Tibet. Banskota's brother, after asking Adrian for a loan of a a hundred rupees "*to help his sick wife*", then said that he could not go with us as liaison officer for the same reason. We were not bereaved. Actually, we had made a specific point of exaggerating the hazards of the trip in order to discourage him. But Banskota's next appointee - a tough-looking, taciturn specimen who had me wondering how he would respond to my unstated possibility of making him sick with medicine at some point on the journey to discourage his curiosity - also asked to be excused as he had "*a heart condition.*" So did a third appointee.

Then we heard that word was getting around the government corridors that we "were a tough outfit and trouble", and that was the real reason the regular liaison officers were reluctant to take the job. Our first reaction was to be relieved, but then the constant nagging anticipation for our return to Kathmandu being as unsullied as Caesar's wife took over, and I said we would have to take a liaison officer even if it meant forcing Banskota to provide one. I could imagine Banskota preparing gleefully for our arrest on our return if we tried to leave Kathmandu without one.

We decided to leave Kathmandu, three months to the day after departing from London, on May 14th. Now, in Kathmandu, as previously in London, we had the organizational problems of preparing for one of the most grueling mountain expeditions in the world without making it obvious that we were going to do so. It meant that all we had in leaving London was the usual television equipment, and normal tropical clothing for filming in Nepal. So, now we had to find high-altitude clothing and equipment in Kathmandu without drawing attention to ourselves. Fortunately, I had contacts among the Sherpa communities and, as they had collected all sorts of surplus equipment as cast-offs from previous mountaineering expeditions and the departure of a large group of American Peace Corps personnel, and with a judicious use of "baksheesh", we quietly assembled what we needed – high-altitude clothing, tents, oilskins, haversacks, waterproof carrier bags for American dehydrated foods, sunglasses, sunburn creams, first aid kits, and medicines - and packed it away from the notice of porters and other watchers of our activities. We were open about buying the normal supplies necessary - flour, *dahl* (nourishing lentils for soup), dried milk, cocoa, sugar and salt. The Tibetans said we would find sufficient meat for our needs on the way - chickens in the foothills, sheep and yaks (the Tibetan buffalo) further north. We were now sufficiently equipped to enter Tibet. It would still be difficult, but no longer impossible.

We were ready to leave on the final stage of our project. That was when my wife's cable arrived to announce that she and the children would be arriving in Calcutta on May 24th and Kathmandu on the 27th and to "please make the necessary arrangements for our arrival." She would arrange to bring a recommended amah (nanny) for the children from Calcutta to look after the children when she was working in the hospital. Adrian also received word from his wife, that she was sick and might require to go into hospital for an operation.

We could not cancel everything at this late stage. Adrian made frantic long-distance arrangements regarding his wife. I arranged with Dr. Anderson for the hospital to find appropriate accommodation for my family in my absence, and she promised to look after them. Then I arranged with the owner of the Imperial Hotel, the Chinese friend, Mung, we had known in Darjeeling, to meet Meg at the Kathmandu airport and tell her I would return as soon as possible. I dared not tell Mung about our plans for entering Tibet, but Meg already knew that was our intention in London, and so would know what had happened if I was not present to meet her.

Mung had arranged to throw a party in the hotel for us before we left, inviting many of the people we had met in the past three months. I didn't feel too well, but thought it might have been caused by the stress of all that was happening. As the evening wore on, the slight nausea increased, and I was unable to do justice to the excellent meal and wines. At midnight I went off to the bathroom to be sick. I even had a passing thought of poison, but there was nothing I could do about it now anyway.

It was three-thirty in the morning before the party ended. I stepped out of my clothes as I swayed nauseously beside the bed, and dropped on top of the sheets. My last conscious thought was how I was going to get up at six and then carry a fifty-pound back-pack for the walking stages of our journey. Adrian, Chris and I had agreed we would each carry that weight of personal equipment to condition us to be able to do that while crossing the twenty-thousand feet passes from Nepal into Tibet. We were in different stages of physical fitness - I reckoned I was twenty pounds over my normal weight after my sedentary professional and social life in London and Oxford - and carrying a fifty-pound back-pack would help to get our weight down before we tackled the high Himalayas.

When Adrian called me in the early morning I could not lift my head from the pillow. I was violently sick and felt like death. To Adrian's worried question as to whether I could make it, I replied that I would be leaving with them as arranged later in the morning - if necessary, to put off the planned departure until afternoon to give the medicines I was taking time to work. I went to sleep for another three hours and, when I awoke, I was clear-headed and free of stomach cramps, but still somewhat weak in the legs. Whatever the cause had been it was obviously clearing. Fortunately, after a short hike, most of the first day was by jeep transport to the town of Trisuli, where we would pick up our Tibetan porters.

But then, suddenly, Adrian had to deal with another crisis. Banskota, still being obstructive for his own reasons, had not yet produced a government liaison officer to accompany us. Adrian, determined that we would not be trapped in this plot, for the present or later, had finally sent him a typed letter informing him that if no liaison officer was ready by the time of our noon departure we would leave without him, but would hold Banskota responsible for the omission in the future.

This had produced an immediate response, but of a completely unexpected kind. We had been using the services of a young university student, Hemantha Misra, as interpreter and general assistant in and around Kathmandu. It transpired quite coincidentally that Hemantha's mother was a relation of Banskota. He was a personable and clever young fellow whose family had good connections with the old Rana regime, and we had found him surprisingly outspoken for a Kathmandu Nepali in some of our involved circumstances in the city. He had expressed a desire to go with us on our expedition, but we were reluctant for at least two reasons: one, he was a friend as well as a colleague and, if we were successful as we hoped, then he would be in serious trouble later; and two, he was a Kathmandu Nepali, unfitted for the tough demands of travel in the high Himalayas. But, apparently, the pressured Banskota had sent for Hemantha, asked him if he wanted to go, gave him official papers authorizing him as a government liaison

Gods and Guerrillas

officer - then phoned to tell Adrian that it was a fait accompli.

Adrian had no alternative in the circumstances but to agree, and hope that somewhere along the route we would be able to think of something that, in his own interests, would keep him from being with us when we made contact with the Khamba guerrillas. While it would be pleasant having him for a companion, and extremely useful in many ways, I could hardly use my secretly obtained and cherished medicines to knock him out as I had intended to do with the others! Hemantha, of course, knew nothing of our ultimate objective of meeting up with the Tibetan guerrillas and crossing deep into Tibet with them on a military action against a Chinese convoy in one of their regular guerrilla operations.

We were delayed in Kathmandu beyond our scheduled departure hunting for suitable equipment to outfit Hemantha - again without alerting him to our eventual goals - because, while we would not have bothered outfitting any government official, we could not leave Hemantha to freeze, or go without adequate bedding where we were going in the high Himalayas.

At last we were on our way. From Kathmandu Valley to Trisuli was forty-five miles, and Adrian had rented two jeep-type vehicles, one American and one Russian, to take us, our equipment, and Tsewang and Trashi, two of our recruited Tibetan team. The first part of the journey to Trisuli was hot, dusty and distinctly unpleasant for me with my lingering nausea. But gradually the last of the nausea wore off, the oppressive weakness lifted, and, as we entered the mountains encircling Kathmandu, I began to enjoy the drive.

The road was only a roughly-built dirt track, pitted, rutted, and corrugated by the passage of many vehicles, winding up and around the lower foothills surrounding Kathmandu Valley, and providing an ever-changing panorama. Lines of women were scything the ripe stalks of rice, singing some Nepalese melodies to the swing of their curved blades, and the men's voices joining in a responsive chorus. When I asked Hemantha what a shoe upside-down on a wooden stake meant, he said it had something to do with keeping off the evil eye that could ruin the crops. Clouds of egrets drifted by the flailing workers. In the villages men and women worked on clay pots and jars, roof tiles and bricks, on potters' wheels and wooden moulds, with hundreds of the products stacked in heaps on beds of straw to dry. The fields were a fascinating patchwork of shapes and greens and yellows and browns according to the nature of the crops. As we claimed higher, stripped stands of the old forest of oak and chestnut and rhododendron appeared, together with glimpses of some wild forest animals.

When we passed over the first ridge we entered a long, twisting drive around and down plunging pine-clad mountains and valleys, but always tilting upwards as we climbed higher into the mountains. Where the variegated greens of the trees thinned, the light greens of fresh rice shoots and darker stalks of maize took over in staggeringly breath-taking cultivation of precipitous, six yards by two yards, terraced fields - from valley bottom to mountain top. Children worked beside their parents, or played, or rode the patient bullocks plodding phlegmatically above some terrifying drops.

It was late afternoon when we arrived at Trisuli, delayed by low-gear driving up steep gradients, and long waits trying to overtake slow-driving trucks on narrow tracks. When we got there, the large and well-appointed guesthouse for visiting officials and travelers was not available, and we had to put up with dirty unfurnished rooms in a dirty unfurnished house, where there were wooden pallet beds and nothing else - no lights, no fire-place, no kitchen. Just to complicate matters a thunderstorm broke, our Tibetans wanted to get away to visit their families in their refugee camp three miles out of town, and we ate a hastily produced supper of damp rice, burned sausages and uncooked onions. However, the tea was hot, sweet and very acceptable.

There were no nails in the walls so we had to improvise with pieces of strings to hang our mosquito nets, and Trisuli had a notorious reputation as a malarial death-trap. It was a hot and very uncomfortable night.

CHAPTER SEVEN

Problems In Communication

Next morning we were up and around at dawn. In the confusion of arrival and the thunderstorm everything had been piled up in a heap wherever there was a space. Until we had a cook organized from among the Tibetans we had arranged to make our own food, but by the time we had found ingredients and utensils, and had prepared a meal, it was almost nine o'clock. Surprisingly, the Tibetans arrived as we finished breakfast, bringing with them a companion, Sedar, who was said to be "a good cook." But they also brought a problem.

Sedar took me aside and said that he had agreed to come but he was concerned because Tsewang had asked to be excused as his wife was sick. "I have a problem, because I do not like the man he has sent as a substitute and I'm afraid there could be much trouble for you because of this."

"What's wrong with Tsewang's wife?" I asked grimly, for this looked like one of those concocted tales one meets with in travel in difficult places. A man will take on a commitment because he can then "sell" the position to someone else and make a profit without going himself. A sick wife, or mother, or grandmother, was as common an excuse in the East as it was in the West.

"No," Sedar shook his head in rebuttal. "It is true that his wife is sick. But he knew she was sick before he agreed to go with you. We all have troubles, and perhaps my wife or children could be sick while I am away. It is not good to agree, then not do it."

I agreed, and asked him if Tsewang was coming in to report this or not, but he wasn't certain. I questioned Sedar about his own background, partly because we might want him as leader as well as cook if Tsewang wasn't going, and partly because he might just be jockeying to get the position of leader for himself. He said he had been a well-to-do trader, of reasonably wealthy parents, before the revolt in Tibet. His knowledge of cooking came from the many travels he had made to many places. He seemed genuine and we decided that, if Tsewang didn't turn up, then we would settle for Sedar in his place.

But I said to Adrian that I would push hard for Tsewang to go with us because it was bad psychology to accept excuses right at the start of a journey, especially one as critical and dangerous as ours. Tibetans would do anything a tough and tested leader demanded of them, but they could sense weakness instinctively and exploit it ruthlessly. We were still discussing the matter when Tsewang himself arrived with a large group of about twenty porters, and we called a meeting.

I told them bluntly, "This is not Tibetan custom what Tsewang is doing. When I was in Tibet I learned the custom that when a man gave his word to do anything, no matter what it cost him he would keep it."

They shook their heads in agreement and murmured approval. One of them said reasonably, "That is true, but Tsewang's wife is sick and he has young children he must look after."

"Was she sick when he gave his word?" I demanded.

"Yes," he agreed. "But now she is more sick and might die, and he must look after the children."

I shook my head. "This I cannot accept. My wife is sick, and attending hospital, and my child is sick and attending hospital. Cowell Sahib's wife is sick and attending hospital. Yet we are here many thousands of miles away from them to help Tibet. We did not go back home. To help Tibet you must be prepared to sacrifice - even if it means wives and children. Many of you have no wives or children because they have been killed by the Chinese. If you want help for your country you must show that you are prepared to suffer. I do not ask of you more than I do myself, and that is why my conditions are hard. We need Tsewang as leader."

I was being weighed and sifted by twenty tough-looking individuals, minds sharpened by years of revolt, oppression, suffering, exile and starvation, and was being judged as to whether I could carry the responsibility of their lives over the next month or more. They did not know our goal, but they knew they were not being selected as porters before Sherpas unless we were going into Tibetan territory. They had seen the equipment scattered around us and could guess that we were going into the high Himalayas. But I had handled tougher Tibetans than these - the feared warrior Khambas of East Tibet - and I suspected that some of their fears were related to their suspicions that we were going into Khamba-occupied country. Khambas were always feared in Tibet, whether as bandits raiding on trading caravans, feuding among their clans, or fighting the Chinese.

I decided that now was as good a time as any to let them know something of our plans, and I described something of my background, and showed them Surkhang's letter of explanation which he had given me before we left London. They reacted with considerable respect and excitement, murmuring his name and some even touching the letter to their foreheads. I told them my Tibetan nickname was "*Khamba Gyau*" - "the bearded Khamba" - and that I had been sent by them to India to get help for their revolt against the Chinese by making a film, with letters from both Kham and Lhasa officials.

I noticed that Tsewang had got up and moved away from the inner circle of Tibetans around me, and was giving orders to those on the outside of the circle regarding the loads. I decided to temper justice with mercy, and said that, if Tsewang went with us, I would send a letter to the United Mission Hospital in Kathmandu where my wife was a doctor, and have her treat his wife at our expense. The refugee camp leader, who had come in with Tsewang and the porters, said he would arrange for Tsewang's wife to go to Kathmandu, and to look after the children in her absence; in which case, Tsewang could go with us as agreed. Tsewang was delighted with the arrangement and soon the Tibetans were busy redistributing loads to be carried.

It was mid-afternoon when we left Trisuli. There were eighteen porters, plus Tsewang the leader; Sedar, the cook; Adrian, Chris and myself; and Hemantha, the Nepali liaison officer. Twenty-four people in all, the smallest loads at fifty pounds, and some of the strongest Tibetans carrying two-hundred pounds. The sun shone, the sky was cloudless blue above the luxuriant greens of the "V" of the valley, but the windless heat was oppressive. Even without a load it would not have been too pleasant walking, but carrying a fifty-pound back-pack for the first time in many years - and still feeling a bit wobbly from the sickness attack - was a disturbing prospect, especially facing several days in the lower foothills before reaching the higher and cooler regions.

It took about two hours to reach and begin to set up our first camp, partly because the Tibetans knew nothing about tents, or, at least the intricacies of foreign tents and equipment. We had brought a large tarpaulin to be erected with bamboo poles as a crude open-sided tent for the porters, and in this they stacked the loads in a long single wall down the center and arranged their sleeping-places on each side, with cooking utensils beside a fire nearby.

The camp-site was on a flat piece of ground beside a clear, brawling small river, with occasional calm pools, and it was sheer joy to dip into the ice-cold mountain water to ease the aches and wash away the perspiration. With a lifetime of experience of living in the open, the Tibetans soon had fires going, cooking pots on, and a delicious meal prepared of chicken curry and rice. We celebrated our departure from Kathmandu and its complexities with mugs of steaming cocoa, and were ready for our sleeping-bags by nine o'clock. We were on our way.

The camp came awake at dawn and for the first time since I had left Tibet fourteen years before I experienced a long-dormant nostalgia. There were murmurings and shuffles as the first individuals got up and began the dawn chores of fire-blowing and stoking, and filling pans of water to boil for the essential tea. And always the low-voiced repetitive religious drones of "*Om Mani Padme Hum*", the Buddhist prayer-mantra, which would be with us all day when they weren't talking to each other. It reminded me evocatively of the beautiful Gaelic, "Peat-fire Smooring Prayer" of Scotland.

We had finished eating, and were preparing to move, when an altercation broke out among the porters as they were sorting out the loads. When I asked what was happening I was bombarded by a gaggle of angry explanations. The chief culprit appeared to me to be a Tibetan called Basang, whom I had already noted as a typical "smart boy" as he glibly and bossily moved among jobs telling others what to do without seeming to do much himself. Now, he was standing beside a large load and refusing to lift it at the command of Tsewang.

"You," I said to him, "pick up that load and get up the trail."

He looked startled at my interjection and began explaining about the weight of the load. I waved him to silence.

"I don't want to know," I stated bluntly. "I give orders; you obey."

"Then I go back," he said mutinously, looking for approval to the others.

I shook my head negatively. "No, you don't. I did not ask what you wanted to do. I said pick up the load and get on the trail. Either that or you get a beating with this stick" - and I waved the stout branch of a tree I was using as a walking-stick. "Yesterday we settled this: you agreed to go, so go."

There was a general movement as the others started to pick up their loads, with glances towards where Basang still stood looking from me to his load to the others. It was clear that he would have liked to push the issue further, and was desperately seeking a way out to save some face. I kept him on the hook, as an example of the discipline we would need during the next month. He screwed up his face, pulled up his shirt, and patting his stomach, said, "Bon-bo-la (honorable official), I have a sore stomach and that is why I cannot carry such a load."

"You should have thought of that sooner," I said ironically. "I'll give you medicine for that later, but for now pick up the load until you drop. Just don't make trouble again."

Muttering to himself, he slung his rope around the load, swung it behind his back and trudged up the trail after the others.

Where we had camped beside the rocky river now gave way to a steeply climbing and rough trail which cruelly taxed muscles that hadn't been used for years, as they were stretched, twisted and jolted under the unusual demands being placed on them. The blazing sun climbed in a cloudless blue sky and perspiration poured down the faces and dropped of the chins of all of us as we labored upwards. The trail left the side of the valley and sloped more abruptly as it zig-zagged, still stony and uneven, across the face of a sheer mountain. Finally, it became like an interminable irregularly-spaced boulder-strewn stairway, on which each step was a major effort on trembling legs as they struggled to carry the weight of body and load. My hair was plastered to my head with perspiration, my breath came in great soughing gulps, and every faculty was concentrated on overcoming the next step.

Fortunately, when all seemed lost in an exhausted haze, the trail straightened out and, rounding a bend, a strong and steady cooling breeze signaled the top of the mountain ridge. Everybody dropped their loads and themselves on to the grassy verge. The silence of exhaustion was crudely shattered by the voice of the pop-musician Cliff Richard singing lustily: "*Let's all go on a summer holiday...*"

Chris had brought his transistor radio, and the syncopated blast roused the recumbent figures. Hemantha, after a shouted "Yippee", even managed to beat out time and a kind of moaned accompaniment to the Elvis Presley record which followed.

After four hours of easy walking downwards, we camped beside a clear stream where the sides of the mountain folded back from the sharp "V" of the valley. The first thing I did was to strip to my briefs and sit knee-deep in the ice-cold water and just soak until I was chilled. By the time I had cooled, the tents were being set up, the fires were lit and the inevitable tea was being made.

The setting sun lit up the narrow valley, laying a lovely yellow patina on the shimmering greenery of moving leaves and the ubiquitous terraced fields belonging to hidden villagers. Birds were caroling their last songs in the cool of the evening. The curling, aromatic smoke from our fires trailed upwards, and the sky faded from its red and yellow to orange-streaked grey to indigo, and then revealed countless flickering points of stars.

The only problem in our world was: who was going to kill the chicken we had bought from a passing peasant? Out of the twenty-four people - including twenty Tibetan battle-hardened rebels - no one was able or willing to kill the bird for various reasons. The Tibetans claimed that their religion did not permit it, or they did not know how. I asked them how they could kill gya-mi ("Chinese") but not gya-mo ("chicken") and they said Tibetans didn't like chicken meat so killing chickens was not in their custom . I said I could not kill it because I was busy writing up my notes. Chris said he could not kill it after carrying it with him all day. Finally, Hemantha said he would do it, and he lopped off its head with a deadly, curved Gurkha kukri.

Eventually it made a tasty dish for us. The Tibetans had come up with a treasure in Trashi, a general handyman, who, among his abilities was a knowledge of how to make excellent flour scones on a bed of hot coals. After stuffing ourselves with his scones and Sedar's cooked chicken and gravy, we appointed him assistant cook with full privileges to eat with us.

As we lay back replete, our satisfaction with the good meal increased by the drifting aroma of wood smoke, the moon broke from behind the mountains and bathed the valley in silver. The suddenness and brightness of the moon's appearing, making every tree branch and leaf stand out in breath-catchingly beautiful silhouette, made me think of Francis Thompson's poem, **The Kingdom of God**:

"O world invisible, we view thee,
O world intangible, we touch thee,
O world unknowable, we know thee,
Inapprehensible, we clutch thee!...

The angels keep their ancient places; -
Turn but a stone and start a wing!
'Tis ye, 'tis your estrangéd faces,
That miss the many-splendoured thing.

While we slowly drank our final cups of tea, savoring the memorable beauty of the night, the Tibetans, after a great deal of discussion, sorted themselves out into two lines beside the fire, pulled their voluminous gowns around their shoulders and, squatting Buddha-wise, launched into an impromptu "prayer-meeting". The flickering firelight played redly on slant-eyed, flat-nosed faces, and their voices rose and fell in haunting melancholy as they prayed to Buddha and the gods for the safety and success of our expedition.

Later Tsewang suggested, and we agreed, that we would not eat as soon as we got up in the morning but only drink tea, then travel for two hours or so in the cool of the morning, and stop for breakfast about mid-morning. After a two-hour break we would walk again until mid-afternoon, camp, have tea, and then have our evening meal at sunset. This was the usual custom when traveling in Tibet and in this way we would be able to make the best use of the day.

The first part of the morning was fairly easy but, as the sun warmed, the trail rose again out of the valley, although not as steep as the day before. After an hour or so it straightened out into a long, gradual slope across the mountainside to the distant lofty white blur of the high Himalayas. Behind us, to the south, the mountains fell away in a diminishing tangle of dark green and ocher ridges, disappearing into a shimmering blue haze.

The early morning summer cramps and stiffness eased off in the increasing warmth and steady rhythm, and the thought of the prospect ahead grew from muted excitement to exhilaration. Away from the stifling artificial life of the cities of the plains and the selfish ambitions of so many, in the mountains of the Himalayas the basic issues were related to people rather than politics - food, shelter, travel, protection.

If a Confederation of Himalayan States seemed an impossible political idea because of the national self-interests of inter-Asian power politics, the idea of these Himalayan countries being homogenous units in unanimous support of a pro-Indian - even pro-Chinese - policy was even more ludicrous as we passed village after village of Mongolian-type inhabitants barely lifting their heads from their fields or their grind-stones to look at us. They wanted peace, and they needed leisure, but they went from dawn to dusk in a ceaseless round of pitiless labor under a growing threat of local corruption and intimidation and exploitation, and the looming threat of a Himalayan war.

The Chinese Communists to the north of the border, who said they cared for the bodies of these Nepalese peasants, if not their souls, had the same shape of faces, the same peasant background, the same unwearying patience - and they were within the same easy reach of the Nepalese villages as ourselves. We could not offer much in the face of the gargantuan Chinese Communist military machine - a film to interest fifty countries of some several hundred million people for a an hour or so; some newspaper articles so long as there was no other catastrophe elsewhere; perhaps a book at some point - but at least it was something, better than indifference, and from smaller mustard seeds greater trees had grown.

I had taken René Sedillot's ***History of the World***, and a paperback copy of ***The Metaphysical Poets,*** in addition to my ***Bible***, with me to read during the trip. And it seemed appropriate that I should read John Donne's words at this point:

> "...On a huge hill,
> Cragged, and steep, Truth stands, and hee that will
> Reach her, about must, and about must, goe;
> And what the hills suddennes resist, winne so;
> Yet strive so, that before age, deaths twilight,
> Thy Soule rest, for none can worke in that night.
> To will, implyes delay, therefore now doe:
> Hard deeds, the bodies paines hard knowledge too
> The mindes indeavours reach, and mysteries
> Are like the Sunne, dazling, yet plaine to all eyes."

We stopped for breakfast about nine-o'clock at the top of a ridge, where the mountain dropped in a giant's staircase of terraced rice-fields to the valley bottom seven-thousand feet below on one side, and the trail continued up and up in a wide sweep on the other.

We climbed steadily until mid-afternoon, when we reached a rounded knoll on which stood a huge tree. Here Tsewang decided we would camp for the night. It was not too soon, for as the porters trudged slowly into camp a few drops of rain fell. As we rushed to raise the tents it began to stream down in heavy sheets, the wind carrying it in a deafening drum-beat against the tent fabrics.

The Tibetans huddled under the tarpaulin, and Sedar and Trashi even managed to produce a pot of hot, sweet tea on a paraffin stove in the thunderstorm. It was a fitting background as Tsewang recounted experiences and stories of Khamba exploits before and during the revolt of 1956-59. The orange-colored material of our tent gave a greenish glow to the faintly discernible faces of the Tibetans, lit by streaking flashes of lightning, the steady drumming of the rain counterpointed by the great rolls of thunder.

It rained most of the night, but the morning was dry. Away to the north there was a remarkable sight. To the west, the almost 27,000-feet snow-covered Annapurna, and to the east the almost 27,000-feet snow-covered Manaslu, towered majestically, with our projected trail somewhere between them. Beneath and around them the lower, also snow-covered, ranges of the Himalayas were visible in upthrust jagged splendor, but they had a tonsure of heavy grey thunderclouds. The slanting rays of sunlight which illuminated the snowy lower slopes disappeared into a heavy charcoal-grey cloud, then bank upon bank of clouds towered in almost mathematical layers of lightening shades of grey to emerge at the crests in smoky white masses edged in blazing gold. This awesome aerial phalanx moved majestically forward over the gigantic peaks, wiping them out from our view to a rolling accompaniment of distant thunder.

Once morning tea had been drunk - and my morning dispensary for cuts, bruises, stomach and bowel ailments, had been completed - we got on our way. When we stopped for breakfast, there was a natural platform of earth projecting behind a large tree and, sitting there, the whole of the next valley lay spread out like a huge map. From the spot, Tsewang, who had come this way several times before, pointed out the direction of our journey for the next few days.

At our feet, the path dropped right away in a series of dizzying spirals and zig-zags to a narrow brown thread snaking alongside the valley river-bed, six thousand feet below. The valley was unusually wide, and heavily-cultivated as usual, with clusters of brown, thatched-roof houses at different places along the winding river. Where the river disappeared, Tsewang said, we had to turn away north over a ridge into another valley. To the north-west lay the large village of Arughat, one of the few market-places on our route, and an official check-point for our permit. Here we would add to our stores what we had not been able to find so far, enough food to last us for the remainder of our trip. Further north still, behind where the morning thunderclouds were now thinning out in the sunshine and blue sky, lay the Tibetan-occupied region of Dzum, our intermediate target, still nine days' journey away.

We had decided to make for Dzum after putting together all the information we could gather in Kathmandu from Tibetan refugees; and then confirmed the decision during our trek from discussions with our Tibetan porters. Gradually, in all the hesitant and cautious conversations, there would emerge snippets of information about the movements of the Khamba guerrillas, and these were usually centered on either Mustang or Dzum. A determining factor for me in choosing Dzum rather than Mustang - in addition to the basic objection that it was a Gyalu Thondup-supported group - was that there were more officials and military personnel likely to be met en route to Mustang than the more difficult route to what was designated the remote and "sacred" region of Dzum. Why it was considered sacred I had not discovered. It was rumored in awed tones in Kathmandu that the Khambas in Dzum went into Tibet on

Gods and Guerrillas

their raids against the Chinese army over the little-known and very dangerous, exposed 20,000-feet Khojang Pass, rearing out of a vast forested tangle of impenetrable surrounding mountain giants.

The Tibetans have a saying: *"Test a horse going up, and a man going down."* After an hour of plunging, boulder-strewn descent, my legs were trembling, aching muscles twitching uncontrollably. I could feel my toes wearing through my socks as they pressed and rubbed against the front of my boots in exquisite agony - and I was carrying only fifty pounds! What the non-sock wearing Tibetans, carrying up to two hundred pounds, were suffering in their leather knee-boots I could not imagine.

It was almost three hours later before we reached the bottom of the mountain, and dropped our loads in breath-expelling relief. I lay back against my back-pack, eyes closed, letting the warmth of the sun ease the pain in my limbs and shoulders, and the cool breeze soothe my sweat-splashed head and shoulders.

After some time I heard Tibetans talking near me and, opening my eyes, saw Tsewang and Sedar reading from a piece of paper. Thinking it was a hand-drawn map of some kind I asked what they were reading. They came over and handed me the paper. I looked at it casually, then with sudden interest.

It was a long piece of rough Tibetan fibrous paper such as was used in their prayer scrolls; but, in addition to the usual Tibetan cursive script, there were two foreign names in capitals - **HEINRICH HARRER, PETER AUF-SCHNEIDER**. These were two German prisoners-of-war who had escaped from a detention camp in India in an epic journey across the Himalayas into western Tibet to Lhasa, later told by Harrer in his book, ***Seven Years In Tibet.*** I knew Harrer personally, and from my Tibetan friends by report, and we agreed that he was a nasty specimen disliked by most Tibetans, while Peter Aufschneider was liked personally and much appreciated for his engineering contributions in erecting buiodings and irrigation projects in Tibet. Harrer's book – which, the director of his publishers told me, he did not write himself but had someone else write - was a mishmash of true and false claims as to his influence while living in Tibet. I knew personally, from both Indian and Tibetan officials, that Harrer had been expelled from Tibet and also from India - and I had even packed his goods to be sent to him at his request. Strangely enough, Peter Aufschnedier was now living in Kathmandu and working as an adviser to an agricultural project. I asked the two Tibetans how they had got hold of the paper, and Sedar said it belonged to him.

"But how did you get it? Did you buy it from somebody," I persisted.

"No," he insisted. "It is my own. When these two foreigners traveled through Tibet they stayed with my parents, and it was my uncle who wrote this. I was only a child at the time. My family and relatives were quite wealthy then, and we gave the two foreigners food and shelter, and my uncle taught them some Tibetan language. Afterwards, they went on to Lhasa."

He had met Peter Aufschnieder in Kathmandu, and he had given him messages to convey to his family, but he told him that they were all dead in fighting the Chinese. He thought Harrer was dead, but I told him I knew Harrer was alive and living in Switzerland, and he asked if I would post a letter to him if he wrote it. I agreed.

The walk along the valley beside the river was easy, but blindingly hot, and perspiration dripped in a steady stream from eyebrows, nose and chin. By mid-afternoon we were close to the end of the narrowing valley, and the trail dropped to wind across the boulders of the fast, tumbling river. At one point it disappeared into a branch of the main current, and we had to wade across, thigh-deep, to reach a flat camping-space for the night. Here we arranged for Chris and Hemantha to go ahead to the large village of Arughat to buy supplies, in order to save some time.

Arughat was only slightly larger than some of the villages we had already passed, but the houses were more substantial, some of them with corrugated iron roofs instead of the normal thatch. It was built on the side of the mountain so the houses rose some sixty feet above the river in several tiers. A rickety wooden bridge swung uneasily above the river, and a steep stairway of large stones led into the one street of the village. The street was cluttered with cackling hens and chirping chickens, lean dogs with ugly patches of mange, scores of hungry-looking children, women with babies - and even standing children - suckling at their breasts.

Chris and Hemantha had arranged for us to sleep in the office of the "Nepal Malaria Education Organization" which, although it had a grandiloquent name and was doing excellent work, was only a mud-and-stone structure with a beaten mud floor. We decided, therefore, we would cook in the main square of the village, on a raised platform under the shade of two large trees, and that the porters would sleep there around our baggage.

But we had a major problem - there was no food in this major marketplace. Chris and Hemantha had been able to find only cups of tea, and no-one would sell eggs, chickens or rice. The rice shortage was a serious matter for the villagers as well as us. It appeared that there had been a drastic crop failure the previous year and there was now a shortage throughout the region. In one of the villages nearby a family of six had died from starvation and many people were living only on roots.

By a savage irony, while Adrian and Hemantha were in the small village post-office waiting to send off letters, the postmaster was trying to dissuade a farmer from sending a letter to his son asking for help - saying that it might cause trouble because the government was denying that there was any shortage. The government should have been worrying about the possibility of the Chinese exploiting the situation by getting rice to the starving people. Yet this was the country of the Gurkhas, the home of Nepal's most famous fighting warriors, whose official indemnity and salaries from Britain and India brought the country its largest foreign exchange.

Tsewang managed to find 21 eggs at a grossly inflated cost, but no rice at any price, and with the eggs scrambled and Tsewang's excellent scones we had a meal at least. But, we were resigned for delay as the porters scattered throughout the nearby area seeking whatever food they could find. We dare not risk going to Dzum, and into Tibet, without having sufficient food in hand, because famine conditions there were even worse we were informed.

I used the time to write up my notes and, as the sun rose, climbed and sank, I read my *History of the World* and my Bible, while Adrian, Chris and Hemantha bent nails, spoon and pins into a fishing line with hooks and spinners to catch fish in the river. In late afternoon we washed clothes and bathed in the river.

Above: The ambush valley
Below left: Truck convoy halted by gunfire
Below right: Chinese soldier fires from behind truck

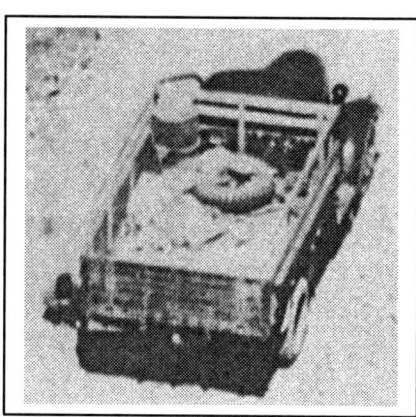

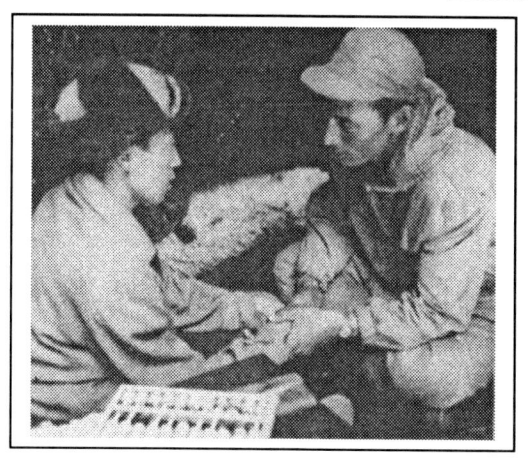

Left: After the raid, Ten-dar (right) questions a Tibetan who lives in the garrison town of Dzongkar.

Above and right:
On the trail with the guerrillas. On the Nepal side of the Khojang Pass the snow was thick and at the top a blizzard was blowing.

Above left: A Tibetan guards the escape valley from the ambush.
Above right: Well camouflaged in his hillside vantage point, Ten-dar waits for the arrival of the truck convoy.

CHAPTER EIGHT

Problems With Bridges, Military Patrols, and Possible Death

After a few days' delay the porters managed to find enough food for us to risk departure from Arughat. But now the extra food meant extra weight, and several of the porters were having to carry double loads which meant a slower pace of travel. We were successful in persuading three local Gurung hillmen to carry loads for a few days for the - to them - princely sum of a US dollar a person a day, but not all the way to Dzum.

Next morning we climbed steadily for two hours, then emerged on to a ridge overlooking a lovely, heavily cultivated valley. The trail dropped away into the valley, then straightened out to follow the course of a spray-tossing river. This, said Tsewang, was the river we would follow all the way to Dzum where it came "right out of the snows of Tibet." The trail led gradually upwards through a pleasant tree-lined slope of the mountain, with the plentiful mint bruised into pungent fragrance by the trampling feet of our porters. But, as the valley narrowed into a gorge, the trail deteriorated into a steep and stony, ankle-aching climb, made torturous as the sun climbed and the heat increased. When we stopped for our mid-morning meal, in a pine-shaded glade in the forest of trees, we dropped to the ground like the dying Buddha, covered with a blanket of fragrant white frangipani petals.

The gorge narrowed until it was only a savage gash between sheer mountainsides. The trail rose and plunged, as it edged around the forested slopes. In some places the mountainsides were so steep that the tops of the leaning trees were only a few feet away from the slopes in which their roots were buried, so sheer was the rise. Hundreds, then thousands, of feet below, the river boiled and foamed around rocks and through narrow channels, while we inched perilously across some smooth mountain face with only inch-wide hand- and -footholds, still carrying our 50-200-pound loads, or we clambered or scrambled wildly across dangerous slopes of loose shale.

Our stopping-place for the night was a ten-foot wide platform, about forty-feet long, under a huge overhang of rock jutting out of the mountain. On every side the mountain plunged straight down into the raging river far below. Even the water supply was a thousand-foot waterfall cascading over terrifyingly smooth rock in a spectacular white spray, ending in a wide and calm pool.

Somebody had found fish from somewhere and it was left to me to prepare the supper. I sautéed it in cooking oil, with a dash of cinnamon and mint, and some brandy from the medicine chest, to celebrate the dramatic setting. As we ate, the moon rose in a clear sky, the firelight danced on the savage splendor around us, and all around there was the deep roar of falling water.

The magnificence of the scene must have affected Adrian and Chris, too, because they decided to begin filming the next day as we traveled. The Tibetans were so thrilled to be "on camera" that we had to threaten them with non-participation to get them to stop hamming it up and spoiling the shots. The scenery was ideal, but the weather was still unpredictable, and we had to be ready for a quick stop to pitch tarpaulin covers for our baggage in the sudden inch-an-hour downpours which churned the trail into treacherous streams of water, loose mud and wet stones.

We squatted under the tarpaulins and ponchos, unable to sit because of the waterlogged earth, trying to keep dry in the curtains of rain. Yet, miraculously Sedar and Tsewang managed to produce a meal, although the food became sodden as we ate. It was too much for the Gurung hillmen, who chose to return to their villages without payment rather than continue in these circumstances. Tsewang said laconically that the conditions waiting for us ahead were worse than anything we had experienced so far, which was a great comfort. Within the hour he proved to be a true prophet.

The mountain grew even steeper to climb, then tilted forward into a long precipitous overhang. The trail wound across this sheer wall, high above the valley floor and the raging river. Ahead, for about two hundred terrifying yards there was no trail at all, and a kind of "trail-bridge" had been constructed out of wooden supports driven into the mountainside, with branches of trees laid lengthwise on the wooden projections, then the leaves covered with a coating of stones and dirt - presumably in a hopeless attempt to keep the awful drop being too visible beneath one's feet. As I negotiated this two-foot-wide "trail-bridge" I had to swing my back-pack away from the mountainside wall so I would not be accidentally bumped over the drop by an outward-leaning tilt, and this forced me nearer the edge in a nightmare shuffle. Fortunately, everybody made it across.

The constant grind of challenges and responses were sorting out the characters among the porters. Tsewang was effective so long as there were no problems of discipline, when he would be reluctant to deal with the culprit, and then be overly friendly in an attempt to curry favor. Sedar was efficient, without being inspiring. Trashi, the handyman, was the best of the lot, as he was last out of a breaking camp, first into a new camp, getting the fire going and tea made, organizing the buying and preparing of food. Basang - the "smart boy" of the first day - continued to be the smartest, constructively, finding chickens where there were seemingly none, buying them at the lowest price, always cracking jokes and raising a laugh - and assisting me when I was handing out medicines. In short, he was a minor Tibetan Chahvan!

We had scarcely started up the trail the following morning when it dropped away precipitously to an unbelievably hazardous bridge, swung obliquely for about sixty yards across the now wider and deeper and angrier river. It was constructed in three sections, the first section dropping at an alarming angle of forty-five degrees to a large smooth rock a third of the way across the raging river. On this rock had been raised a six-foot palisade of branches lashed together with tree fibers and filled inside with heavy stones to keep it "stable" on the rock. The first angled section reached from the mountain on our side to this makeshift support. From the far side, three sets of three large tree-trunks had been projected outwards in a cantilevered span, and this formed the third support on the far section.

In the space between, poised above the roaring fury of the river's central channel, two tree trunks were placed with only lashed bamboos and tree branches as a footway all across the span. As each Tibetan stepped on to this contraption it swung crazily under his weight, and we had to hire some local hillmen to carry the loads of others who were unwilling to risk crossing such a nightmare with loads.

It was too good an opportunity for filming to miss, but the Tibetans were disgruntled when, seven of them having crossed over the wildly swaying nightmare, Adrian and Chris asked them to do it again to make certain that it was, as they said, "in the can." Naturally, Basang was the first to volunteer - both ways. Now that we were approaching our objective, more and more time was taken up with filming, and this, with the deteriorating condition of the trail, was slowing us down.

The next day continued the "firsts". The day before it had been the first nightmare bridge. Today was the first sight of our snow-mountain goal. Previously, we had seen distant glimpses of Annapurna and Manaslu to the east and west as we climbed between them; but now, as we climbed out of the forests and valleys we reached stone highlands and, in the rising "V" ahead, the snow-crowned high Himalayas of the Nepal-Tibet border. For the first time, too, the hill people we met were bilingual and spoke Tibetan as well as Gurkhali; and the houses were no longer stone-and-mud plastered, with thatched roofs, but stone-built with flat roofs of fibre-matting held down with large stones.

It was also the first time to report at an Indian-army radio check-post known as Setelvass. This place was listed on our permit as the last place to be visited, and we not only had to be unsuspected here, we had to be so lily-white regarding our intentions they would not radio our presence back to Kathmandu. We had planned to return by a different route, but, still, in any questioning about our trip, we would have to be ultra-careful not to give anything away.

The officer-in-charge of the check-post was a friendly Indian, with two junior officers, one of them Nepali, and a few soldiers. While the Tibetan porters went off to find chang, the Tibetan millet beer, and to keep out of sight, we drank sweet Indian tea and chatted with the military men. The officer-in-charge had spent twelve years in various Himalayan check-posts, and he said that there had been an unusual number of refugees coming from Tibet recently. He chattily volunteered the information that there were only ten of these small check-posts along the eight hundred miles of high Himalayan border of gigantic mountains, remote valleys and heavy forests. What went on in the next valley was unknown, much less what was taking place five days' journey northward to the border crossing. It was only recently that refugees had come into this region at all, because there was no recognized "Pass" crossing from Tibet to Nepal in this area, although it was rumored that there was a regular flow of refugees coming from Tibet into Dzum from somewhere.

We kept the officer chatting volubly, until our permits were stamped showing that we had entered and left Setelvass as agreed, and slipped away without him noticing that we had given no information regarding our subsequent movements. We did not stop in the village for the night but, rounding up our obviously tipsy porters, we left as if going to the west towards Mustang, but, out of sight of Setelvass, we turned north-east and headed for Dzum, now three days' journey away. We had now been traveling steadily for fourteen days since we left Kathmandu and, if we calculated another week or so in Dzum to make contact with the Khamba guerrillas, and at least a week to arrange to travel inside Tibet with them, it was going to take us at least six to eight weeks to complete the assignment away from Kathmandu. That was long enough to attract undue official attention to us, with awkward questions and obstacles to getting our film out of the country. It was also an unconscionable length of time for my wife to be in Kathmandu with no knowledge of my whereabouts or time of return!

Although we pushed ahead as quickly as we could out of Setelvass, considering that our porters were beer-happy enough to be singing cheerfully but tending to stop off for more drinking from hidden supplies and subsequent consequences, we had to stop shortly to camp for the night. As we sat around the camp-fire a local hillman arrived from the north who said he was heading for Setelvass after being

Gods and Guerrillas

to Dzum for trading. We persuaded him to stop with us for the night while we plied him with questions.

He said that thousands of Tibetan refugees had recently crossed over the border under Chinese pressure along the northern Tibetan border region with Nepal. They said the Chinese were confiscating their herds of yaks, sheep and goats, giving them nothing in return. and transferring them away from their ancestral homes. Many had died of starvation, many of them had mysteriously disappeared, some even while working in local Chinese garrison and other constructions.

Were there any signs of Khambas near Dzum? I asked him as innocuously as I could. He was uneasy with the question, but he said that there were signs of Khambas around Dzum, but the locals didn't like to speak about this as the Khambas were dangerous, armed, and very fierce warriors. He didn't know how many, nobody ever said. They were only seen in groups when they came to Dzum for supplies of some kind, or for important religious festivals in the monastery with the famous idol. The Khambas lived outside Dzum in some of the remote valleys. At the festivals, when they got drunk, they would talk about some of their raids against the Chinese, but no local Tibetans ever went with them on the dangerous sorties.

Regarding the trail from where we were to Dzum, he said it was very difficult, and even dangerous in places. He only made the journey because he made good profits from his trading in cigarettes and "down-country goods." He and a tipsy Tsewang got into an argument about an alternative trail which I could partly understand, although it was conducted in the local vernacular of part Gurkhali and Bhotia-Tibetan. It seemed the hillman was advising against a circuitous "easy" route for reasons I could not follow, and was proposing going almost directly over the intervening mountain ridges into Dzum by a hazardous, unknown, but possible trail.

The next morning the argument was settled, when we met another hillman coming from Dzum, and he had just come the same direct way. He agreed it was difficult and dangerous in places, and also he had come south downhill which was easier than going north, he said. After some persuasion, and a generous offer of "baksheesh", he agreed to return with us as a guide to Dzum. Our porters weren't happy, but the issue was settled.

The start was not auspicious. The slope ahead was at least forty-five degrees, almost completely bare of shrubs or trees, with a single-file, hairline, path snaking upwards across the shifting shale plunging straight down three thousand feet. One false step, one slip, one momentary loss of balance, meant certain death. Even where there were patches of grass, these were short, springy, smooth and covered with a thin layer of dried pine needles, making it treacherous underfoot. The Tibetans had even stopped their constant prayer-mantra of "*Om Mani Padme Hum.*" We were like cats on a broken glass-topped wall as we gingerly picked our way forward.

After negotiating this hazard, the path dropped dizzyingly downward in straight drops of a hundred feet or so. Where it was not straight down, it angled across the precipitous face on a terrifying insecure carpet of pine needles which hid whatever was underneath - if anything. We had to "prod" our way forward with stripped branches of trees, to make certain that there was enough substance underneath to take our weight, and not drop us into the raging river far below.

By midday we turned a bend in the mountain and saw the petrifying hazard of yet another "bridge" crossing the river. The mountains on either side had narrowed into a dark sunless menacing gorge, and the two-thousand-feet drop and half-mile forward to the bridge, was a series of plunging drops and steep angles to a point where the two mountainsides curved inwards into a narrow sixty-foot knife-gash spanned by - wait for it! - two tree-trunks. This was the "bridge".

If it looked paralyzing from two-thousand-feet up the mountain, it was positively mind-numbing when standing beside it. Both eyes and ears were bombarded with the horror of sight and sound of that treacherous span across the madly roaring and echoing river assaulting eyes and ears. No wonder the Tibetans had not wanted to come this way!

The approach to the tree-trunk span was across a smooth projecting rock with only a few shallow depressions on the slick wet surface as footholds. At the edge of the rock, where it curved and dropped away into the knife-gash chasm, two smaller tree trunks bound together with fibers served as a tilting, unstable causeway on to the main two tree-trunk crossing. This was about twenty or thirty feet and was without hand-holds of any kind. There were only crudely-cut gashes cut into the tree-trunks as flattish "steps" to help in attaining balance. Sixty feet below, the river was a dark, sullenly roaring menace waiting to receive the unwary and unfortunate. We not only made it - in a sepulchral silence - Adrian and Chris even filmed it from both sides and the center.

The up-slope on the far side rose even more steeply than the down-slope. Then, at one thousand feet, we moved on to a seventy-foot rock face to climb straight up on footholds that were only shallow depressions and thin runnels to keep us from falling to certain death beneath. We were still carrying our loads of varying 50-200-pounds of television equipment and personal effects, and, unlike a mountain-climbing exercise, we were not roped together. A brisk wind had arisen, too, and blew on us dangerously in sudden gusts as we labored upwards.

Incredibly, our Gurung hillman guide had obtained a goat from somewhere in those nightmare conditions and he was leading it, or carrying it across his shoulders, as we traveled. He offered it to us for sale as food, no doubt at considerable profit to himself, and we didn't haggle over the price. He even killed it and skinned it for us, and we celebrated our safe survival with a royal feast - half of the body to the television team, half to the porters, and the head to the hillmen. Tsewang even cooked a Tibetan delicacy, mo-mos, or steamed dumplings with fillings of herb-spiced meat and wild onions.

Next morning, after climbing another two thousand feet straight up the mountain - description palls with repetition - we stopped for breakfast and, switching on our radio, we heard the news that Prime Minister Nehru of India had died. For me, it was the end of a memorable decade of confrontation with the charismatic leader of India, over the question of Tibet and his pro-China policies. Despite our highly publicized disagreements, I had respected him as a worthy representative for his nation.

Throughout the day it was sheer climbing and tortured limbs, our most lasting memory the sight of the straining calves of the man in front of us, and the sobbing, whistling breaths counter-pointing the rising sound of the wind. Each step literally carried with it the possibility of an ugly death - the sudden lurch, a vain grasp at slipping grass or air, and a hurtling, bouncing, bone-shattering, flesh-lacerating drop to eternity.

Ironically, the previous evening I had just been reading George Herbert's poem "Death", in The Metaphysical Poets book I carried with me:

> *"Death, thou wast once an uncouth hideous thing,*
> *   Nothing but bones,*
> * The sad effect of sadder grones,*
> *Thy mouth was open, but thou couldst not sing.*
>
> *For we consider'd thee as at some six*
> *   Or ten years hence,*
> * After the losse of life and sense,*
> *Flesh being turn'd to dust, and home to sicks...*
>
> *For we do now behold thee gay and glad,*
> *   As at dooms-day;*
> * When souls shall wear their new aray,*
> *And all thy bones with beauty shall be clad.*
>
> *Therefore we can go die as sleep, and trust*
> *   Half that we have*
> * Unto an honest faithful grave;*
> *Making our pillows either down, or dust."*

It was not just a morbid reflection. We were conscious that we were going into a situation where we could easily die from the fighting that was involved, and not just from the dangers of Himalayan mountain travel. We had even had discussions about whether we should be armed as we went into battle with the Tibetans. I had told the others that the Khambas had an agreement among themselves that, if they were badly wounded in battle, they should be put to death by their comrades rather than be left to the Chinese. We had decided, on personal as well as professional grounds, that we would not carry arms during the filming assignment, and that we would accept the same conditions as the Khambas - that is, if we could persuade them to take us on a raid with them.

The next day we met two Tibetans on their way from Dzum to Kathmandu. We stopped to share drinks and information, and, in answer to our queries, they said that, yes, there were Khamba guerrillas in the vicinity of Dzum. They had recently returned from a foray across the border into Tibet, where they had shot up a Chinese convoy, killed the Chinese soldiers, and brought back guns, ammunition and other bounty from the convoy. They had also rounded up herds of yaks confiscated by the Chinese from Tibetans.

The information from the two Tibetans was a relief, because we had only been traveling on the slightest items of news about the presence of warring Khambas in these remote mountain regions. Now the only remaining challenge was to persuade them to take us with them.

CHAPTER NINE

"Sacred" Dzum's Talking Idol And Deadly Khamba Guerrillas

The approach to Dzum up the sheer slopes of the intervening mountains came between us and the towering 20-30,000-feet snow-crowned giants comprising the border between Nepal and India, shutting out all sight of them. We twisted and turned, struggled upwards and stumbled downwards, but always in a tangle of precipitously rearing mountain slopes.

At the end of the day before we were due to arrive at Dzum we reached a massive overhang of rock bulging out from the mountain, leaving a narrow shelf about sixty feet long, but only about four feet head-room in front and a foot high at the rear, commanding an unobstructed and incomparable view on three sides. As the sun set above the encircling mountains in its nightly glory of reds and golds, we were perched like eagles in an eyrie scanning a magnificent panorama of endless giant snow mountains and plunging valleys, green forests and silver rivers. The approach to Dzum was hidden by the sheer sides of the valley beneath us, and the river which swirled and roared in a tight curve. In ths dramatic setting some unknown devotee had carved and painted a gigantic sitting Buddha on the rock-face across from our camping-spot.

Dzum, we had been told, was not a single village, but comprised a sprawlingly occupied region of small communities just under the snows of the high Himalayas. We discovered this the next day as we arrived at one community and found that it wasn't Dzum, and that there were other scattered communities before we came to the village of Dzum itself. These communities had possibly sprung up, or at least expanded, with the arrival of the many Tibetan refugees fleeing from Tibet. The first refugees had kept going until they reached Kathmandu, or India; but, as news of unhappy conditions there spread backwards through the valleys to the mountain borders, the later arrivals became reluctant to be confined to the often dreadful circumstances in some of the camps in the heat of the foothills and plains of Nepal and India.

The occasional few houses we now passed were of Tibetan stone, flat-roofed design, and the people were definitely either Himalayan Bhotias, a kind of mixed Tibetans and locals, or native Tibetans. They were dressed as Tibetans, in the loose-ankle-length maroon gowns, caught at the waists with tightly wound colored scarves, and the women with gaudily-colored aprons. On the open spaces around the houses there were *dzos* grazing, or cross-bred yaks, instead of the sheep or goats of lower regions.

Along the trail were piles of mani stones, seen all over Tibet. These were crude shrines of stones with either chalk or chipped inscriptions of the Buddhist prayer-mantra, "*Om Mani Padme Hum*." We had just climbed a long incline with a raised pile of these mani stones when we found ourselves approaching a large village called Chokang.

Ahead lay a breath-catching beautiful valley, with green fields bathed in the morning sunshine, and bending away to the left, where the first houses of Chokang were visible. There were scores of large fields of tall, gently waving stalks of barley, interspersed with clumps of trees in varying shades of green. The mountains encircling the valley were dark with pine forests, and, for the first time, we were able to see, unobscured, the full pristine glory of the high Himalayan snow-covered giant ranges. The ever-present

Gods and Guerrillas

wind whispered with cooling susurrus through trees and grain, and the river was a background murmuring harmony.

As we entered the village we were met by a huge individual in Tibetan dress, but his maroon colored gown was not ankle-length; it was caught at the waist to form a knee-length "kilt", the chest part pushed off one shoulder, revealing a crossover shirt of vaguely-familiar patterned green-brown silk. It was made from a parachute!

"Khamba," Tsewang whispered to me nervously.

"Is he the headman?" I asked him, puzzled. I thought, from what we had heard, that the Khambas were supposed to be hiding in the valleys. This one didn't seem to be bothered by the arrival of strangers, just normally curious. Tsewang was too nervous to do more than shake his head negatively.

The Khamba was joined by other Tibetans, and from the deference they showed him he must be the headman or leader. He had a few low-voiced words with Tsewang, pointing to a house further up the street, and then led the way there. As we walked I could hear the villagers asking among themselves, "Have the Chinese arrived?"!

Adrian fell into step beside me. "What is happening?" he asked.

"Either we are being taken to his house, or we will be taken to a campsite," I replied. "I can't sort out whether he is a village headman or a guerrilla leader. But Tibetan custom is to first provide visitors with tea, talk about travel conditions, and then work around to what is the purpose."

I laughed at Adrian's expression when I mentioned drinking Tibetan tea. They had sampled some in Kathmandu, and the rancid butter concoction had been hard to take. The Tibetan tea was made from bricks of Chinese tea, put in a churn with a lump of rancid yak butter, salt and often a pinch of soda to make it "draw". When taken as a gravy rather than tea it was actually very pleasant, and in the icy cold of Tibet it was a warming appreciated drink.

The Khamba led us to a wide patch of ground on the outskirts of the village, just beneath a house which he pointed out as his own, and with a wonderful view of the whole valley. He said this was where we could camp, and when our porters were preparing the site, the Khamba invited us to take tea with him in his house. I thanked him and asked him politely to excuse Adrian and Chris as they would have to supervise the porters, and said I and Tsewang would be happy to go with him. I asked him his name, and he said he was Abu Jampa, the "Abu" a usual Tibetan designation for headman or chief.

From the ensuing conversation, while drinking endless bowls of butter tea, I gathered that Chokang was the central village of the Dzum region, that there was no actual village called Dzum. I made no attempt to ask about Khamba guerrillas in the area, but kept it open by describing my own experience of living among Khambas in East Tibet for three years and for another eleven years among Tibetans on the Indian-Tibetan borders. He was thrilled that I could use the Kham dialect, and chatted away amiably. Custom required that only a vague outline of plans should be discussed at this stage so we exchanged general information only. After a while we excused ourselves and went back to camp.

We discussed what gift should be offered to Abu Jampa, according to Tibetan custom. The arriving guest was given every local hospitality - including the offer of the headman's wife or daughters or whoever! - and in return he would be given what would be considered luxuries to the host. We decided to present Abu Jampa with rice, Indian tea and cigarettes.

This time we all went in a group to pay our respects - Adrian, Chris, Hemantha, Tsewang and myself. I made a short formal speech, apologizing as was customary for the poor quality of the gift offered, and thanking the headman for all the help provided. He replied that the gift was unnecessary and lavish, and that he was happy to be of any assistance.

On this occasion tsamba, or roasted and ground barley flour served as a kind of oatmeal, and dried meat of indeterminate vintage, was served, as well as butter tea, and we got down quickly to details. With Tsewang elaborating, I outlined our plans as wanting to film and photograph Tibetan life and customs in the valley and beyond. Also, to get into touch with the Khamba guerrillas in the area; and, finally, with their cooperation, to go with the Khambas on a raid against Chinese convoys across the border in Tibet.

It was quite a list, and Abu Jampa listened impassively until we had finished. He asked Tsewang about our credentials, and Tsewang went into a long explanation about my background of help for the Tibetan cause, and I handed him the two letters given to me in London from Surkhang and Yangpel. After reading them we discussed in detail how the project would be handled.

On the way to Dzum, Adrian, Chris and I had held private talks away from Hemantha and Tsewang regarding what we were going to do about the final arrangements. We decided that there was no way the project could be handled without the two of them finding out about it in some way, even if it was only in our extended absence inside Tibet with the Khamba guerrillas. We concluded, therefore, that we would be frank about most of our plans and then, only at the end of the assignment on our actual trip into Tibet, and a hopefully successful raid, give an adequate summary. Since we did not know ourselves what the raid plans were likely to be they would naturally be safe until that time.

Abu Jampa proposed he should go personally to the next village of Rajen, where the largest monastery in the area was located, and arrange for us to film the monastery and lamas there. He would also send a letter and messenger to a large encampment of between five hundred and a thousand nomad refugees who had just fled across the border from Chinese oppression, and who were living about a day's journey away from Rajen. Finally, he would inform a group of Khamba guerrillas to see if they would agree to meet with us for a discussion of our plans. It was as much as we could hope for - far more than I had expected to accomplish in such a short time.

We all had an uneasy night's sleep for, despite our seventeen-day climb to accustom us to the elevating altitudes, we were now at fifteen-thousand feet, and experiencing the usual insomnia, stomach cramps, nausea and diarrhea. I told the others that it should pass in two or three days, but that they would have to learn to walk and do other activities more slowly or they could have black-outs.

Immediately after breakfast the following day, Adrian, Chris, Hemantha and Tsewang left to begin filming in the village and valley. I wanted to write up my notes, and had just sat down in the warm morning sunshine, my back against a large rock overlooking the valley, when there was a rustle of movement as the lounging porters got to their feet respectfully or moved out of the way.

A tall figure, preceded by Abu Jampa, strode up to where I was sitting and gave a smart salute. The easy, independent carriage, the magnificent six-feet physique, the broad facial features, all indicated another Khamba. But, most significant of all, he was dressed in khaki shirt, wool-lined yak-skin trousers, bound by khaki puttees and leather army boots. I had made direct contact with the Khamba guerrillas at last.

I asked him to sit down beside me and ordered Trashi to bring tea, and we chatted casually for some time. He was interested in how I had come to speak the Kham dialect, and that led on to where I had been in Kham province and who I knew that he might know. He was fascinated to hear of my hilariously opportune meeting with the famous Khamba chieftain, Topgyay Pangdatshang, and my subsequent friendship with him and the Pangdatshang family. He had none of the characteristic servility of the Tibetans from central Tibet, who were accustomed to accept the role of serfs in a feudal society. The Khambas had their independent tribes and chieftains, and their relationships were based on respect and not fear.

This Khamba was cautious in talking about himself and I sensed instinctively he was normally an uncommunicative, cold and ruthless individual, although a decidedly handsome one. He was from Litang, in central Kham, he said, but had left there almost twenty years before, some time before I had arrived in that 13,000-feet-high, famous monastery city, of East Tibet. His face was inscrutable as we talked, his eyes only occasionally flickering with interest if I mentioned a name or place that was familiar. Sometimes a flashing smile would light up his otherwise somber face. His name, he replied to my question, was "Tendar."

We had been talking for some time when he mentioned that one of his group had had frostbite, was in extreme pain and was in danger of losing his foot and his life with gangrene. Could I give him medicine for this? I replied that I had not brought many medicines, but I certainly could help him.

"When should I go?" I asked him casually.

"Tomorrow - or today?" he replied, watching me closely.

"Today is better," I said, "as it will mean one day's less pain for the man."

"Will you come now, and alone?" he asked.

I didn't know what was behind his question, but guessed he meant it wasn't with the others, and not for any filming. "Yes," I agreed, "but I will need to take medicines."

"I will have some food at Abu Jampa's, and then we can leave," he said, getting to his feet. Then added, to my surprise, "Later we will discuss the films and photographs and other matters." He saluted, and strode out of our camp, with only a casual nod of acknowledgment to the respectful porters.

Adrian and the others returned before I left, and I quickly explained the situation. They agreed that it was too good an opportunity to risk losing with premature pressures. But, when the Khamba returned to our camp and saw them there, he changed his mind for some reason and said that they could come with us and made no objection to their film equipment.

The trail wound through fields, then out on to a boulder-strewn slope high-lighted by a spectacular waterfall. The Khamba went ahead of us with long, tireless strides, into another valley of fields with Tibetan women working and singing; then away from the fields, towards the snowy mountains. We skirted a village, crossed a makeshift bridge over a small river, into a narrow valley - and a Khamba encampment of black yak-hair tents pitched on a grassy platform, with the forests and mountains forming a magnificent backdrop. As we approached several men came out of the tents and came towards us and saluted us smartly.

They were a striking-looking group, only one of them under six feet in height - and he looked the deadliest of the lot. All were dressed in the knee-length, loosely-tied, yak wool-lined gowns, parachute silk shirts, riding-boots or army boots with puttees, wool-lined trousers, and a variety of headgear. They escorted us to the tents, and on the way

Tendar, who was obviously their leader, told them of our meeting.

Inside what appeared to be Tendar's tent - which could hold at least a dozen people comfortably - there were three raised and carpeted dais around the sides, and a small altar with idols, fruit, rice, butter bowls with burning wicks, and a picture of the Dalai Lama, draped with the traditional white muslin or silk scarves. I was led to the seat of honor beside the altar, and Tendar and the others ranged themselves in the Buddhist lotus position on the carpeted dais. Tendar finished his account of our meeting and the smallest, but deadliest-looking, of the Khamba guerrillas, who had been looking at me closely throughout, said suddenly, "*Dik-ba kur!* (a popular Kham expletive, "By my sins"!) I have it! You were the foreigner who came to Litang with Topgyay Pangdatshang about fifteen years ago. You rode the grey horse with a demon and I watched you race afterwards!" He launched into an excited description of that event fifteen years before to his Khamba companions.

Now, as I looked at the small but deadly Khamba from Litang, I showed as much amazement as shown by his listeners. I had hoped that my knowledge of the Kham dialect would help us with the Khamba guerrillas, but I never thought of meeting someone who knew me when I lived in Kham amongst them. He had seen me race, and shoot in their rifle-shooting competitions, and he was now reciting these events with great relish. I interpreted his enthusiasm to Adrian and Chris. For the next hour or so, as we drank the usual tea, and then a meal of tsamba and dried meat, the conversation was of mutual acquaintances and places in Kham.

Only when we had eaten did Tendar call for their companion with frostbite to be brought - yet another tall, powerful Khamba. His leg was a horrendous mess of suppurating gangrenous stinking flesh. His toes were lost in the spongy black excrescence - except for the projecting white of exposed bone. I would have to cut it all away to give the man any chance of recovery - and that was remote. But at least, it was a chance. As he was now, he was certain to die, and painfully.

I called for boiling water and said I was going to cut away the infected flesh, and told Tendar to get the man drunk with chang, or Tibetan millet beer, as an anaesthetic. Adrian asked if Chris could film the operation, and, after some discussion, the Khambas agreed. so Adrian and Chris set up their equipment. When I lived in Tibet I had done many operations because there was nobody else to do them, and had acquired a considerable reputation as a doctor among the Khambas. But, it had been some years since then, and I had no surgical instruments with us on this trip. I had only a safety razor-blade, which I had to fit into the top of an expertly whittled piece of wood as a makeshift surgical knife by one of the Khambas.

Meanwhile, the suffering man had been plied with bowl after bowl of chang by the jokingly sympathetic Khambas, as they got him drunk quickly. I gave him four sleeping tablets to help the numbing process later, if not during the operation. I also asked two of the Khambas to hold the man down while I operated. For the rest, I had a disinfectant, a British antibiotic powder, clean gauze and bandages.

It was a gruesome experience, and I don't know who was the more exhausted when I had finished, the sick man or myself. Both of us were covered in perspiration despite the high altitude cold. I removed his toes and the gangrenous flesh all the way back to where there was pink raw flesh of his foot. The sick man groaned and twisted in the powerful hands of his friends, grimacing in his agony, but he didn't pull away from the cutting process except instinctively when the pain was excessive. I gave him some antibiotic tablets to prevent septicemia and said I would be back in two days to have a look at his foot.

I was too exhausted for any further discussions with the Khambas, and we agreed that we hold our talks when we returned in two days. The return to our camp in the Chokang village was something of an anti-climax after the recent excitement. The evening meal of slaughtered meat was being prepared enticingly around two campfires; flames crackled and pans of vegetables hissed, men talked and laughed; several villagers were gathered around our radio, listening with awed looks on their faces to the music and voices. Down the valley, smoke curled lazily against the darkening green of the trees, and the last rays of the sun turned to yellow the tops of the high forests and the snows. People on the roofs of houses called to others working in the fields; women and boys returned from the stream with buckets on their backs, singing haunting songs; birds sang in a burst of evening joy. Lulled by the melancholy sound of the Tibetan porters' evening prayers, and a comforting sense of one-ness with destiny, I fell asleep.

The following day we held a strategy meeting. Abu Jampa had mentioned casually that in fifteen days there would be a celebration of the Dalai Lama's birthday, when Tibetans from all around the immediate region would be coming to the nearby monastery. The important question was: did we try to pressure the Khambas to take us with them on a raid into Tibet before that time, or wait until afterwards? The trouble with the latter option was that it was stretching our time out of Kathmandu to very suspicious lengths. Also, Hemantha's family might be sufficiently worried to initiate a search for us, and we would be exposed in a forbidden region of the Himalayas before we could return safely with the film.

Hemantha himself was thrilled with the adventure so far, but understood the consequences of being involved too closely with our intention to cross into Tibet. While he was an official appointee of his government I suspected that the corrupt Banskota had probably fixed the official reports to show that he had sent someone other than Hemantha on the expedition to cover his own delinquency. There was no way we could expose Hemantha to the dangers of a raid across the Himalayas into Tibet.

On the day of our proposed return to the Khamba guerrillas' camp to see their sick companion's foot, they sent my former Kham friend - whose name was Assang - to escort us back there. We had decided that it was in Hemantha's interest not to be closely associated with any aspects of the raid, and he was not going with us. When the deadly-looking Assang strode into our camp, however, Hemantha was present. In his usual friendly fashion Hemantha commented on the fine fur hat Assang was wearing, and asked through me as interpreter if it was from a Tibetan animal. Assang replied laconically to me, "No, Chinese. I shot him for it - but don't tell the Nepali that. He might faint."

When we arrived at the Khamba camp again we found that, in addition to their regular black yak-hair tents, they had erected a ceremonial tent in our honor. This was like an ancient Crusader's tent, white with red, blue and green piping, and elaborately embossed black scroll-work on top. Inside, carpets had been scattered around the sides of the tent, with low tables set in front of each person.

One thing we did not have to worry about was food. Because of the success of their raids and the subsequent bounty of herds of yaks and sheep and goats, the Khambas had access to plenty of animals. The smells of rich meat cooking was overwhelming as we drank the usual initiatory butter tea. The conversation remained general until Assang brought out a 35mm Canon camera. I looked at him quizzically and asked: "Did you shoot a Chinese for this, too?"

He laughed uproariously. "No, I bought this in India a few years ago. Is it any good? Please ask your friends."

Adrian and Chris confirmed that it was a good camera. and in good condition. Had he taken any photographs, they inquired interestedly, on the Khamba raids into Tibet? And he replied off-handedly that he had, but he had now run out of film. Did they have any to spare? Adrian said they could let him have some from our stocks. This led naturally to a discussion of our filming cameras, and Adrian and Chris took the Tibetans outside to show them the zoom lens for long-distance work, and casually introduced how it was possible to film close-up of fighting without actually being right next to the people fighting. Chris also showed them people working at a distance and how they could be recognized without them knowing anything about it. The Khambas were deeply impressed. I told Tendar that this was how we hoped to film them fighting the Chinese, if they agreed to take us with them on their next raid. He was noncommittal, but his usually expressionless face lit up with an appreciative smile. I left the matter there, knowing that there would be no substantive discussions until after the feast they had prepared for us.

I suggested I examine the man with the gangrenous foot in his own tent, as I wanted to get the experience out of the way before sitting down to our meal. The Tibetans agreed and we walked to one of the distant black tents. Inside the air was foul, but I was pleasantly surprised by the appearance of his foot when I had removed the bandages. It was certainly a whole lot healthier, and the man himself was cheerful and optimistic, insisting that he was now "well". I re-dressed the foot, and said to keep on the bandages until I came to see it again. I also showed the Tibetans how to make a simple crutch which would help him to keep his foot off the ground. He was grinningly grateful.

It was the best meal we had had since before leaving London, dish after dish of fragrantly spiced meats and vegetables, served with bowls of freshly brewed beer. There was another guest present, called Gyen Lamala, a visitor from the Khamba guerrilla group operating out of Mustang, who had come to Dzum for operational discussions. It was the garrulous Assang, and not the taciturn Tendar, who informed me that there was tension between their two groups. According to Assang, the Mustang group was too much under the suspect influence of Gyalu Thondup, the Dalai Lama's brother. The Dzum group did not trust Gyalu Thondup for many reasons, not the least of which he was trying to get them to send down a highly respected golden idol in the local monastery which the Dzum Khamba group had successfully brought out of Lhasa. The golden idol was what had given to Dzum its reputation as a "sacred" valley.

The idol was several centuries old, and one of the three patron images of Tibet. It was claimed that it had never been "made", but had been miraculously "created by the gods" (I had sudden visions of Aaron's similar explanation to his brother Moses regarding the golden bull-image made by the Israelites while Moses was away on Mount Sinai!), and its miraculous powers had been demonstrated many times in the past. On two occasions in Lhasa it was said to have talked, making prophetic utterances, and it was also said it would speak a third time on a matter of supreme importance to Tibet. It had become a Khamba symbol of defiance and triumph against the Chinese, and it was now identified with the return of the Dalai Lama to Tibet. The Dzum Khambas took it as their responsibility to look after the idol, and they suspected that Gyalu Thondup wanted to remove it to India to increase his own influence - and wealth, they added, as it was draped with strings of precious jewels in addition to being made of solid gold - and not in the true interests of Tibet. He, in turn, punished the Dzum group for their stubborn refusal to release the idol, and did not send them money or goods or arms like he did with the Mustang group of Khambas. Now, Gyen Lamala was here to persuade them to release the idol to be taken to India for the Dalai Lama's birthday celebrations, in exchange for a plentiful supply of weapons, but they would not agree.

After the excellent meal was finished the Khamba leaders raised the subject of our accompanying them on a raid into Tibet. Tendar was obviously a leading commander of the Dzum group, as Gyen Lamala was the Mustang representative, with Assang as Tendar's second-in-command. They talked easily and freely, saying that they very much appreciated our coming to help, whether it was agreed to go on the raid or not. The feast today was an expression of their appreciation of all that we had done in seeking them out, and consideration of help for the Tibetan cause at their hands. Later, they would like us to receive a freshly killed sheep also as a gift.

I folded my hands in the Tibetan gesture of thanks, but said nothing, as they were not finished talking.

"About the raid, the Chu Zhi Kang Druk (a sub-group of Kham guerrillas) leaders here ask if you have fully considered how serious the consequences of such an attack might be? Everybody may be killed or captured, because the Chinese troops are both skilled and ruthless. This is a known risk to ourselves, but it would be much more serious if it happened to you while with us. It will bring international attention to us here and put a stop to all our activities. Or we might be accused of killing you for your equipment as 'Khamba bandits'. If you are captured, the Chinese will torture you, and make propaganda against you and your countries. Before we talk more, we need to know if you have considered any or all of these possibilities, and we hope you understand that we offer the suggestions as friends."

I interpreted their remarks for Adrian and Chris, and I addressed the Khambas with our reply:

"We have discussed what you have said and we deeply appreciate your concern, and the consideration which you have given to our proposal. We have given this matter great thought for many months. The Tall One (the Tibetan name for Adrian) and I are married - he has one child, I have three - and we have made statements before legal people in Britain regarding our possible deaths here. We are not young irresponsible people looking for money or fame. Let me explain."

I held out the palm of my hand. "Look, here is India, and here is China, with Tibet in the middle, so Tibet is important. In politics this is known; but in publicity - that is, letting the world know - it is not so well known, because of the many lies told by leaders of some countries."

They nodded, sitting forward with hunched shoulders, as they concentrated on what I was saying.

"We have come here so that the world may know about Tibet - its suffering, its importance and its courage. We can film and photograph Tibetans in refugee camps to show something of the suffering, but that is not true Tibet. Tibet is defending their religion against a godless country. Tibet is five million people refusing to submit to over a billion Chinese and Indians. Tibet is a few poorly armed Khambas fighting against the world's largest army of well-equipped Chinese. Tibet is between two countries who may soon be at war with each other. That is what we want to tell the

Gods and Guerrillas

world. We want to show that there are Tibetans, like yourselves, who are not accepting the nonsense being spoken by China and India that you are living in peace and contentment with Chinese invaders. We want to show that there are groups like you who are not only fighting the Chinese, but are defeating them. We want to show that the Chinese military roads in Tibet, like the Chinese military, are vulnerable to Tibetan attacks. If we can show this on our film, it will help your cause in the eyes of the world."

I sat back, finished, and they began talking among themselves, while I gave Adrian and Chris a summary of what I had said. Finally, Gyen Lamala said: "We understand, and agree with everything you have said. If you wish to go with them on their next raid, they are happy to agree. They have just returned from an attack against a Chinese military convoy in which they destroyed nine trucks out of fourteen, yet no-one in the outside world will know of this because there was nobody to tell them about it. We are doing this all the time."

I asked them where the previous raid was conducted and Adrian brought out his ever-present map. They described how the Mustang group operated to the north-west of them, and the Dzum group operated over the nearby Khojang Pass. They described the Chinese outposts, garrison positions, and troop and patrol dispositions. They had volunteer spies, and paid informers in many places among the Chinese military and civilian people, but it was very difficult obtaining quick information because of the nature of the terrain. So, usually they were dependent on the gods to inform them of the best time and place for their attacks.

I knew what they meant, but I gave a brief explanation for the benefit of Adrian and Chris in the historical aspects of Tibet's unique form of Lamaistic Buddhism and the tantric practices of the shamanistic Bön sect. The Lamaistic

Buddhism of the predominant Gelukpa sect was a corrupt form of Mahayana Buddhism, in that it had incorporated a variety of Hindu and native gods into its pantheon. The other major sect was the Nyingmapa, which could be broadly characterized as a mixture of the corrupt idolatrous Buddhism with tantric practices taken from India and Mongolia.

Both of these sects predominated in the monasteries throughout Tibet, identified by the casual observer as "yellow hats" and "red hats". The Bön sect was small by comparison. The lamas, or monks of the two main sects were analogous with the priests and pastors of Catholicism and Protestantism of Christianity, in that they performed the traditional liturgies and ceremonies on behalf of their lay fellow-believers in the monasteries, or as official ecclesiastical representatives of the monasteries in homes, local councils or government bodies.

But, outside of them, and infinitely more influential than either of them in the lives of the people, were the tantric adepts, the *chod-gyad*, secret masters of the paranormal whose influence in the lives of every Tibetan, from the lowest peasant to the Dalai Lama, was proportionate to the supernatural powers they could display. They provided charms to stop sword and bullet wounds, they invoked rains for harvests, they cured diseases, they even raised dead corpses for initiation purposes in a ceremony known as *ro-lang*, ("raise corpse"), by activating it with a "spirit-being". These tantric adepts were prepared to have an acolyte swing a razor-edged sword at their exposed necks and not be harmed, as evidence of their being possessed by an alien spirit. Their faces and voices changed under possession by an invoked deity from the underworld, while the supplicant discussed with the invoked deity the "miracle" they wished to be performed. Their invocatory performances were public for all to see and their powers were feared everywhere by everybody. I had helped film a *chod-gyad,* with Prince Peter of Greece and Denmark, who could call on nine different "spirits" with different facial and vocal expressions, a film Prince Peter donated to the Uinersity of Copenhagen.

The tantric adept always required some form of stimuli to invoke the demon, or familiar spirit. It might be a secret mantra communicated to him by his "guide" when he was an initiate; or it was a sung tonal invocation; or a musical accompaniment, such as a human thigh-bone trumpet; or certain ceremonial clothing; or ornaments, such as miters or aprons of necklets made of human bones; or bone or skin relics of past master-adepts.

Adrian and Chris were fascinated with the procedure and wondered whether we would be permitted to film it. I advised against raising the question at the moment, but said that it might be possible nearer the time of the enactment. The *chod-gyad,* whom I had filmed with Prince Peter had agreed to be filmed under "trance-possession", as it is called in the West, for a generous payment of money. This was unusual because one of the strong beliefs of these adepts was that the secrets of their expertise were never supposed to be divulged for any reason, least of all for money. Later, this *chod-gyad* had died mysteriously. So, I thought it unlikely that permission would be given to us here in Dzum.

For the present, it was enough that they agreed we should go with them, that we should ambush the important north-south military road, and that it should be sooner rather than later. They would now go to the monastery and inform the priests of the proposal, and ask them to consult the gods for their approval on the venture. Adrian delicately proposed a gift "for the monastery", so that it would not look like a bribe to the gods, and the Khambas said that would be appropriate.

CHAPTER TEN

Attacking a Chinese Convoy inside Tibet

The monastery was located at the foot of a towering rocky mountain that dropped sheer from a sharp, triangular peak, behind which loomed the snow-covered Himalayan mountain range. It was surrounded by a cluster of houses and nomad encampments scattered across the wide valley floor. There were hundreds of Tibetan men, women and children moving around the houses, tents and fields.

The monastery itself was not remarkable in any way, but inside was the famous golden idol, one of the three patron deities of Tibet. I had seen many larger, and more impressive-looking, idols when living in Tibet. This one was only about ten or twelve feet in height, with an expressionless, pock marked, roughly hammered, gold face. What I had not expected, despite various conversations with the headman and Khambas, was the incredible wealth with which it was garlanded; neck, arms, lap and extensive plinth were draped with gold, silver and precious jewels of every description. No wonder Gyalu Thondup had wanted the idol brought down to India!

On a wide platform in front of the idol were piled rice, fruit, vegetables and butter image simulations. Then were tiered rows upon rows of brass bowls, hundreds of them, with lighted wicks flickering in liquid butter. Men, women and children were crowded around, their voices mingling in the prayer-mantra, "*Om Mani Padme Hum*", accompanied by the click-and-whisper of their rosaries and prayer-wheels. Many of them were weeping openly as they gazed with awe at the unresponsive face of the idol above them. Behind them, the monastery lamas were seated on rows of low platforms at right-angles to the idol, their prayer-invocations rising and falling, broken only by the occasional break in the litany to ring small brass bells, play the tenor trumpets or sonorous blast on the twelve-foot long trumpets. Percussion accompaniment came from the small hand-drums, the large skin-drum on a stand at the rear, and a huge brass gong struck with a resounding blow.

It might have been our generous gift that persuaded the monastery monks to agree unusually to having the "secondary" divination process filmed. This was a less arcane practice than the *lha-babs*, or trance-possession, process, which interestingly had a striking similarity to the ancient Jewish ritual of *Urim and Thummim*. The Tibetans put two pieces of paper with positive and negative indications inside two flour balls the size of golf balls, and swirled them around in an open bowl. A blind-folded monk then chose one of the flour-balls, and when this was broken open the "decision of the gods" was derived from the positive or negative answer. The Jewish practice of *Urim and Thummim* was to have a black (negative) and a white (positive) stone inside a pouch, and the priest chose one without seeing either, and this was taken as the *"answer from Yahweh"*. Every great Jewish leader from Moses to David had used this method at some time, with great success.

The Dzum monks drew a positive reply from the gods and said that the gods had decreed we should plan for the attack to be held on June 6th and there would be a successful outcome. I had a sudden recollection of a similar experience by King Croesus, who consulted the gods regarding his planned war with the Lydians and was assured by the Delphic Oracle that *"a great empire would fall."* Unfortunately for Croesus, it was his own empire that fell in the war. But the Khambas were elated, and we were relieved that we had permission for the raid. My own divine assurance of survival and success sprang from my personal communications with God; that was why I was there, and why I believed we would have a successful outcome..

We had an "official" meeting with the abbot, who thanked us courteously for our gift, and said he hoped we were enjoying our visit. He said the monastery would pray for the success of our project, and to convey his greetings to the Dalai Lama when we met with him. We assured him we would, and then left quickly for our meeting with Tendar.

We had arranged with Tendar to meet away from both the Khamba camp and our own, because we did not want to involve ourselves with explanations to Hemantha. With this in mind, too, we had arranged for Chris to take Hemantha on a "filming expedition" so he would not be aware of Adrian's and my critical planning meetings with the abbot and Tendar. Tendar had described the meeting-place at a prominent tree on the mountainside above the village, and he was squatting under the tree when Adrian and I arrived. He stood up at our approach and walked around, scanning the surrounding mountains and forests behind us, presumably as a precaution against any suspicious observers. Satisfied, he sat down beside us without explanation. It was just part of his natural caution which had kept him and his companions alive until now.

Tendar took a piece of folded paper from his pocket and opened it to reveal a roughly drawn map. He put it on a flat stone that he had prepared before our arrival, and spread it out, apologizing for its crudity compared with ours, but said that it had been drawn out of their own experience of the country. It showed a rough diagram of the terrain between Dzum and the winding Chinese military road inside Tibet on the other side of the Lhokang Pass, with double wide lines indicating valleys, narrower double lines indicating gullies, large jagged inverted "V"s the Himalayan border with a prominent "X" at the 20,000-plus-feet of the Khojang Pass, and smaller "v"s lower mountain ridges on both sides of the Himalayas.

He pointed to a spot under the "X" of the Khojang Pass, and said that we would camp there on the first night, to be in a position to cross the dangerous Pass quickly. He casually remarked that there was a Chinese outpost on the far side of the Pass, and that would be the first of many dangerous obstacles on the way before we even reached the ambush site. He said he had already sent out scouts to find out what Chinese patrols were moving on the far side, and they would report back to our camp-site below the Pass. From the Pass camp-site he would send out other scouts to keep us informed of what to expect ahead of us.

The Chinese knew the Khambas were using this route to attack their convoys, but they were in the difficult circumstances of not being accustomed to move quickly, or much at all, in high altitudes. The more heavily armed they were, the more difficult it was for them to move. So the Khambas used the tactics of moving quickly, striking suddenly, and retreating rapidly.

The ambush point, "chosen by the gods", was located in a valley in a natural fork between two sheer mountains, and with a large river flowing between. The military road ran in a winding curve down the valley between the river and the mountains on this side. Checking Tendar's map with our own, this looked like the upper reaches of the Tsangpo River, which became the mighty Brahmaputra as it left Tibet for India. Tendar would lead his Khambas to where a low ridge of mountain led out of the sheer mountain to near where the military road curved round its projection.

First, Tendar said, he would place us in positions behind rocky formations on this ridge on the far side of the road and river, and above them, to keep us out of the Chinese returning fire. There we could set up our cameras behind the rocks, and he would then go and arrange his men in their attack positions. He would place the machine-guns beneath us so that we would have the safest covering-fire during the attack. He would have scouts out further up the valley, and also down the valley, to keep a watch for unexpected Chinese reinforcements.

Should the convoy be too numerous, Tendar said, or too heavily escorted, the Khambas would let it pass; but, if we wanted, we could film it safely from our camera positions. Should the convoy be a size they could handle easily with our safety in mind, then the scouts had a prearranged signal and Tendar would give the command to attack. We would then be on our own until the action was completed.

Tendar picked up the map and, folding it, slipped it into an inside pocket of his khaki jacket. He looked at me keenly, and asked, "I know you can move at high altitudes, because you have lived in Tibet. But what about your friends? They will be like the Chinese, unable to move quickly the higher we go. My men will be carrying their arms and ammunition, plus food, and we always carry away what weapons and ammunition we find at a raid, so we will not be able to carry extra loads for your friends. We do not take local porters with us, even if they were willing, because they are more a hindrance than a help . We will guard you as much as we can, but we cannot carry your equipment."

I interpreted what he said for Adrian, and Adrian said that he understood. He didn't want to promise what he didn't know he or Chris could perform, except to say that they would not expect the Khambas to be responsible for them. They would take the risks involved. Tendar gave a nod and what for him was a slight smile, and stood up.

"I will arrange for three men to come to your camp before dawn tomorrow. They will help to bring you and all your equipment to our camp. There we will see what equipment and stores we have to take as well as our weapons and ammunition. Do not let the Nepali official see them, or say where you are going. May the gods be with us."

He gave an unexpected illuminating smile which transformed him from a ruthlessly efficient guerrilla commander to a recklessly handsome daredevil, and our discussion was over.

That night, as I read in my Bible, I came across the words of God to Paul regarding a dangerous event in his life: *"Do not be afraid...for I am with you and no man shall attack or harm you...Paul said (to his companions), 'I now bid you take heart, for there will be no loss of life among you...This very night an angel of God said: 'Do not be afraid, Paul, you must stand before Caesar, and lo, God has granted you all those who will sail with you. So take heart, men, for I have faith in God that it will be exactly as I have said..."*

Our story to Hemantha was that we expected to be away filming in the high Himalayas, for which he was not equipped, and would be away several days. If he didn't believe it, he was too polite to say anything. Our withholding of information now would work to his advantage later, when he could truthfully say to the Kathmandu authorities that he knew nothing of some of our activities.

With Hemantha and Chris out of the way, Adrian and I re-organized our loads for the raid: high-altitude clothing and sleeping-bags, packaged soups, dried eggs, adequate number of film stock, no toilet requisites of any kind (no paper, no toothpastes, no soaps, to leave evidence for the

Chinese that foreigners had been there!), medicines especially for bullet wounds and high altitude problems, camera equipment with all surfaces dulled so that they would not reflect sun-glint and reveal our positions to the Chinese, film stock with all containers removed beforehand for weight and evidence reasons.

I took Tsewang aside for a final important briefing. Would he be prepared, I asked, to leave ahead of us on the return journey to Kathmandu, after we returned from Tibet? I explained. If our mission to Tibet against the Chinese were successful, and we were able to film the Khamba attack on one of the most strategic roads inside Tibet, then we were going to have in our possession filmed evidence of such importance that the Chinese would be prepared to do anything, literally, to recover and destroy it. To outwit the Chinese - and the Nepal and other governments, who might be subject to Chinese pressure, or reluctant to have the films widely shown because of their own policies - we would like him to go ahead of us, carrying the films. He would then enter, and pass through Kathmandu check-posts as a single refugee-like Tibetan simple individual going to sell and buy goods in the city. In Kathmandu he would go to a friend of mine, carrying a letter from me instructing my friend to pay Tsewang a large sum of money for their safe delivery. I didn't say it to Tsewang, but I knew he would be thinking of his wife and family, and that their medical treatment would continue to be dependent on his cooperation with us. We would still have the much more difficult problem of getting the films out of Nepal and on to London, but that stage would have to await our arrival. For the present, we had to get them out of our own possession when we arrived at the Kathmandu check-posts because they were certain to be alerted by the authorities to expect our return. Tsewang was happy to agree. We were ready to go.

www.classictravelbooks.com

We were awakened before dawn next morning; had a quick meal of Tibetan barley-flour "scones" and boiled mutton and, as dawn was breaking, we were on the way. The Tibetan porters who had come with us from Kathmandu were unusually silent as they watched our departure. Tsewang said that they had had "special prayers" for us the previous evening. They knew nothing of the details of the raid, but they were aware that something important was afoot in our association with the Khamba guerrillas. As they folded their hands in a gesture of good-luck, Tsewang dipped his fingers in a bowl of water and flicked it on us also as a sign of blessing of the gods.

At the Khamba guerrilla camp there was a greater bustle of activity than on previous visits. We were met by Assang, and another guerrilla officer, Lama-la, and served the usual scalding hot butter tea by Nyima - of the gangrened foot, now cheerfully propelling himself around with the aid of his crude crutch as he anticipated living again and not dying in agony and stench. Assang said that they were sending pack horses ahead with the heavier weapons and ammunition loads to a camp-site beneath the Khojang Pass. They had also agreed to have three extra Khambas who would carry our extra loads and help us; if they were needed at the ambush they would be armed and fight, but otherwise they would be responsible for helping and protecting us.

Two hours after the pack-horses left, we followed. It would be a long day, Assang warned, as we would not be at the camp-site until sunset. After today, each day would be worse, not so much because of traveling distance but because of the tension of look-out for Chinese patrols as we moved through them.

By mid-day we were out of the high grasslands, with their scattered refugee nomad encampments of black yak-hair tents, and into a savagely split tangle of barren precipitous gorges where the trail rose steeply around the sheer sides of the mountain in a narrow, stony hairline; or wound treacherously across sheer stone or slate slopes which strained ankles painfully and slid away frighteningly in gathering landslides to the river far below.

In the early afternoon we emerged on to another wide grassy plateau with a magnificent backdrop of snow mountains, and the inevitable black tents of the nomad encampments. Tendar led the way to one of them and when we entered there were some of the Khamba guerrillas we had met at the lower camp, and others we had never seen before but who were obviously of the same group from their familiarity with each other and their easy acceptance of the coming raid.

Inside the tent, the ground had been covered with a layer of aromatic tree branches, with the usual colorful Tibetan carpets, so this was not the normal refugee community. This conviction was further strengthened when we were served a simple but substantial meal of bowls of fresh yoghurt, then rice and savory meat. When I commented on the amount and variety of the food to Tendar he observed laconically that we better make the most of it because it was the last we were likely to have for several days.

When we finished eating, Adrian and Chris went outside to do some filming and I remained inside with Tendar. The nomad hosts and the other Khambas had drifted away on their own interests. Tendar and I were reclining against the piled goods behind us in a companionable silence. In the past few days I had come to like this tall, taciturn Khamba commander very much. He was still cautious and uncommunicative, given to long brooding silences, and I often caught his glance resting on me thoughtfully. But, recently he had smiled more often, was more relaxed, and I wondered whether it was because of the gods' approval.

After a time he said, "We have had to change our plans a little. Yesterday was too cloudy for our scouts to make a careful survey, and I decided to wait here instead of just under the Pass as we arranged. That spot is very good for a quick strike over the Pass, but it very exposed for a long delay. I have sent out six men to spy out the three trails leading from here into Tibet and the area of the ambush. We have to weigh carefully whether to risk the Pass as the easiest of the three, or by-pass that by taking one of the other two much more difficult and dangerous crossings. I am sending a seventh scout to survey the site of the ambush to make certain that it is as we have noted in the map you saw. On these raids we cannot be too careful, because the Chinese are very cunning and very ruthless, and each time we are successful they produce something different. We have survived so far because we have always been very careful, as well as having the gods' help."

"How will this affect our timing?" I asked curiously. "Didn't the *chod-gyad* say that the gods wanted the raid to take place on the 6th?"

Tendar shrugged. "The *chod-gyad*'s interpreter could not confirm to me whether we had to leave on the 6th, or be at ambush site on the 6th, or attack on the 6th. As commander I have to make a military assessment and decision within what the gods say." He smiled sardonically and added, "We don't have a calendar here like you. I'm not sure whether yesterday was the 6th, or today, or tomorrow. I don't think the *chod-gyad* would know, either - but the gods would. So you could say that I am approximately obedient to the *chod-gyad*'s approximate message. The outcome of the raid is in the gods' hands but the arrangements are in mine."

I grinned at him. This was the most revealing he had been and he was showing me a side of himself with which I could delightfully identify. In my own service for God I, too, had often to come to terms with what appeared to be ambiguous commands. Even my presence on this assignment had been a cause of great dispute between me and God. Tendar was a man who had been stripped of every relationship except the one between himself and his gods. As far as I could see, he had no close friends among the Khambas. He was respected and admired for his leadership expertise and successes over many years of fighting, but he usually sat and walked alone.

"How are you with traveling at night?" his slight smile was provocative. "We will leave here right after midnight, take a quick meal of tsamba and tea, and then travel as far as we can before dawn. I should have more reports then about the situation on the trail ahead, and will decide whether to remain until dark or move cautiously in daylight. We will be doing a lot of moving in the dark and that's why I'm asking."

"I did a lot of that while I was in Tibet," I said dismissively. "Adrian probably did a lot in the jungles. But how are we going to travel in darkness on the kind of rocky trail we came over today? Is the trail ahead easier?"

His eyes lit up with a full reckless smile at some inward thought, then he looked serious again. "The trail ahead is much more difficult. We have one very high Pass with heavy snow, and some smaller Passes with many dangerous places. On this side of the Pass, we will use flashlights occasionally when I think it is safe; but on the other side we must not use flashlights at all. They would be seen too easily by watching Chinese."

"What arms do you have?" I asked with interest. I had heard rumors of secret supplies from India, had heard of plane-drops by Americans and Taiwanese, and seen scores of Tibetans wearing the green-brown, camouflage, parachute shirts among the Khambas in this region. The supply of guns from clandestine sources was a source of the antagonism shown towards Gyalu Thondup, who was said to use them to bolster his own influence rather than for the Khambas's strategic advantage.

"You will see our guns shortly when the others come back," Tendar said soberly, avoiding the Gyalu Thondup quarrel issue. "Most are old, of different makes, and ammunition is difficult to find. A-lay!" he sighed in sudden bitterness and regret. "When I think of the guns and ammunition we handed over to the Indian officials when we arrived in India with the Dalai Lama I could weep. We had modern machine-guns and mortars and automatic rifles we captured from the Chinese, but the Indians would not let us keep them. Now we have to use old weapons, and raid the Chinese military convoys to improve our supplies. It is so little to fight against so many."

I told him of my own earlier secret meetings as interpreter with America's intelligence agents in their discussions with the Khamba leader Rapga Pangdatshang. Rapga had wanted to have a large and assured supply of weapons delivered to a bridgehead in south-eastern Tibet, where the Khambas dominated thousands of square miles of territory in the savage mountain region where the Chinese were either unable or unwilling to engage them. But instead, America had chosen to send a few obscure Tibetan individuals to the USA for radio and some other fiddling battle training, drop a few radio and other supplies from airplanes over rugged terrain to unknown individuals, and, with India's approval send a restricted supply through Gyalu Thondup to Mustang. It was a pathetically inadequate effort, and Rapga had dismissed it with contempt.

Tendar lapsed into one of his moody silences, and I considered his handsome features in the darkening gloom of the tent.

"What were you before the revolt in Tibet?" I asked him suddenly. While he had the magnificent physique of the tough Khamba warrior, he had the ascetic features and thoughtful eyes of a scholar. His eyes, which had been so watchful, were now turned to me, unguarded, and with a jolt of surprise, I realized that this was a man who must often have wept. There were no signs of tears in his eyes now, but they were dark with a personal grief that caught at my own throat. I recalled the words of the Russian Marxist-turned-Christian philosopher, Nicolai Berdyaev:

"The suffering that has once been lived through cannot possibly be effaced...The man who has traveled far in the realms of the spirit, and who has passed through great trials in the cause of his search for truth, will be formed spiritually along lines which must differ altogether from those pertaining to the man who has never shifted his position and to whom new spiritual territories are unknown...I am enriched by my experience even if, to cross the abyss which lay before me, I have been forced to address myself to powers other than human...."

I felt an unusual rapport with this recently met Tibetan. His ways were not my ways, and his gods not my God, but the fire of his personal vision and commitment was no less intense than my own.

"I was not born for this kind of life," Tendar spoke suddenly, sitting up and hunching forward in his concentration. "I wanted to live in peace, to practice my religion. I was the steward in a large monastery in Kham and I loved the life. As a lama I had no wife, but I had brothers, a sister, parents and relatives. They are all dead - killed by the Chinese. The Chinese plundered my family home, destroyed my monastery, took away my friends and lama colleagues, to build their roads, starve and die. I was left with nothing but to fight for my country, religion and the Dalai Lama. Later, I married a wife, and so apostatized completely from my religious vows. She, too, was killed by the Chinese, and now I have nothing but what you see here." His bitter protest was like a raw wound in the grey-dark tent.

I sat silent. There was nothing one could say to assuage such private grief, and any trite comment would have been a gratuitous impertinence. I knew that he felt my sympathy or he would never have unloaded that suddenly unbearable, lonely outcry of protest at circumstances which had turned a sensitive man of peace into a ruthless instrument of war.

"So now I know little beyond fighting Chinese in these mountains," Tendar continued reflectively, "and how to handle guns and men. It is now five years since I and these men entered Lhasa and brought the Dalai Lama safely to India, and I have been doing nothing else but killing Chinese all this time. Sometimes I despair, but what else is there for me to do? I cannot live in a refugee camp. I am too old to go abroad for studies. I can only fight for the freedom of my country and the return of the Dalai Lama."

He had been facing forward, his thoughts inward, and he turned now to face me. "That is why I am doing this raid for you. You are one of us, sent by your God to help us, and so I have agreed to take you on this mission. In a few days we could all be dead, but it will have been in a good cause. I have given orders that, whatever happens in the attack, you three must be safeguarded in a rearguard action. Your film must be made, your newspaper articles and book written, so that the world may know of our deep desire for peace and freedom to worship. This will be my most important attack since we brought the Dalai Lama out of Tibet, although it will be small by comparison, for so much of importance depends on its success."

The others returned, some of them bringing bundles of wood for the fire, and the leaping flames soon lit up the tent. Others brought in weapons and they were all soon disassembling guns, cleaning and oiling them with yak butter. The weapons gleamed dully and wickedly in the flickering firelight as they were turned over in obviously expert hands, the greased faces of their owners intent on every detail of the preparations.

Tendar was a different man from an hour before. The most expert of all, he had words of advice to each of the others, about correcting previous mistakes in sighting, gauging, and trajectory. His own weapon was an American Springfield rifle, and it was like an extension of his own arm as he turned and twisted it lovingly in his hands in demonstrations of tactics.

"We will use hand grenades this time," he said suddenly. "We will try to blow up the trucks with them; but, if we cannot, we will at least blow holes in the road."

Puntshok Thondup, the youngest but tallest and most powerful of the Khambas, was the machine-gunner, and he gave a delighted laugh as he pulled a hand grenade from the fold of his gown, made an imitation throw with it as he fell face forward. The others laughed at his mock display. With his crossed ammunition belts, bulky Tibetan gown, and god-box he seemed to fill half the large tent himself. Two of the others beside him, Dorji and Lonzong, were also machine-gunners, and they looked more menacing than any Hollywood-type gangster.

Assang, my friend of earlier Kham travels, was his usual smiling, deadly self. He was obviously enjoying every minute of this hit-and-run guerrilla life, knew nothing of the soul-torture of Tendar, enjoyed the excitement of preparing for battle, and the thrill of killing during it. He was only held in a measure of restraint out of his respect for the superior intelligence and even greater fighting efficiency of Tendar.

Gesang, the tall, quiet, friendly one, was cradling his rifle lovingly in his hands like some weekend sportsman. Tsambala, short, stocky and thug-like, but cheerful and friendly as a puppy, was feeding bullets into his automatic weapon with a vicious, "Jih... Nyi...Sum...(One...Two...Three..)", as if counting dead Chinese. Gaybo, the oldest of all the Khambas, was said to be the best marksman, deadly accurate at almost any distance. His main task was make certain to shoot to kill the leading drivers of the Chinese convoy to stop them and block any bypassing by the other vehicles coming behind, and kill the drivers at the rear to block any retreat.

These, and others whose names were not known to me, were not only a motley collection of individuals, they were also clothed in a variety of dress. Tendar, from his captured Chinese military cap and jacket to his khaki puttees and army boots, could have passed for a Chinese officer. All of them had the same basic Tibetan maroon gown, girdled at the waist with a colored scarf, and worn at knee-length, but some of them had acquired earth-colored cotton khaki robes which they wore on top of their maroon gowns, presumably as camouflage. Their head-gear ranged from standard Tibetan fur hats through plundered Chinese military caps of various kinds to Western wide-brim hats.

They had been fighting together against the Chinese since 1952, first in Kham and then, as the revolt spread, across Tibet, and now from Nepal. None of them had families with them, or even news of their families in Kham, and they were a tightly-knit group of seasoned warriors who viewed each other as family.

www.classictravelbooks.com

We were awake at midnight and the Khambas went about their activities with practiced skill. Fires were lit, tea and tsamba prepared, loads adjusted, guns and ammunition checked, and within an hour we were on our way. The night was pitch-black - an unexpected gift from the gods, Tendar said - and the going was easy as we crossed the wide valley at a rapid pace. Flashlights were carried by approved individuals, and were flashed occasionally at difficult places, but otherwise we proceeded in the dark and in silence.

We had been going for about two hours, and had reached a wooden bridge over a brawling river, when one of Tendar's scouts appeared from the other side. He and Tendar had a low-voiced discussion, then moved on again without any comments to the others.

We climbed steadily across the side of a steep mountain, keeping our feet with difficulty in the darkness. At an opening in the mountainside Assang, who was ahead of me, moved away towards a darker shadow and a dog started barking savagely. Yak-bells began tinkling and the sound of animals moving could be heard. Other dogs began barking, and voices were raised, and the moving bodies of yaks were all around us.

The Khambas threw themselves down behind boulders around us, and I fell behind an inadequate thorn-scrub. My throat went dry as the black shape of a huge Tibetan mastiff slid past in the darkness. If it was anything like the dogs I knew in Kham they were killers when they were unleashed. I had been shown how to jam a short sword or stick in their open, snarling mouths as they jumped in attack, and then how to kick upwards against the sword or stick to break their jaws so that they couldn't savage me to death. The problem now was that I couldn't see them come at me in the dark.

Assang returned with a low-voiced explanation that it was an unexpected nomad camp. He had his short sword in his hand and, with him in front, another Khamba with his sword out and held ready, behind me, we moved around the settling yaks and guard dogs until we left them behind.

When the blackness of the night gave way to the quickly lightening grey of a new day, I saw we were in a narrow valley whose steep sides reared ahead of us to reveal palely glimmering snows. Almost filling the "V" against the now reddening dawn sky towered the snow-bound barrier of the over-20,000-feet Khojang Pass leading to our objective. I also noticed that, at some point in the darkness of the night, we had been joined by more armed men - presumably some of them the scouts who had been sent ahead.

When we stopped for a rest, there was a sudden break in the low-voiced conversations as some of the Khambas pointed up the mountain to the right of us. I could see nothing and, after a while, I asked Tendar what was happening.

"Four deer," Tendar whispered, smiling. He spoke to Assang, who slung his rifle to an easier position on his shoulder - and then went up the sheer slope at a fast pace after the animals.

"They aren't going to shoot them, are they?" Adrian asked me in surprise. "What if the Chinese hear?"

"Apparently," I replied. "They must either be very confident or very clever - or know something we don't."

We watched the progress of Assang as he angled across the mountain to where the deer could be seen grazing. When he was about two hundred yards away from them, with hardly a stop for breath, he unslung his rifle, sighted it standing upright, and in one smooth movement fired. One of the deer dropped to the ground. The sound of the shot echoed loudly around the enclosed valley, then diminished into silence.

"Well, at least we know they can shoot," Chris said sardonically. "If the Chinese don't shoot us first."

"And, remember, he's not their best marksman," I reminded him.

The Khambas treated it matter-of-factly. Tendar said, "A good shot," approvingly, then detailed a man to go and help Assang skin and carry the animal. As soon as we reached a suitable spot near the river we stopped to light fires and cook the deer. I fell asleep as it was cooking and awakened to a glorious mouth-watering odor of fresh venison. This was a healthy sign that my nerves were in good condition, anyway.

When we had finished eating, and were sitting back replete, Tendar called for a discussion based on reports from the scouts. The scouts each gave their varied reports, and then the others all contributed their thoughts or proposals in the context of what had been learned. This was Kham tribal custom. They were prepared to be led by a strong leader, but he had to prove himself and not just impose his will, so Tendar listened quietly as each man had his say.

I lay in the sunshine and let the discussion wash over me, while Adrian and Chris went about quietly filming the engrossed men. I would be told when the plans were completed. An hour or so later I was called over to the circle of Khambas. In the center they had built a model of rocks, stones and dirt, to resemble the mountains and valleys of the place of ambush, from the information gathered among them. The proposed plans were that we would be placed on the far side of the river, so that even if the Chinese saw us they could not reach us. One man would be with us with a rifle, and two others would be there to help carry equipment. At a given signal to stop all action they would withdraw, taking us with them. As we were on opposite sides of the river the party would regroup at a point half-way up a long valley leading back to the Khojang Pass and into Nepal.

It was excellently conceived as far as I could see - but it had one major flaw. Our position was too far away from the action to take effective films and photographs. Adrian asked if there was no nearer point, and there was renewed discussion. Tendar insisted that our safety was the chief consideration on this occasion, and not the amount of vehicles destroyed or Chinese soldiers killed or weapons and ammunition recovered. The film must be safeguarded and shown to the world. Some of the others argued that it was too much of a risk to place us near where the Chinese could capture us and the films, because then nothing would be gained. Finally, it was agreed that we would be placed around and above the ambushing group on a lower rise about twenty yards from the point of attack. When this was decided, the Khambas looked at us with a new respect. To them, we were going unarmed into the field of combat with only our cameras.

With the place of attack decided Tendar ordered an immediate departure, with the scouts going ahead. He pointed to where the nearer mountains were a tumbled mass of massive and precipitous boulders, before disappearing into the white-draped gigantic serrated majesty of the eternal snow-line. "Beyond that," he said wryly, "there are another two steep climbs, with snow and ice all the way. Then we reach the top of the Pass."

CHAPTER ELEVEN

Night Journey inside Tibet

With the discussions satisfactorily completed, we broke camp about mid-day, and for the first hour or two the going was comparatively easy. At one open spot, Tendar even gave permission to Puntshok Thondup, the young giant machine-gunner, to warm up his trigger-finger by firing two or three rounds at a black stone about six inches in diameter some two to three hundred yards away. He nicked it top right first burst, bottom left next burst, and the third round shattered it to pieces. I supposed it was some comfort as far as establishing accuracy was concerned, but it seemed to be a lunatic risk in disregarding security. However, Tendar - whose every action and decision appeared to be the result of careful, thoughtful calculation - did not attach much importance to this. When I mentioned the danger of the Chinese overhearing the sound, he seemed to feel it was more important to give Puntshok "gun-confidence" now rather than later.

We climbed the final ridges of precipitous ledges and massed boulders to where the eternal snows began and passed into the snow-line with laboring breaths - permanent snows were usually at about 17,000-feet - and our earlier climbing activities were puny in comparison. We climbed for about a hundred yards, lifting first one foot high out of the snow and then the other, stopping for a breather; and every five hundred yards or so, we would sit down for about ten or fifteen minutes. But we were now exposed to the unceasing, sub-zero winds sweeping off the peaks, and sitting was a doubtful relief.

By mid-afternoon we reached a vast, saucer-like depression tilting upwards deceptively like a giant curved and smooth screen towards the top of the Pass, but it dangerously concealed crevasses hiding fatal "snow-bridges", precipitous ice-fields and glacial climbs and descents where we could all disappear in the blink of an eye. Looking backwards the way we had come, a magnificent panorama of snow-peaked mountains, and forested lesser mountains, fell away beneath our feet. The westering sun laid a golden sheen on heavily moving white and grey masses of cloud formations.

I looked uneasily at those masses of clouds, pouring like some gigantic cotton-wool waterfall over the now not-so-distant Pass, and at the nearby massive curtain of snow descending above our heads. I saw Tendar also looking at them thoughtfully, and he gave a sudden command to move on quickly to the Pass, with himself taking the lead on to the steep curved slope of virgin snow. He sank almost immediately to his thighs but plunged confidently forwards - or rather upwards, for the slope to the top of the Pass was at an angle of forty-five degrees or more.

One by one the others followed in his steps, each succeeding footprint making it easier for the one behind to follow in an ice stairway. It was grueling work, and as we labored slowly upwards, I wondered what we would do on the return journey on the other side of the Pass if the Chinese soldiers were close behind and we could not stop for a rest every fifty yards as we were now doing. For, although the Khambas were stopping, I knew it was more on our behalf than their own, and that they had reserves of strength that neither we - nor anyone not born in those high altitudes - could match. One good thing about the physical effort was that it removed to a great extent the fears of lurking Chinese frontier soldiers on the other side of the

Pass. In discussing this with Tendar he hadn't given a clear explanation - or I hadn't grasped it properly. I understood from him that it was difficult to say where they were likely to be, because they were never at the same place twice, either because of the climatic conditions or military strategy. Tendar seemed to accept the uncertainty fatalistically as just another military hazard. I was reminded of a friend of mine in Scotland, who was partial to tossing off sardonic bon-mots, saying, "Thank God for the troubles you have today, for the troubles you'll have tomorrow will be worse."

Late-afternoon, breathing slowly and painfully in deep chest-laboring gulps, we approached the top of the Pass through billowing masses of thick grey clouds and snow driven by a howling blizzard. At this height in the Himalayas it was not uncommon to have winds of over 150 miles an hour and more. The blizzard drove into our faces cruelly, with the icy particles striking exposed skin like thousands of sharp needles, freezing breaths around our mouths and beards into a grimacing mask. It hid not only the top of the Pass but also the Khambas at the front of our long, single-file column.

Laboring upwards, and drawing in great sobbing breaths at every step, I was suddenly surprised to find the Khambas ahead of me gathered in a group and setting up colored "wind-horses", Tibetan prayer flags, a symbolic act of worship and thanks to the gods which was usually performed by Tibetans crossing high Passes but one which seemed crazily bizarre in our clandestine circumstances. My first thought was that it was a rash gesture of religious bravado, a taunting reminder to the Chinese that the Khambas had once again "been there, done that." But there was no sign of machismo among them, their faces solemn and thoughtful as they stood in silence and prayer around the blizzard-snapping flags. This was their witness to the Chinese that their commitment to fighting to the death was not just empty patriotism and duty like the Chinese occupiers of Tibet, but a witness to their spiritual allegiance to the gods and to their Dalai Lama.

I stood among them with mixed feelings. For the first time in fifteen years I had returned to Tibet, but there was nothing to be seen on the far side of the Pass because of the howling blizzard which caked my eyebrows, dark glasses, and beard with ice. We were a puny group in this raging merciless vastness, leaning into the gale to keep from falling; and somewhere within the radius of a few hundred yards or less there were hundreds of Chinese soldiers much more potent than a Himalayan snow-storm. The words of Stephen Spender came to mind:

"*...Near the snow, near the sun, in the highest fields*
See how these names are fêted by the waving grass. And by the   streamers of white cloud
And whispers of wind in listening sky.
The names of those who in their lives fought for life
Who wore at their hearts the fire's center.
Born of the sun they travelled a short while toward the sun,
And left the vivid air signed with their honor."

Tendar stepped away from the group around the prayer flags and looked along the long stretch of unbroken snow disappearing into the billowing clouds sweeping through the Pass. There was no sign of a trail in that deadly white tablecloth forming a funeral shroud over crevasses, gulleys and precipitous drops, into which a thousand men could easily disappear.

Then, after a few minutes' silent contemplation, he struggled over the shoulder of the Pass, hunched forward against the buffeting of the howling wind and driving ice particles, and was gradually absorbed into the curtain of thick cloud and snow. We followed in his path, in waist-high snowdrifts even after his and others' trail-blazing. At one point there was only a narrow ledge jutting out over a sheer drop, and the short, stocky Tsambala had to stand as an anchor against the force of the wind while each of us slid and fell against his body to keep us from rolling over the edge in a killing avalanche.

Going down was even steeper than the climb up had been on the south side. Not one of us could keep our balance on the precarious slope as we lay backwards on our heels to compensate for the steep angle, for as soon as we lifted one leg we either shot forward or fell back. To increase the difficulty, we had to keep in sight of the man in front, for visibility was nil in the snow-and-ice maelstrom around us. To lose sight of each other might mean being lost for ever, death by frostbite and starvation. I had a sudden thought that this was what had happened to the man whose toes I had removed.

Suddenly there was a loud yell, and a Khamba, holding his jolting gun and ammunition belts, shot down the slope on his back in a cloud of snow. At first I thought he had fallen, but he was laughing as he was yelling, enjoying the chute effect. He was followed by another, and another, and another, until all of them were plunging down the sheer mountainside like a winter lark in a park, all of them shouting the "Yee-hee-hee" war-cry of the Khambas. Only Tendar was left standing, watching with an amused half-smile – and Chris, with his ever-present camera filming the bizarre episode - as the shadowy shapes hurtled past in an apparent release of tension. Our only consolation was that not even the suspicious Chinese would believe that the noises they heard were those of a raiding party at this time, in that kind of way. They were more likely to believe that it was Abominable Snowmen!

When we finally rested a few thousand feet down the mountain my boots, trousers, stockings and underside of fur-lined coat were stiff and soaked with caked ice and loose snow. We were still in clouds and wind, but there were gaps and sheltered spots and, through the drifting openings we could detect snow-less spaces. It was difficult to believe that any of the Khambas knew where we were, and I was about to offer Tendar my compass when he rose to his feet and asked confidently if we were ready to move on.

It was incredible, but true. Not only Tendar but most of the others seemed to know that the regular trail lay over to the left of where we had rested; and, after another hour or so of angling and scrambling downwards on rocky and trail-less slopes, we came out of the clouds altogether and there was a trail - and Tibet - in front of us.

It was a memorable sight. We were still in the shadowed mountain, but for hundreds of miles ahead of us the multi-green forested mountains fell away to barren brown and yellow valleys and plateaux, softened now in the late afternoon sun in a unparalleled panorama of vast splendor. All around us majestic snow giants towered serenely, the snow-and-ice maelstrom of the peaks now only a muted sound and cloudy distant memory, their sun-bathed heads with cloud formations matching in grandeur the dying beauty of the sky. In all that glorious vastness there was no sign of a single inhabitant or animal moving. We were numberless miles from nowhere. The words of John Milton in his "*Paradise Lost*" leapt to mind:

"These are thy glorious works, Parent of good,
Almighty! Thine this universal frame,
Thus wondrous fair! Thyself how wondrous then!

Unspeakable! Who sitt'st above these Heavens
To us invisible, or dimly seen
In these thy lowest works; yet these declare
Thy goodness beyond thought and power divine."

"The trail," Tendar said quietly at my elbow," lies beyond that snow mountain where the sunshine lies in the valley. Are you glad to be back in Tibet?"

"Yes," I said, and sighed, "but I wish it had been in happier circumstances. In the sunshine, beneath that snow mountain, men will die in the next few days."

"In that sunshine, beneath that snow mountain, many men, women and children have died, are dying, and will continue to die, and be tortured, until the Chinese oppression is removed from our country," Tendar said reprovingly. I nodded gloomily in acknowledgment, and we moved forward together in silence, thinking our own thoughts and drinking in the incredible, austere beauty of this tragic country.

During this comparatively easy stretch, where the wide trail made it possible for two or more people to walk together and talk, Tendar cleared up a mystery which had been puzzling me. Earlier, talking with him and other Khamba leaders, I had been puzzled by the lack of evidence of, and lack of interest in, loot from Chinese convoys. They were so obviously short of arms, ammunition, clothes, food, and goods, yet, except for a few items of each of these, there was little to show for the many claimed attacks on Chinese convoys, garrisons or armed groups. Had it not been for the many indisputable statements by the hundreds of inhabitants in the Dzum region, the presence and many stories of the thousands of refugees who were pouring in from Tibet, the obvious, awe, admiration, respect, and even love shown by them to the Khambas, we would have doubted many of the accounts of raid successes which we heard.

But now Tendar spontaneously volunteered the explanation, pointing to the heavy loads of food, arms and ammunition being carried by the long line of Khambas ahead of us. Were it not for the necessity of carrying so much to the scene of an attack, he said, they could benefit a great deal more by bringing away plunder. To insure the success of a raid, each Khamba had to carry enough ammunition for an unknown number of Chinese enemy, plus spares for a possible retreat action; and, as the essence of their success was their superior mobility at high altitudes, they dare not take undue risks by overloading themselves with the much-coveted loot. If only they had strong horses, he sighed regretfully, what they could not do to the Chinese and for their own people, but they only had a few pack-ponies useful around Dzum. But anyway, he shrugged, there was really very little valuable plunder on the military convoys other than weapons and ammunition, and the same was true of the Chinese garrisons they attacked.

We now plunged downwards into a valley lying at right angles to where we had come off the pass, and the Khambas move ahead with their tireless strides, eating up the miles. My own legs were rubbery at first, after that nightmare drop through steep snow slopes, but soon I was also settled into the steady swing that I thought I had forgotten in jostling city streets. It was dangerous, mind-taxing, strength-sapping stuff this, but I was thoroughly enjoying it when I thought about it. I guessed from the fact that I was having to fasten my belt-buckle in more notches that I was losing a considerable amount of excess weight.

By seven o'clock we were still pushing forward, and we had been moving for eighteen hours since leaving the nomad camp just after midnight. The small stream we had seen near the top of the pass had grown into a small river, and Tendar called a halt beside it for a meal. I thought it was for a few hours' sleep, but, when I asked him, he shook his head firmly and said that we had to keep going quickly as long as there was no sign of Chinese. If we met Chinese patrols we might have to wait until they passed, or engage them in a fight, and that would delay us on the way to the ambush site. If possible, he said, he would like to get to the ambush site before dawn the next morning, and that meant going on through the night!

I couldn't believe that they were really going to go into battle with a Chinese convoy after over twenty-four hours without sleep - and then a retreat over the way we had come to avoid capture afterwards. These conditions might be all right for the phenomenal iron men of Kham, but Adrian, Chris and I were soft with several years of city life. However, Tendar knew this, was aware that we - or, at least, the exposed films - were important enough to get away safely, and I was content to leave the decision to him. But after the quickly snatched meal - tea made over a low fire and butane burner with Tibetan flour bread and cold hard-boiled eggs - I snatched a quick sleep for about an hour until we were ready to leave.

Now began our long dark night - but of the body, not the soul. No flashlights allowed. Twenty-three men moving into position between two known concentrations of several thousand Chinese troops, between two known garrisons of several hundred troops, and several known check-posts, and an unknown number of possible scouting or hunting patrols. It was another moonless night, and each man followed the barely discernible head or rifle outline of the man in front.

At least, that is what I did. The Khambas seemed to have cat's eyes and feet, and I strained every sense to interpret the sway and dip of the man in front in order to anticipate the kind of path underfoot. Scrub and widening path gave way to a steadily climbing, rock-strewn one, which in turn gave way to heart-stopping loose shale slopes dropping straight down to the growling river far below. No word was spoken, and during the rests only low-voiced necessary remarks were allowed by the cautious Tendar.

We went on through the night, pausing at every sudden bird-call, every suspicious sound, every blacker shadow ahead, to interpret what they meant. Tendar was everywhere. Ahead, behind, beside us on the trail, observing everything; Assang, his menacing lieutenant, equally shadowy and ubiquitous. We tripped over stones, blundered into boulders, slipped into bushes where sharp thorns filled our hands even through thick gloves, scrambled back on to narrow ledges after tumbling over edges and being grabbed by anonymous hands from behind.

The fur-lined, heavy coat which had served me so well in the blizzard on the Pass was now a thing of torture - hot, heavy, an intolerable encumbrance. I stumbled on, increasingly weary, laboring, despairing. It was impossible. The Khambas might - could - make it. I never could at this rate. Adrian and Chris were in the same ultra-fatigued state, I gathered from our whispered conversation during rests.

Tendar slid in beside me as I lay panting after one rough stretch. "We still have some hours to go to reach the place of ambush," he said quietly, "and we have about two hours of this climb to the top of the small Pass between us and there. Do you think you can do it?"

I shook my head negatively and replied, "No. Or, if we do make it to the place of ambush, we can never make the return journey feeling like this."

He was silent for a few minutes, then he said decisively, "We must lay up for the night and tomorrow, and then attack the next day. When we have come this far we must not miss the opportunity. If you have a sleep will you be able to carry on?"

I passed his query on to Adrian and Chris, and they agreed that this was the only possibility, and I gave our decision to Tendar. He squeezed my arm in the darkness, rose, and gave a few whispered commands to the others.

We went on for another short distance, then, in an open space between clumps of shrubs, where the dry and ice-covered grass crackled underfoot, he whispered that we would spend the night there. In the morning we would move a short distance further on, where there was a narrow cleft in the mountain, and spend the day there. This was Chinese patrol territory, he said, and it was too dangerous to risk drawing attention. The Chinese used dogs for trailing, while nomads used dogs for guarding.

The Khambas dropped where they were, untying their girdles and pulling their bulky gowns over their heads in exhausted lapse into sleep. I took out my poncho, folded it around my arctic sleeping-bag to give me more protection from the icy cold, climbed in with all my clothes on, and dropped off immediately into a deep exhausted sleep.

But it was a restless and uncomfortable night. The night grew colder, frost and ice gathered on clothes and sleeping-bags, and lay thick around my exposed face and beard. The incredible Tendar and Assang seemed to be awake or moving around every time I awoke. Before dawn everyone was up, taciturn, stiff and shivering, and we moved quickly upwards to a naturally hidden gully in the mountainside. There, the Khambas made a small fire around which we all huddled, watching the sun rise with agonizing slowness to thaw us with its heat. It was so bitterly cold I sat wrapped in my sleeping bag and, even when the sun did reach us, I remained fully clothed inside it.

We lay there, unmoving, for the whole day, except for the Khambas taking turns at keeping watch. Tendar sent two of them ahead to scout out the terrain and the place of ambush. Tendar gave orders to reduce our loads to the minimum, keeping only what we would need for the ambush and leaving behind in a bundle hidden deep in the bushes what we would need for the return journey to Dzum.

We waited until late afternoon when the two scouts returned with a report that the trail ahead to the ambush site was clear. While waiting, the Khambas went over plans for the attack once more. Tendar proposed that if it were a large convoy of twenty trucks or more that it would be allowed to pass, but we would film it. If less than twenty vehicles, they would attack it and fight the Chinese while we filmed the action. Then we were to withdraw and retreat with the films to safety back up this valley, and the others would cover our retreat and all rendezvous with us at this spot. If less than ten trucks, they would try to knock them all out and then call us down to the road to film the Khambas looting the vehicles.

There was some low-voiced but heated disagreement with the plan, especially from the oldest Khamba, Gaybo, the marksman and most experienced guerrilla among them, who wanted to shoot up the convoy whatever the size. But Tendar finally convinced him that on this mission it was the films and photographs which were important, not the number of vehicles destroyed or Chinese killed.

We moved over the top of the smaller Pass in the early evening on to a wide, easy downward-sloping trail. One scout was ahead, and one behind, to keep us from being surprised. Tendar walked beside me, free to talk again.

"It is sad to think that we need so little, yet we cannot get it," he said, without rancor. "Some warm clothing, for instance. You saw how we had to sleep in our gowns. With tents, sleeping-bags and, as I said yesterday, riding and strong pack horses, we could launch more effective attacks against the Chinese in their garrisons as well as convoys. We could move so quickly that the Chinese could never catch us in these mountains."

"How many attacks do you average?" I asked him.

"Too many to count. This will be the fifth attack in five months."

"Have you lost many men?" I inquired.

"None," he said promptly. "Thanks to the gods. There are many hundreds of us - four or five thousand - in these mountains, and in the hundreds of raids we hardly ever lose a man. This is deliberate policy, for we now have to conserve every man and every gun as much as we can. Our strategy is to use surprise and speed in attack, returning to the mountains where the Chinese cannot follow easily on foot and we have the advantages. It is the best we can do until we get the help we need from our Tibetan leaders in India."

It was soon dark, and the silently groping experience of the previous night was repeated. I found I was developing an unexpected skill for moving quickly in the dark, by adapting my reflexes to the movements of the man ahead. But, surprisingly silently as we moved for so large a group of so many large and heavily loaded men, it was still a tense, suspense-packed journey. Every so often we would stop at a whispered command up the line while Tendar, Assang or Gaybo listened, or went ahead to check on some suspicious sound or object. A bird would rise unexpectedly from beneath our feet, its startled call splitting the night with sudden, throat-constricting clamor, and we would halt until it had settled and the dark valley was silent again but filled with a greater waiting menace. Had some Chinese sentry heard, and were rifles already being lifted quietly somewhere up ahead?

We went on for four hours like this, and then stopped for a rest. There was a whispered consultation somewhere and Tendar slipped in beside me.

"Have you a flashlight?" he asked in my ear. "Please lend it to me. Gaybo says that there is a deserted monastery about half an hour away. If there are no Chinese billeted there we will stop, make tea, sleep for three hours, then move on to the ambush spot before dawn."

I gave him the flashlight and he disappeared as quickly and silently as he had come. We moved off again, more slowly, more cautiously, than ever. A few hundred yards away a light flickered on then off again, and my breath caught in my throat as I waited for a high-pitched Chinese voice to call out - or a burst of unannounced gunfire. The night remained black and silent, and we walked on.

The light went on again, and this time remained on for an agonizing few minutes, which seemed like an eternity as we remained frozen and tense in place.

"Gukpa rang-ray! (The bloody fool)", Tendar, beside me, swore softly through gritted teeth. "What does he think he's doing? That light will be seen for miles." He lunged quickly but silently up the trail. After a bit the light went out, and the line of men moved on.

Tendar returned beside me and whispered, "Follow me closely, and quickly. The monastery seems empty, but we are checking all the rooms in case there is someone in them."

I followed him down a long slope, picking my way in his shadow, then over a rubble-strewn courtyard, through a dark doorway beside which stood a tall figure with his rifle held at the ready. I had thought the night dark outside, but inside the doorway it was like walking into black velvet. Tendar's hand guided me forward over another step - and then I was suddenly blinded by the light of a flashed flashlight. This time there was no rebuke from Tendar as one of the men reported that the monastery was empty.

It was an eerie, unforgettable sight. It had obviously been a fairly wealthy monastery for it was solidly built and the wall murals had been elaborately and freshly painted - except where they were smeared by vandals and darkened by smoke. The monastery had been gutted and looted by the Chinese. In the flickering light of the flashlight as we went from room to room, images were seen to have been desecrated or destroyed, thrown to the floor, burned black with soot. Religious scrolls and rich silk hangings had been piled, with Buddhist scripture manuscripts, on the floor and set alight. Smashed glass and painted wood cupboards lay scattered everywhere.

There were murmurs of dismay, and muttered curses, from the Khambas, and I suspected that the Chinese would be made to pay a higher price tomorrow. No, today, I suddenly remembered that it was after midnight. I picked up a few objects as mementos of the occasion that I could put into my back-pack - a few burned pages of Buddhist scriptures, a chipped ochre-colored idol, a trampled hand prayer-cymbal, and a discarded Chinese chopstick - to remind me of the somber occasion if we all survived. I did not wait for tea to be brewed - in the middle of the monastery floor where the Chinese had made their destructive fire - I climbed into my sleeping-bag and immediately fell asleep.

We were awake and on the way again after three a.m., now traveling even more slowly and cautiously as we neared the critical military road and ambush site. Two hours later we halted in unrelieved darkness and Tendar said we were there, and that the three men he had assigned to us would take us to our appointed places on the hillside above the road. He was going to place the others in their firing positions.

Our guard with the rifle, Tseten, turned up the mountainside to the left and began a steep, almost vertical, climb up shifting shale to where there was a four-foot high, rocky outcrop, like a rampart, which would form an excellent cover for our filming activities. As the night around us lightened we could see the slaty brown hillside, with its scattered, stratified and grotesquely-shaped rocks, lent itself admirably as camouflage for the necessary apertures for our filming cameras. By six o'clock, when the sun was just beginning to touch the highest peaks all around us, we were ready for the attack.

CHAPTER TWELVE

The Ambush, Tragedy And Retreat

It was a magnificent setting for an ambush. From the northwest the road curved toward us in a series of sharp bends, following the line of the river. Just beneath us, the mountains on either side of the river closed in, and the valley became a lazy "S", a three-hundred-yard double bend. The military road, which followed the contours of the river, was only about fifty yards from our hideout, on this side of the river. On an exposed point, where a shoulder of a nearby mountain met the valley, just above the road and commanding a view of the approaching convoys someone at some time had built a dugout, and I could see one of the Khambas preparing his shooting position there - Assang, I think. He is going to get the best photographs of us all there, I thought suddenly, remembering his request for films to take photographs on his Canon camera. I could see none of the others, but our guard said that three of them were directly beneath us and to our right, and the others in a short arc beyond them. The guard said they had all smeared their faces with dirt, and had put branches from scrubs in their headgear to make them blend even more into the surroundings.

We settled down to wait for the Chinese convoy as the sun climbed above the mountains peaks and warmed the valley. The Khambas had told us that, on average, most of the convoys from north to south passed in the morning, and most of those from south to north in the afternoon.

In the first two hours we were tense with expectation and excitement, but gradually, as the sun rose and bathed us in its heat, we became less tense and even drowsy. The slope was so steep that we had to jam our feet against embedded stones to keep from sliding down into the valley in an avalanche of loose shale, and this did not lead to easy slumbers.

At first I was uneasy lest we all sleep and miss the convoy, but as the Khambas around us all seemed alert I let myself drift more deeply into sleep. At one point I was awakened by one of our guards warning us to be alert. A Tibetan herdsman appeared, driving a small herd of yaks down the road from which we expected the convoy, and we watched and listened to the tinkling bells around the necks of the yaks until they disappeared into the distance. Chris filmed the unwitting herdsman and animals from behind his camouflaged rampart to get the feel of the distance, and then we settled down again. There was no sound anywhere, except for the rise and fall of the wind; even the river was silent from where we were.

I had dozed again when a guard wakened me at 1:30 to say that another Tibetan was on the road. Did we want to film him? Adrian and Chris shook their heads negatively, and we went back to a dozing silence.

I awakened suddenly, trying to sort out the unusual whine from the moan of the wind. Was it truck engines? I turned to look questioningly at our guards who were also tensely attentive. Tseten looked cautiously over the edge of the rampart, nodded his head affirmatively - and the first rifle shot rang out! This was followed by a fusillade of shots and the battle was on.

During one of our earlier discussions I had asked Tendar what methods they used in stopping a convoy, and he had looked puzzled. "Methods?" he asked. "What do you mean?"

I explained how, during the war in Europe, or in other popular uprisings, the civilians would either put explosives of some kind on the road, or place an innocent plate on the road, and when the vehicle or tank stopped - they dared not take the risk that the plate was innocent - the hidden civilians would throw flaming petrol-bottles or hand-grenades into the stopped vehicles.

Tendar was very interested but he had never heard of this, let alone used the methods. "We just shoot them," he said casually.

"Yes," I persisted. "But even if you do kill the first driver with the first shot, what happens when the second driver accelerates, and those behind him, to pass the first truck?"

"We shoot them, too," he replied simply, puzzled by my naiveté.

I knew from experience the astonishing, even legendary, marksmanship of the Khambas, who learned to shoot almost before they learned to walk; but to accept this expertise so calmly when the success of the raid - and their lives - depended on those first few shots, was almost beyond belief. However, I had swallowed my arguments at the time, and remained silent. It was just as well. For, as I looked over the rampart at the scene below, the first driver was already dead, and the others dead or dying as their feet instinctively had hit the brakes - because the trucks were still in line and hadn't even had time to swerve let alone accelerate past.

I stole a quick glance at my watch to check the time - 1:50 - then grabbed my cameras and scrambled to my filming position beside Adrian on one side and Chris on the other.

Just below us, the four Chinese trucks on the almost straight, middle length of the lazy "S", had all stopped within one hundred yards of each other - three together and the fourth about fifty yards away. With no cover anywhere, the Chinese drivers and soldiers in them who were still alive had jumped down and were underneath or behind the trucks firing at the Khambas hidden on the mountainside around us.

Suddenly, I could scarcely believe my eyes! Through the zoom lens of my camera there was Tendar walking - yes, walking! - towards the first truck. So far as I could see there were no Chinese under the truck firing at him, but there were certainly Chinese under and behind the second truck less than ten yards away from him. It seemed suicidal, especially when he turned his back on the second truck and looked over the tail of the first truck, presumably to see what load it was carrying. He had said he would find out what he could in the trucks for us to film, but I had meant at the end of the action, not right at the beginning while presenting himself as a target.

While the guns kept up a rolling thunder from both combatants, the narrow valley with enclosing mountains acting as a monumentally reverberating sound-chamber, Tendar disappeared around the far side of the first truck and I turned my camera on the action elsewhere. The Chinese under and behind the second truck were still returning fire, as were the Chinese beneath and behind the third and fourth trucks.

From the corner of my eye glued to the eye-piece of the zoom lens I saw Tendar appear again, making towards his firing position on the hillside, when he suddenly stopped, turned, swung his arm and fell face downwards on the ground. He's hit! I thought sickeningly. Then there was an explosion near the second truck, and I realized he had thrown a hand-grenade at some hidden Chinese There was a raised burst of firing from the Khambas at the exposed Chinese bodies which resulted, and then all movement ceased.

Another Khamba appeared from our side of the valley heading for the third truck, swung an arm and another explosion followed, a blue-black cloud arising from beside the truck, and all firing stopped there.

Some Chinese underneath the fourth truck suddenly broke away and made toward us, firing as they ran. One of them fell as he was hit, then struggled to his feet and ran on. Another disappeared under an overhanging ledge right beneath us. One of our guards, who had been watching but not firing, according to Tendar's instructions, now lifted his rifle and loosed off three rounds at the Chinese advancing on our position. Then, remembering his orders, he signed urgently for us to leave.

"Go now," he ordered. "Immediately. Pack everything." I looked at my watch - 2:10 - twenty minutes of non-stop action! The gun-fire had become less concentrated, but was still sounding in short staccato bursts.

We threw cameras, films, and discarded clothing into the back-packs, the three Tibetans slung them over our shoulders, and plunged suicidally down that vertical mountain slope in a long, sliding, striding, mad dash for the narrow valley beneath.

Reaching the stream at the bottom, without pausing for breath, we strode at a fast pace up the trail we had come down so cautiously before dawn. Having seen us on our way, Tseten, our armed guard, left us to return down the valley to help cover our retreat, while the other two urged us to keep going quickly, assuring us that the others would catch up with us.

Sure enough, half an hour or so later Tseten re-appeared, moving swiftly, accompanied by the tall, gangling Gesang. They waved to us to wait for them. When they caught up with us Gesang said urgently to me, "Bon-bo-la (Boss), get some medicines quickly -------- has been shot."

"Who?" I asked, missing the name, and recalling the collapsed movement of Tendar during the action.

"Gaybo, the old one," Gesang repeated. "He has been badly shot and requires medicines. Tendar, Assang and Tsambala are with him."

"Where is he shot?" I asked, as I unpacked one of the back-packs where I kept my supply of medicines.

"Here," Gesang said, pointing to the region of his heart. "I think, but there is large hole back here," he pointed over his left shoulder. "He has also been shot in the face."

I felt a wave of hopelessness sweep over me. The man could not live, if the report was true. How could he travel over the trail we had come, including one 20,000-feet Pass and two smaller but more difficult Passes, with open chest-wounds like these and the loss of blood involved? I said nothing of this, however, but asked the men to build a fire quickly as I would need lots of hot water.

They looked surprised at this, but I said we must have fifteen minutes at least to dress the wounds. If the Chinese followed, they would just have to fight them off until I had finished.

We had a fire going and water boiling, with my medical supplies laid out on a flat stone. I had no forceps, or surgical instruments of any kind, only ordinary scissors, and I hoped that I wouldn't have to dig shrapnel out of the wounds. I could only bind him up, keep down infection, and hope that he would survive. While we waited for his arrival I had a sudden flashback of the Scriptures I had read before we left Dzum: "...There will be no loss of life among you...God has given you all those who sail with you..." I wondered if the Khambas were thinking, too, of the favorable prophecies of their *chod-gyad* that the gods would safeguard them.

But when Tendar, Assang and the others appeared I could see by their faces that the worst had happened.

"He has gone," Tendar said starkly. "We could do nothing. He was shot in the heart, shot in the face and had lost lots of blood. It was impossible for him to live, and he asked us to shoot him so that the Chinese would not find him alive. We refused, but he insisted we leave him to die while we saved ourselves, and bring the foreigners and films to safety. He died in my arms."

They had neither time nor equipment to dig a grave, so they had placed his body under a heap of stones, and hoped that the Chinese would think it was just another roadside mani shrine.

There was a heavy silence around the sputtering fire as I gathered together and packed my equipment. Tendar was lost in his thoughts. It was Assang who said harshly, "All right. Let's get going or the Chinese will find us and kill us all."

"Will we have time to film and take some photographs of the monastery we slept in last night?" Adrian asked me to find out. "It will serve as evidence of Chinese destruction of monasteries."

I asked Assang and he nodded curtly, taking over easily during Tendar's moment of dark grief at Gaybo's loss. He directed a few men to go with us, and Tendar, while others went ahead with him. He was limping, but he waved away my inquiries, saying only that he had twisted his ankle.

On the way to the monastery Tendar briefly described what had taken place. They thought they had killed all the Chinese, but one soldier had run from behind the fourth truck down the embankment of the river and Gaybo had left his hideout to go after him. There was an exchange of fire between the exposed Gaybo and the hidden Chinese soldier, and Gaybo went down, then struggled to his feet holding his hand-gun. He caught up with the Chinese and tried to shoot, but the gun must have been empty, because he reached for his dagger - and found that he had dropped it. The Chinese had shot him again, and then struck him on the face with his own empty gun. By that time Tendar was on his way to help him and when he reached Gaybo the Chinese soldier had disappeared. Tendar guessed he was still alive and in hiding, but he had called off the action to get help for Gaybo. It was possible that, if the Chinese was alive, that he might be able to get telephone or radio help from the trucks to call in reinforcements. In which case, we had to move really fast.

I thought of the three Passes to be negotiated before we could consider ourselves "safe" - and even then it was relative. The first Pass was just ahead of the monastery, at about 15,000-feet as near as I could guess. Then there was a long dip down, and a sudden rise to about 17,000-feet and a second saddle-like Pass, where I had walked and talked with Tendar on the trip into Tibet. This, too, dropped down for several hours, past the point where we had laid up for the night and day, and then swept on and up to the terrifying 20,000-feet Khojang Pass into Nepal.

We only remained filming in the monastery for about fifteen minutes, the Khambas impatient to be gone although acknowledging the importance of having filmed evidence of the desecration. When we had finished, Tendar set a cracking pace up the valley to catch up with Assang and the others. We could see them distantly ahead and above us on the trail on the left-hand side of the valley, but a bend in the valley behind us hid what might be happening on the military road. Now that the thunderous echoes of the ambush gunfire had died away the usual silence seemed even more profound.

During our rare rest-stops Tendar said that there were three main garrisons behind us in a wide arc: Tsang to our extreme right in the northwest; Dzongkar behind and slightly west; and Kyerong on our left to the east. Between these, there were unknown numbers of concentrations of troops in forests and caves, checkposts, scouting parties - or even other convoys on the road which would quickly alert all troops everywhere. If the Khambas had the advantage of mountain mobility, the Chinese had the advantages of fast road transport, modern radio and telephone communications, although these would be of decreasing value the higher we climbed.

We were making for the Khojang Pass, between the three garrisons, in a gamble that we could reach there by superior timing, mobility and personal strength, before the Chinese. If, however, the Chinese guessed our intentions, they could throw sufficient troops into a flanking movement to our right and left which could cut off our route of escape to the Khojang Pass. In which case, Tendar said calmly, we would be forced to work our way backwards through the Chinese troops and enter Nepal from alternative, and even more difficult, Passes around them. What worried me was that the Khambas seemed to take it for granted that we would be able to accomplish these miracles of survival as easily as they said they would.

The Khambas took it all matter-of-factly, as if it were some academic game of chess. They obviously enjoyed this battle of wits and were supremely confident that in their own mountains they were the masters. But what did bother them, and cast a cloud of gloom over the group, was the death of Gaybo. Any death would have bothered them, but what upset them most about this episode was the fact that the optimistic prophecy of the gods had failed in the death of Gaybo. Time after time they returned to this in their conversations.

We topped the first Pass, and the first set of dangers from our flanks was behind us. We were not out of danger by any means, but it meant that if a large Chinese force had arrived at the place of ambush immediately after we left and had launched a flanking manoeuver they would have been here to cut us off, so we had escaped the first snap of the Chinese dragon. A larger force, a wider bite, and we could still be swallowed at any of the difficult stages ahead.

Except for the steep climbs, I was still moving easily and lightly on my feet and knew that I was good for several hours. Adrian and Chris seemed the same, although we rarely spoke, saving our breaths for the task of moving quickly. By late afternoon, moving more slowly now after that strength-sapping pace from the ambush site, we had passed our sleeping and lying-up culvert of the first night where we picked up the things we had left behind, topped the second Pass safely, and turned into the long valley leading to the dreaded Khojang Pass. We were on the last lap.

We stopped for a quick meal of several bowls of scalding hot soup and some tsamba, a quick readjustment of some loads as we got rid of anything not absolutely necessary, and we were on our way again as the sun set. As the Khambas moved around swiftly, saying little beyond what was necessary and obviously engrossed with thoughts of our extreme situation, I recalled the words of Robert Browning:

"*Fear death? - to feel the fog in my throat,*
  The mist in my face,
When the snows begin, and the blasts denote
  I am nearing the place,
The power of the night, the press of the storm,
  The post of the foe;
Where he stands, the Arch Fear in a visible form,
  Yet the strong man must go:
For the journey is done and the summit attained,

And the barriers fall,
Though a battle's to fight ere the guerdon be gained,
The reward of it all.
I was ever a fighter so - one fight more,
The best and the last!..."

We finished the hasty meal and moved on again, a repeat of our journey to the ambush site, but moving more swiftly, taking more risks, keyed up with the excitement and tension of possible pursuit. At first the trail swung downwards in a long angle, winding around the projecting mountainsides, soon dropping all the way to the valley floor where we had to pick our way upstream among increasingly larger boulders and tossing spray. While this made our path infinitely more difficult and wearing as we slipped and struggled between and over the boulders, it had the distinct advantage that the noises of the large stream - more like a small river - covered the many small noises of our passage.

The brawling river had another advantage I had not thought of until then, the noise hiding whatever sounds we made stumbling in the dark. We had stopped to take off boots and stockings and roll up trousers to cross the river at one of many points, and somebody mislaid a boot in the thick darkness. To find it, somebody else flashed a flashlight. There was an immediate order from Tendar and Assang to put it out, but not before a distant sound indicated a barking dog. Were the Chinese trailing us with dogs, or was it just some nomad dog barking at a night sound?

It energized us to attempt an even quicker pace up the uneven trail. It was not just a question of keeping ahead of pursuing Chinese, but also of the Chinese border troops billeted on the Pass ahead being possibly alerted by radio to meet us coming towards them. Would our strength be sufficient to stand the unimaginable strains being imposed on our bodies? Or would we have to surrender exhausted on the icy slopes above to the overwhelming power of the Chinese? We had only been cat-napping spells of sleep for the best part of three nights, while climbing up and down the highest and toughest mountains in the world.

The Khambas were determined to make it the quickest - but also the infinitely hardest - way to the Pass. They went straight up, and because of the almost vertical angle it meant we had to move five paces to the right, then to the left, then to the right, in zig-zag fashion, as we progressed up the face of the sheer slopes. At first we would go for a hundred yards or so, then stop, standing still for another breather, sitting down almost every third stop for a few minutes. These stages became less and less, and the sitting stages longer the higher we climbed.

Drifting masses of grey wetness in the darkness indicated that we were rising above the clouds; also, there was an eerie lightness around us as we entered the regions of eternal snow. Fortunately, there was little wind on this return journey, but what wind there was was paralyzingly cold in sub-zero temperatures when we stopped for a rest.

Soon we were a staggering, stumbling line - silent, except for the soughing of great sobbing breaths. I passed from vaguely hallucinatory flashes of recalled scenes of Napoleon's retreat from Moscow - blindly stumbling figures, endless snows, mutilated bodies, shadowy wolves - to a numbed exhaustion of fragmented flashes of half-remembered phrases - *"in a minute pay glad life's arrears of pain, darkness and cold...", "the elements' rage, the fiend-voices that rave...", "Why be afraid of death as though your life were breath?...".*

I could no longer lift my head to look upward at that black immovable outline against the now shell-grey sky that was the top of the Pass. I only existed in a twisted world of agonizing breathing, of painful automatic movements of leaden legs, of a deep, blazing inner intensity of compulsion which kept me going when everything else within me cried out to stop.

I was vaguely conscious when the figures around me dropped to the ground, and I, too, fell flat on my face. I remained immobile - even at times falling into a deep sleep or unconsciousness despite the piercing cold - and only coming stupefyingly awake when Tendar called out, or pulled me to my feet, to stumble on.

If I had any capacity for wonder left, it was for Tendar. He had said earlier that he had a cold and a headache, and had asked for some medicine to keep him from coughing in the night, as a security precaution. When he spoke to me I could hear how hoarse he was, how thick with cold, yet he was ahead and behind as before, and most often beside the three of us, watching and encouraging us to go on.

Now that we were in the snows, the Khambas used the flashlights more often, throwing caution to the winds as they sought the best way through the glassy ice-fields and treacherous snowdrifts. The snow was so thick we could no longer sit down, and we dropped our tortured legs from clinging snowy step to snowy step. My mouth was parched and I broke off an icicle and ate it hungrily, despite Tendar's warning admonition that it might give me stomach cramps. I was past caring.

Later, much later, I noticed that it was lighter. Tendar said, "It is dawn," and I looked around, seeing the dark outlines of the Khambas disappearing over that hitherto unreachable rim.

We had reached the Pass, and there were no Chinese. But it still did not mean that we were safe. There were no Nepalese or Indian border patrols or checkposts to stop them from crossing deep into Nepal after us, and the Khambas were intent on putting space between them and us.

But, as I dragged myself up to the Pass to where I could see the other side into Nepal, with Tendar standing beside me as the Pass winds roared and we had to lean forward against them to stand upright, I was conscious of a scene of indescribable splendor. To the north, south, east and west stretched range upon range of snow-capped giants, their iridescent peaks hovering in multi-colored majesty above the clouds as the sun rose to unfold the purple forests of lesser ranges of mountains around them. In that awesome sight everything became still and the world, the problems, the Chinese, the dark night of agony, fell away, and the words of William Wordsworth's poem came to mind:

"What soul was his when from the naked top
Of some bold headland, he beheld the sun
Rise up and bathe the world in light: He looked,
Ocean and earth, the solid frame of earth
And ocean's liquid mass, in gladness lay
Beneath him: far and wide the clouds were touched
And in their silent faces could be read
Unutterable love. Sound needed none,
Nor any voice of joy; his spirit drank
The spectacle: sensation, soul and form
All melted into him; they swallowed up
His animal being; in them did he live
And by them did he live, they were his life.
In such access of mind, in such high hour
Of visitation from the living God,
Thought was not; in enjoyment it expired.
No thanks he breathed, he preferred no request;
Rapt in still communion that transcends
The imperfect office of prayer and praise,
His mind was a thanksgiving to the power

That made him: it was blessedness and love."

I stood with Tendar, our arms around each others' shoulders, with a sense of closeness rarely if ever experienced. We had shared danger and grief and vision; and there, at 20,000 feet on the roof of the world, we stood together with God and the breaking beauty of a new day and a new lease of life. Mountains and valleys, snows and forests; and, beyond them, nations and governments and armies, politics and selfishness and greed. They seemed puny and contemptible that morning. I felt immortal.

We moved away from the summit without talking, dropping down several thousand feet before Tendar called a halt. "We are safe now" he said. "It would have been good if Gaybo had only lived. We lost a good friend, and a good gun. He was a brave man and we shall miss him very much. When we tried to lift him to carry him the blood poured from his wounds, and he said it was impossible for him to go on. He said he was an old man, that he knew the time of his death had come, and that we must leave to get you and the films back to Nepal safely. We still said we would carry him, but his mouth was dropping open and his eyes turning upwards. 'Shoot me,' he said to me, and I refused. I could not do this for him. 'You shoot me,' he said to Assang.' I will shoot you," Assang promised," if you will allow us to carry you first and see if the Chinese follow. If you are a hindrance to us, then I will shoot you.' He did not answer. His head fell back and he was dead."

The others listened in silence, their thoughts far away. In another few days, with some of the five thousand Khambas scattered among these mountains, they would be taking part in similar actions along the thousand-mile stretch of Nepal's frontier with Tibet against overwhelming Chinese forces occupying their country, and Gaybo's fate waited for them somewhere in the snowy wastes of their lost land. It seemed a hopeless cause.

Yet, was it? Something lived in Tendar, in the Khambas, in me, in Adrian and Chris, which had grown a little more, had blazed a little brighter. The physical evidences of despair were overwhelming wherever we looked, yet our very existence in the midst of them, our presence there with the Khambas in their cause, despite all the odds, added up to something. Not something negligible, but something profound and far-reaching. There was no greed, or selfishness, or arrogance, or exploitation, or injustice, or hubris, here among them. Comradeship, love of country and each other and their religion, and a willingness to die for them. To them, commitment even to a hopeless cause was of greater value than the complacent hypocrisies of political expediency.

I remembered the words of Lord Byron in his ***Triumph Of The Defeated***:

" *They never fail who die*
In a great cause. The block may soak their gore;
Their heads may sodden in the sun; their limbs
Be strung to city gates and castle walls;
But still their spirit walks abroad.
Though years elapse and others share as dark a doom,,
They but augment the deep and sweeping thoughts
Which overpower all others and conduct
The world, at last, to freedom."

When we were out of the snows around the top of the Pass, and striding easily down the trail on the far side, Tendar fell into step beside me and talked about the ambush. I asked him what he was doing when he came out of his hideout and ran to the trucks. He said he wanted to see what the truck contained; if there was anything worth filming. When he got there he saw a Chinese lining his rifle to shoot him, and he went round the truck as cover. The Chinese - whom we could not see from where we were - followed him, and Tendar pulled open the door of the cabin and slipped around the front of the truck to shoot him. Nothing happened he said, then he laughed.

"I was never so frightened in my life. I went back around the side of the truck and there was the head and shoulders of a Chinese soldier slowly appearing out of the cabin and beside the door. I shot immediately, the body fell - and there behind him was the Chinese I had been stalking. He, too, was so surprised that he just stood there, and I had time to recover and shoot him dead. What had happened was that I must have killed both the driver and his companion with my first long-distance rifle shot. When I opened the door, the driver's companion's dead body must have started sliding sideways, so that when I looked around the front of the truck, it seemed as if he were looking around the door at me. I shot a dead man! No wonder the other Chinese was surprised. It gave me time to shoot him, though."

"What about the hand-grenade?" I asked him.

"That was to flush out the Chinese from beneath the second truck. They were proving difficult for the others to hit, so I threw the grenade, they ran, and Assang and one of the others shot them."

"Weren't you afraid that you would be hit when you walked towards the first truck at the beginning of the action?" I asked him. "After all, one of several Chinese could have shot you in the back at that stage."

"None of the Chinese could shoot me," he said simply, with supreme confidence. "I carry the Dalai Lama's gift and mandate, and although the bullets were going past my face and shoulders like bees" - he grinned recklessly - "as well as my back, I knew that none of them could harm me."

We walked on, talking, in easy companionship while the sunshine crept down the mountainside to warm the green lower slopes of the valley in a rose-yellow glow. Far below we could see smoke rising from the last campfire at the same site which we had left a few days before. Some of the Khambas had arrived ahead of us and started the fire for the inevitable tea.

"We'll sleep for a few hours there after we have eaten," Tendar said, "then we'll go on to the nomad camp at Kaloon. I don't think the Chinese will follow us there, but in the past they have crossed the border claiming they were 'chasing Khamba bandits', and I don't want to risk staying too close to the border and risk your films. Do you see that snow-peak up there?" He pointed away to our right. "Just to the left of that, and a little down on the other side, are fifteen Chinese soldiers, and a large checkpost, watching that Pass, scouting the mountains, and watching us with binoculars. They came there after a previous raid, when we used that route."

"How do you obtain such accurate information?" I asked curiously. "For instance, how do you know that there are fifteen and not ten or even twenty?"

Tendar gave one of his rare laughs. "Because we have one of our people working for them. We have a Tibetan who they think is very useful and important to them as a guide and informer. The Chinese have to have someone like that, because they do not speak Tibetan or any of the Himalayan languages. These people send us reports of the Chinese and their activities through relatives and friends."

At the nomad camp, where we had stopped on the way north, we stopped again and had a wonderful meal. The nomads killed a sheep to celebrate our safe return and we had boiled mutton with rice, spiced vegetables, yogurt and tsamba, washed down with bowls of hot yak milk. When we had finished eating we stretched out on the aromatic, shrub-covered ground of the tent as we were, and fell into the deep, dreamless sleep of the contented and exhausted.

CHAPTER THIRTEEN

Miraculous Deliverances And Plans

Next morning, we were still eating when one of the Khambas called Tendar out of the tent. He was away some time, and when he returned he brought with him a short, stocky Tibetan. He introduced him to me as a trader, and then said:

"This man has brought news which should interest you. He was traveling from inside Tibet to Nepal, and was just to the south of our ambush point two days ago when he was stopped by Chinese soldiers. There were three trucks, packed full of soldiers, all with arms at the ready, patrolling the roads and searching nearby mountains. They detained him for questioning about his movements, and asked him if he had seen any armed Tibetans, and when he said he hadn't they let him go. The important point of his information is that this was less than an hour after our ambush, and on the road to the south of where it took place, so that more Chinese trucks and soldiers must have arrived at the spot less than an hour after our departure. If we had not picked up the wounded Gaybo when we did, and if you had come down to the road to take pictures, we would all have been killed or captured. It was the gods' goodness to us that we left when we did, because of Gaybo; but it is a pity that Gaybo had to die. If we had tried to carry him with us as we first thought, we would have been captured, too. The gods were with us, except for Gaybo's death."

I agreed, but I felt unhappy as I recalled, not only the responsibility we shared in Gaybo's death, but also that I, too, had been so confident that all of us would return. We had been so remarkably successful in our project up to that point I naturally thought we would be equally successful in every way during the raid. But Gaybo had died, and, to the sadness of his death was added the disturbing factor of apparently unfulfilled supernatural promise regarding favorable outcome with no loss of life. It created a cloud of uncertainty, but I pushed the problem away for the time being until I had both time and quiet to give it more thought.

Later, yet another informant arrived to report on the Khambas' previous raid into Tibet and the consequences. There had been fourteen trucks attacked in that convoy, ten of which had been damaged; of the ten, two were complete write-offs and left beside the road, three had been towed to Kyerong for major repairs, and five had been taken all the way to Lhasa for repairs. Twenty-three Chinese had been killed, and more badly wounded. He had been in the Chinese garrison at the time and had been told that the men in bandages had been in "a motor accident."

Following on that attack, thirty-three truck loads of soldiers had scoured the nearby mountains for three days and nights, under the command of a high-ranking Chinese officer. This officer had been angry when they returned to their garrisons to report that they could not find "the Khamba bandits".

He also reported that the Mustang group of Khambas had successfully attacked a large troop of Chinese on horses, and killed over a hundred of them, with none of the Khambas killed. The Chinese were so angry when they could not capture the Khambas that they tortured and killed many local Tibetans.

Another interesting item of information from the informants was that the day previous to our ambush a convoy of twenty-five trucks packed with soldiers had gone down the road; which meant that, if we had not been so exhausted that night and had arrived at the ambush site at the time we had first anticipated, the Khambas might have attacked it anyway out of devil-may-care bravado - with unimaginable consequences! I could see Tendar, like me, struggling with the mysteries of divine intervention.

The informants' reports made everyone uneasy about still being so close to the Chinese on the other side of the Pass. We had carefully hidden the obvious signs of foreigners - egg shells, chocolate wrappers, toilet paper - and especially evidence of filming, which would give us away to the Chinese and would know that it was not just the usual Khamba raid. If they guessed that there had been filming, then it was even more likely they would risk crossing into Nepal after us. Another thought was that the local Chinese would report their suspicions to their top officials in Lhasa, who would radio it to the Chinese embassy in Kathmandu, and they would have their people on the lookout for our arrival in the city. We could not let our guard drop until we had got the films safely out of Nepal. With this in mind we gave the canisters of shot films to Tendar for the Khambas to keep safely until we were ready to leave. He handled the film canisters as reverently as the Buddhist scriptures he was in the habit of reading.

If the Chinese authorities decided that the publicity would do them real damage internationally - after all, we had broken through the so-called impregnable frontier, attacked them on one of their famous military roads close to three of their largest garrisons on the borders, exposed the fallacy of their claimed "peaceful and contented Tibetans" under their occupation, had filmed evidence of a desecrated and destroyed monastery and the massacre of their vaunted troops, and escaped successfully - then it was more than likely they would lodge a serious protest with the Nepal government officials in an attempt to have them confiscate the films and have us arrested.

I had made tentative arrangements with Tsewang for him to leave ahead of us carrying the films hidden in the normal large woven containers used in the lower Himalayan region to take vegetables and chickens to market. But there were seventeen days' travel between Dzum and Kathmandu, with several military and civilian checkposts, the most serious being Setelvass, Dotang and Arughat before reaching Kathmandu. If anything happened to Tsewang during that time, and those places, we would not be able to do anything about it. It was a huge gamble - and a greater headache! - requiring some kind of supernatural help if we were to get the films through all the intervening offiicial agencies primed to stop us succeeding

We wanted to remain in Dzum to film the local Dalai Lama birthday celebrations, which were to be especially joyous on this occasion because of the recent successes of the Khamba raids across the border. The necessary filming requirement involved persuaded us to postpone sending the films by Tsewang until later.

If our Nepali colleague Hemantha was suspicious of our absence for several days "filming nomads in the snows" he was too polite to mention it, and his only concern was the delay occasioned by the Dalai Lama's birthday celebrations, and what this would mean to his family. He had never been away from home for so long in the past.

We had decided to do some local "color" filming shortly after our return from the raid into Tibet, when Tendar and a Khamba companion suddenly appeared, breathless and agitated. I only caught a few of his gasped words "Gya....arrived in Kaloon."

"What did he say?" Adrian asked anxiously.

"I think the Chinese have arrived in Kaloon," I said, and Adrian looked as stunned as I felt. Kaloon was only several hours' walk away, the nomad camp where we had stopped after leaving the Khamba camp.

"Wait, wait!" I said to Tendar, who was unusually excited as he talked with the headman Abu Jampa and other local Tibetans about the incident. "What was it you said?"

"Gaybo has arrived at Kaloon," he said slowly, smiling widely.

"Gaybo?" I said stupidly. "Our Gaybo?"

"Yes," Tendar confirmed with a laugh. "The man who was shot, is alive and has arrived in Kaloon, where we spent the night. This man saw him and brought the news." He indicated the Khamba who had come with him.

"But I thought - " I began, and Tendar finished, "He was dead. Yes, so did I - and Assang and the others. But he has arrived in Kaloon, very ill, but alive. You must come quickly with your medicines. I have asked Abu Jampa to get some horses. We will ride there and fetch him from Kaloon."

It was a rough, jolting trip as we rode on the small pack horses, with Tibetan wooden saddles, over the narrow rocky trail up to the high grasslands below the snows. We still had not come near Kaloon, and were riding through a small group of stone houses when Gaybo suddenly appeared through the swirling cloud- mists in front of us.

His face was a horrific mask of caked lacerations, dirt and streaks of sweat. His head was a bloody mess of tangled hair and blood. His woolen sweater, originally grey-white, over the green-brown parachute shirt, was now mostly black with dried blood and dirt, with a jagged, two-inch gaping hole ominously in the middle and left of his chest.

Tendar walked up to him, wordlessly, and turned him around. High up on Gaybo's left shoulder, surrounded by a filthy, bloody tangle of sweater, shirt, blood and dirt around a much larger - three-inch or more - gaping hole where the bullet had exited.

Tendar turned him around to face us again. "What are you doing here?" was all he could say to Gaybo. "I thought you were in Kaloon."

"They wanted me to stay there," Gaybo said unsteadily, "but I said I was fit to walk on here - even to the camp."

"You will sit down here," Tendar ordered him firmly, " and Khamba Gyau" - he nodded to me - "will give you medicine and dress your wounds." He turned to the small circle of wide-eyed villagers gazing at Gaybo with awe. "Bring tea and hot water to us."

But I decided that if Gaybo had survived this far, he would be able to travel another hour on a horse to our camp in Chokang, where I could treat him properly and where he could rest and relax. So I filled him full of pain-killing drugs and, after some bowls of tea, we mounted him on Tendar's horse, while Tendar said he would walk beside him. I also got the villagers to give Gaybo bowls of beer and rice-wine instead of tea, to help anaesthetize him on the journey and the treatment later when we arrived.

He was reeling in the saddle, and supported by the inexhaustible Tendar, but he grinned at the welcome from his excited and exuberant fellow-Khambas as we entered the camp near the Dzum monastery. Somebody had run ahead and informed the lamas, and they streamed out of the monastery in a laughing and cheering crowd. They were wanting to hear his story but I insisted I dress his wounds first.

While I was preparing my medicines and bandages - and hunting for scissors - Adrian and Chris set up their filming equipment. I had to cut him out of his sweater and parachute shirt, while Adrian and Chris filmed the process, and they gasped as the full horror of the wound was exposed. The bullet had entered at a sharp angle fortunately, and had ploughed upwards to come out through the large well-padded shoulder muscle, somehow avoiding fatally injuring heart and lungs. But the wound in the back was huge, gaping, filled with pus and dirt - I even took out fragments of metal and a half-inch broad thorn - angry-red and swollen. After I had washed it with hot water and then disinfectant, I used the scissors and a long piece of metal like an ice-pick to explore the wound for pieces of shrapnel and soil. Another bullet had also made a deep furrow along his chin and cheek. His forehead was a mass of bruises and scars where he had been beaten in his face-to-face struggle with the Chinese soldier, and his left hand was swollen and red with livid scars.

During it all, Gaybo never uttered a moan - he even carried on a conversation with the other Khambas who were holding him down in anticipation of his struggles against the pain, watched by surrounding lamas and villagers. When I asked if I was hurting him, he said, "No," and added that he was grateful for my help.

When I had finished, and had given him a hefty dose of sleeping-tablets and the last of my antibiotics, I was more exhausted than he appeared to be. Now that I was finished I was free to listen and interpret for Adrian and Chris what had happened.

He remembered all the events leading up to his urging Tendar and Assang to shoot him, and then unconsciousness. Recovering, he recalled the Chinese soldier who had run for the river embankment jumping out on him and catching him unaware. In the ensuing struggle he had been shot in the chest, then when both of them were left without ammunition they tried to finish off the other.

He did not remember being "buried" under the stones with which Tendar and Assang had covered him, and had a bad time trying to figure out what had happened and how to get out. Fortunately, none of the stones had been too large or heavy and, eventually, he had worked his way out of them.

He had gone to the stream and had a long drink of water, and then staggered up the narrow valley after us. He kept falling unconscious, but always managed to drag himself into some sort of cover before he passed out. At one time he was aware of Chinese voices and, proceeding cautiously, he saw about fifty Chinese soldiers had reached the monastery where we had slept the previous night. It was still light so he reckoned they must have arrived soon after the ambush. He didn't know if the fifty he saw at the monastery were all of these arrivals, or if they were only a group form a larger party up ahead of him.

When night fell he slept in a clump of bushes and, as soon as he could travel, he staggered on up the trail to the Khojang Pass until he saw Chinese troops were ahead of him. He retreated and swung away to the east , coming around in a wide circle to attempt another Pass to the southeast, the Sulba Pass. Here again the Chinese either had a regular garrison or a group had arrived because there were about another fifty Chinese soldiers guarding the Pass. He had then retreated again and worked his way to the north and come over the mountain range between two other unnamed Passes, which brought him eventually to Kaloon.

It was an awesome performance, even for a fit man, but for one in Gaybo's wounded condition, with a small-fist-size hole in his chest, it was next to miraculous. Certainly, time after time the listening Tibetans said, "It's a miracle," "he came back from the dead", "the gods helped him."

Now they felt they had cause for a real celebration and they put even more enthusiasm into their preparations. I was reminded that the etymology of "enthusiasm" was *en theos,* meaning "God within." The reason I was there on this "impossible" assignment was because I believed "the God within" had sent me to help the Tibetans; and their own indomitable commitment as individuals or as a Tibetan people was inspired by "the god within" them.

While Adrian and Chris were busy filming the celebrations of the Dalai Lama's birthday in the Dzum valley, I wrote up my notes of all that had been happening. During the years I had spent in Tibet I had participated in many celebrations: the making, ornamenting and raising of tents; the preparation of clothes and food of all description; the family, relatives, friends, and community parties in tents or around fires; the endless rounds of drinking cha, "tea", chang, "beer", and arakh, "rice wine"; the gun-shooting displays and competitions; the horse-riding contests; the card and mahjong games; the joyous singing and dancing.

In between, when I wasn't being drawn into the celebrations, Tendar would join me to talk over the possible fate of Tibet. "What do you really think of the future of Tibet? Do you think Tibet will ever be free of Chinese? Will the Dalai Lama ever return? What would you advise us here to do?"

I tried to explain to him what I had been proposing regarding a Confederation of Himalayan States, but told him that it was unlikely to happen for many reasons. Tibet would never be independent so long as there was a Communist government in China. It might be possible for the Dalai Lama to return under certain arrangements. The old Tibet, as we had known it in the past, I said regretfully, was gone for ever.

We were both silent for a long time after I had finished speaking. I guessed he was thinking of unending battles against Chinese convoys, of other Khambas than Gaybo being shot and not surviving, of fighting without hope of freedom for their country and religion.

"I may not live to see my country free," he said finally, "but I will not feel that I have altogether wasted my life. If I do live, and if Tibet becomes free, I would like to meet you again sometime. Do you think this is possible?"

"We will make it possible," I promised. "After this past few weeks and days, even these past few years, you must continue to believe with me that all things are possible if only we believe."

As the birthday celebration ended the Himalayan monsoon rains began. The hundreds of Tibetans who had come to Dzum valley to celebrate in black, white and brown tents dismantled them and departed to their own distant valleys and villages and encampments. We, too, were now ready to leave Dzum.

The parting with the Khambas was surprisingly difficult, considering that our acquaintance had been so short, but it had been intense in supremely challenging circumstances. The words of George Eliot's poem, "*A Minor Prophet*", came to mind:

> *"The earth yields nothing more divine*
> *Than high prophetic vision - than the Seer*
> *Who fasting from man's meaner joy beholds*
> *The paths of beauteous order, and constructs*
> *A fairer type, to shame our low content...*
> *The faith that life on earth is being shaped*
> *To glorious ends, that order, justice, love,*
> *Mean man's completeness, mean effect as sure*
> *As roundness in the dew-drop - that great faith*

www.classictravelbooks.com

*Is but the rushing and expanding stream
Of thought, of feeling, fed by all the past.
Our finest hope is finest memory....*

*Even our failures are a prophecy,
Even our yearnings and our bitter tears
After that fair and true we cannot grasp;
As patriots who seem to die in vain
Make liberty more sacred by their pangs."*

We left behind with the Khambas our stocks of food, a radio, binoculars, what extra high-altitude clothing we had, the butane stove, storm lanterns, and they were extremely grateful. I had used up the last of my medicines on Gaybo, who was recovering remarkably, as was Nyima of the gangrened foot, and both of whom refused our invitation to have them medically treated in Kathmandu. They stood in a line with the other villagers - as tough, ruthless, ferocious and attractive a group of men to be found anywhere - their hands raised indomitably in a parting military salute. Tendar left them to walk some distance with us, holding on to my hand. Finally, he stopped, and saluting, said, "The gods were good to us in sending you here. *Ga-lay-peb* ('walk slowly' - the Tibetan farewell)."

We had made our final plans for departure, given our last gifts, said our last farewells. We had discussed, and decided, what to do about the safety of the films. There were three important factors to be considered, we reckoned: one, the monsoon rains sweeping up from the plains of India in great grey clouds and sheets of rain, swelling the already thunderous rivers and threatening to destroy the frail bamboo bridges on our return journey to Kathmandu; two, the negotiating of the military and civilian checkposts after our extended stay in the high Himalayas, to dampen suspicions enough to preserve the secret of our films; and three, to arrive quietly in Kathmandu without anyone knowing, until we had successfully got rid of the films.

There was nothing we could do about the monsoon rains, except to try and cut down on our travel time as much as possible. While we were discussing this possibility Adrian came up with a proposal where we would pay our Kathmandu Tibetan porters on a sliding scale of performance. If, instead of seventeen days for the journey, they did it in, say, seven, then they would receive top rates plus generous bonus; if eight days, less, and so on. At first there were protests from the porters that it was not possible to do it in seven days, but after we had haggled, and pointed out that the loads would be progressively lighter, they agreed with increasing enthusiasm to aim for the seven days and highest rates.

To circumvent the possible suspicious scrutiny of the military and civilian checkposts en route, we packed the films and accompanying notes into as innocent packages as possible and put them into the load of the most intelligent and trusted of the porters. When we approached the first of the checkposts at Setelvass it was arranged that Adrian, Chris and some of the Tibetans would go ahead of me to survey the reception; and then, if all went well, one of them would return to inform me and the porter carrying our critical load of films. If there was a suspicious response at the checkpost I would get the porter to bypass the checkpost in some way, while I would report with some reason for coming in behind the others.

Our porters set a really fast pace on the relatively easy trail, in anticipation of the difficult stretches ahead, made more difficult by the monsoon rains. The worst of the rains struck us late on the second day when we were almost at Setelvass. It was fortunate in a way, because it meant that there were very few people around to see from which direction we approached the checkpost. But it also meant an incredibly blinding, slithering scramble down the treacherously flooding steep mountainside to the wildly swinging, perilously wet, tree-trunk bridge over a raging river now in full flood. Even some of our Tibetan porters were so petrified that they had to be assisted over by the more courageous of the others.

When they had gone on to the Setelvass checkpost, I waited in the slanting downpour, high gale, and increasing darkness, on the far side of the bridge, with the porter carrying our films. Eventually, one of the porters returned as arranged to inform us that all seemed to safe for us to proceed to the checkpost.

When I got there I found Adrian, Chris and Hemantha in the military quarters affably drinking tea with the officers, who were only casually interested in discussing a few innocuous incidents of our travels beyond Setelvass. We left them a welcome gift of several packets of cocoa. However, we decided not to push our luck by staying overnight with them, and we pushed further down the trail to a wet and miserable camping place instead.

The next day the monsoon rains were even worse, getting under our oilskin ponchos and, with the perspiration, unpleasantly soaking our clothes to the skin. The trail up which we had come several weeks before was now submerged in many places under the wider and more savagely raging river, and we had to scramble up the steep mountainsides to make a way through boulders, bushes and trees where there was now none of the previous trail at all.

And with the rains came the leeches. The inch-to-two-inch upright, revoltingly-swaying, blood-suckers were everywhere and unavoidable. Underfoot on the trail, within seconds one or more had attached itself to our boots and undulated their obscene way through eyelets or over the top of boots and attached themselves greedily to our skins. Weaving from the stone-clad sides of the trails they clung to the clothes and loads, then made their way inside shirts, under pants. Dropping from the overhanging branches of trees on to the hats or hair of those passing underneath. Millions and millions of them, it seemed, we dare not stop for a minute before there were battalions of them swaying and undulating towards us. Soon, we were streaming blood from a hundred leech-sucked punctures, stockings and boots squelching blood and water. Repellents and salt were of little use, and the only effective deterrent appeared to be the red-hot tip of a cigarette applied to the grotesquely-gorging creature. The days were bad enough; the nights were wakened nightmares.

On the third day we reached a spot where the swollen river had taken a wide sweep to inundate the trail we had walked on coming up the trail. Now it was a boiling cauldron for almost twenty yards, cutting off any progress down country. This was what we had feared, and we had been told that, when conditions were like this, even the local hillmen would refuse to travel for any reason or money. But we had to get through somehow.

Even the Tibetan porters were pessimistic. But they became more hopeful when I suggested that it might be possible to rig up a "rope-bridge" such as was used to cross unbridged rivers in East Tibet when I had lived there. Fortunately, we had brought some climbing equipment with us in case of emergency - an ice-axe, pitons, long nylon rope, metal spring clip for tying the rope to the waist so that it could be paid out - and we now took these out of the loads. One of the Tibetans scrambled up the sheer mountainside to a tree that looked strong enough to carry weight. But, then, we had to get the rope to the far side of that boiling, boulder-tumbling river somehow. The river was wide and full of rocks, but not too deep - waist to shoulder-high - but it was moving fast, turbulent and menacing.

Adrian as the tallest volunteered to go first. He stripped down to his pants, tied the rope around his waist, with the rest of us as "anchors" paying out the rope as he advanced, took two long sticks, one in each hand, and stepped into the ice-cold torrent. It was a nerve-wracking experience, as at every step he would either stumble on some unseen underfoot obstacle on the rocky bed, or stumble as wave after wave of roaring water hit him. But, eventually, he reached the far side safely and, in a short time, he had fixed the rope around a stable boulder, adjusted it so that it fell in a descending dip to just above the river, and shouted that it was ready.

Tsewang offered to go next to test it for the others. A shorter rope was tied around his waist, passed through the metal spring-clip, which was then threaded on the rope, and he was ready for the upside-down dipping trajectory to the other side of the river. There were three dangers - at least. The first was that the person on the scarily dipping rope would travel too fast and be smashed against the boulders on the far side; to avoid this we arranged for yet another length of rope to be tied to the person going over, and for some of the porters to "feed" this while others kept the overhead rope on which he was sliding from slipping and dropping him in the river. The second danger was that the dip in the rope would increase under the weights and one or more of the people going over would be carried away by the force of the current. The third danger was that, as more people went over to the far side, there were fewer people to help the person going over, so it became progressively more difficult to negotiate the passage. And I was due to go over last. However, we all made it safely.

The porters proposed that we bypass the large market village of Arughat where we had been delayed on the upward journey so that they could still make it to Kathmandu in the seven days. It meant taking a much more difficult, and unknown, route; but the advantage to us was that it keep us away from the more popular, and officially scrutinized, trail.

It was a murderously difficult and utterly exhausting march through the oppressive heat and continuous rains of the lower foothills, in what was virtually without a marked trail, but despite several misjudgements and diversions, we reached Trisuli, the last stop before Kathmandu on the late afternoon of the sixth day. Here we arranged for the porter who was carrying our films to go ahead of us, alone, and reach Kathmandu before we did. We gave him two letters: one for any policeman who might stop him on the way suspecting him of being a thief, and authorizing the porter to take his goods to Kathmandu; and the other letter was for Mark, the Imperial Hotel manager, to say that we expected to arrive shortly, that we had sent this man ahead to inform him of this, to reserve our rooms, and to please take the man's load and keep it safely until our return.

We paid off our porters in Trisuli, retaining only Tsewang, Trashi and Sedar to travel into Kathmandu with us. We had Tsewang hire an old truck on our behalf, so that we would arrive in Kathmandu we would look like a nondescript tourist group instead of a reputable British television outfit. Impressive groups, or well-equipped expeditions, drew the attention of officials who used their authority to cause delays and extort baksheesh. The final stage of our odyssey would begin in the morning.

CHAPTER FOURTEEN

Crisis And Arrest In Kathmandu

Our arrival in Kathmandu was something of an anticlimax after all our fears and speculations. Nobody gave us more than a passing, incurious glance as we arrived at the city police checkpost in a roaring thunderstorm, after dark, and the sheltering officials waved us through without checking.

We drove straight to the Imperial Hotel to find that our advance porter had also had no trouble, and he and Mark were waiting for our arrival, with the films in safe custody. With that established I found out from Mark where my wife was staying and arranged for a taxi to take me there right away.

While waiting for the taxi, Mark told me that the Hospital had arranged for my wife to live in the home of the British Council official, who was on leave in Britain at the time and who had offered his house to the hospital. Unfortunately, it was located on the outskirts of Kathmandu, about six miles away and had no telephone, so I could not inform her of my arrival.

I arrived at a darkened house at midnight. Between the hotel and the house, the enormity of my wife's circumstances in Kathmandu overwhelmed me. It was not that I was only just now thinking about them. I had thought about them every day while we were away from Kathmandu, and when we were not grappling with our own problems. But I had assumed that the Hospital would have made all the arrangements to accommodate her and the family requirements. Now, driving for several miles through the darkened countryside of Kathmandu I had cause to wonder about those arrangements.

Also, arriving after midnight outside the city, in the dark, at a house whose servants didn't know me, was not exactly a cause of celebration. So I asked the taxi driver to wait with his car headlights on full beam while I knocked loudly on the door of the darkened house. Lights went on in the servants' quarters and a voice shouted questions in Nepali, which were answered by the taxi driver. Then lights went on in the main house, first the bedroom and then downstairs.

A servant opened the door and, in the hallway behind him, stood Meg, in her dressing-gown, looking puzzled and concerned. It took a few moments for it to register that it was her husband and then her face lit up in relief and welcome. "Patla! (my name among English-speaking Tibetans) I didn't recognize you, you have lost so much weight! Thank God you have come back safely." Then she was in my arms and I was back in my normal family world.

Later, Meg explained her lack of immediate recognition as being due to my deep sun-and-snow tanning, and that my figure was now convex instead of concave! I had been vaguely conscious as we traveled that I was losing weight, but it was only when I arrived back in Kathmandu and weighed myself that I discovered I had lost thirty pounds in thirty-six days of travel. So it was no wonder that Meg had not immediately recognized me on arrival.

She had been having her own problems in my absence. Arriving in Kathmandu, a strange city in a strange country which she had never visited before, with three children under five, one a baby of five months, she knew no one except Dr Anderson of the United Mission Hospital. She knew our Chinese friend, owner of the Imperial Hotel, Mung Hsueh, who met her on her arrival at the airport; but Mung knew nothing of our plans to go to Tibet, only to inform Meg that I was away on an expedition and would be back "shortly". Meg, of course, knew what our plans had been before we left Britain, but she had refrained from mentioning this to anybody in Kathmandu.

The British Council official's house which had been provided for her was a spacious, lovely home, but it was remote from the city, and the Hospital did not provide her with a car, only picking her up in the morning right after breakfast and dropping her off at night. This meant that she had to leave the three young children in the care of unknown servants all day. To complicate matters further, the Anglo-Indian nanny she had brought with her from Calcutta, on the recommendation of a doctor friend, had turned out to be a sadist who disliked children, and after discovering the children were terrified by her Meg had to get rid of her and find another more suitable one locally.

Fortunately, the British ambassador, Anthony Duff, and his wife, had befriended her; but even this had its complications, because, in discussing our unexpectedly delayed absence, she could not give any hint that we expected to cross over into Tibet with the Khamba guerrillas. When I returned she had been so concerned about our long delay that she was considering informing the ambassador what we had intended doing.

Before leaving Adrian and Chris the night before, we had arranged that the first item on our agenda was to get rid of the films, and we had developed several possible plans. On the Edgar Allen Poe principle of the most obvious being the most likely to succeed, we planned to see if we could get them through Customs in the normal way. To obviate the possible risk of discovery we prepared a false set of film canisters, weighted with mud and stones, in a single package, and recorded as "sixty canisters of exposed films." We prepared a second package of the real films, also recorded as "sixty canisters of exposed films", and our strategy was for Adrian to test the Customs' response to the first package. If there was suspicion, then nothing was lost, because we still had the real films in our possession.

Meanwhile, we had rented a jeep, and Chris and I were in the jeep with the real package of sixty genuine film-stock, in the airport parking lot, while Adrian was seeing the first decoy package through Customs. If he had problems then he was to give us a signal, and we would leave the airport vicinity immediately. Afterwards, our back-up plan was for Adrian and Chris to take-off quickly in the jeep and drive to India and try to get the films across the more lax land-border inspection.

However, in Customs, Adrian was having no trouble at all. With the Customs' inspectors about to sign and stamp the clearance papers, Adrian pretended to have suddenly remembered that he had more films in a second package in his jeep outside, and could he bring them right away before the documents were signed? The inspectors looked dubious and said that the plane was due to leave, but if it could be done quickly he could bring it. Adrian collected the package from us, the inspectors signed and stamped the documents, and then rushed the two packages on to the waiting plane while we watched the disappearing plane with relief and triumph from the parking lot. A further bonus was that the plane was going to an unsuspecting Pakistani, and not suspecting Indian, destination, so there would be no possible Indian collusion with Nepal authorities. The beauty of this strategy was that we could not be held for any violation of the laws of Nepal, because we had the officially signed and stamped documents to prove that we had brought in 120 canisters of unexposed films, and had sent the same number of officially approved films out. Any violation of this requirement would have subjected us to indefinite delays, fines, and even imprisonment.

Now we had to face the consequences of our success. First, we had to see the British ambassador and report to him what we had done, and give him our assessment of the critical situation facing Nepal on the northern border with Tibet. The ambassador had been friendly and helpful - that is, in our "legitimate" filming program of "Tibetan refugees" - and we felt professionally responsible to give him an account of what was happening on the Nepal-Tibet border which would impact on his diplomatic relations with Nepal. We had no similar compunction about leaving the Nepal officials uninformed, because of all their selfish interests and petty manoeuvering before our departure.

Before meeting with the ambassador, Adrian and Chris made arrangements to leave Nepal immediately afterwards by the road to India. Very few people chose to do this because of the tedium and difficulties of road travel, and we anticipated that it would give them time and opportunity to get out of the country. I would remain to face the consequences of what we had done, partly because I had created them and partly because my wife and family were still committed to being in the country until the end of her temporary contract with the Hospital. I would join Adrian and Chris for the next film in Burma when I could get away.

We were concerned regarding what to say to the British ambassador regarding our trip as we felt we had to give some report without jeopardising our project. We decided that Arian and Chris would leave Kathmandu quickly and quietly and I would speak to the ambassador. After weighing all possibilities, we reckoned that the usual Nepalese government bureaucracy could not move that quickly, and it would take some time for them to find out Banskota's ploy of substituting Hemantha for a government liaison official. When we warned Hemantha, he suggested that he go with Adrian and Chris to Calcutta, on a "pleasure" visit, and this would delay inquiries longer. It would make my situation worse, but I was accustomed to be in these crisis situations with angry officials.

When I met with the ambassador, (later to be knighted and promoted to Head of British Intelligence!) as I anticipated, he was annoyed, to put it mildly. However, as I also anticipated, he accepted the situation as a *fait accompli*. We had a long discussion about what we hoped to accomplish by publicizing the situation on Nepal's border with Tibet in our film. Would it not harm Nepal, while not helping the Tibetans? Would it not just help the Chinese? It might provoke the Chinese to confront or even invade Nepal while eliminating the Tibetans in the high Himalayas.

I pointed out that until we went to the north, the Nepal government had not even been aware that there was a critical "situation" on the northern borders. What they accepted - and informed other governments, who also accepted it - was that there were only a few harmless Tibetan refugees who had settled down peacefully in the mountains. In the final analysis - just as with the Indian government ignorance over the situation in Tibet five years before - the political and military initiatives and advantages were all with China. Any publicity that we could provide, therefore, would only cast light on what was already unknown to friends of Nepal and would not be of any advantage to China. Hopefully, it would provide them with a major political headache.

China certainly knew that there was a large, well-armed concentration of several thousand Khamba guerrillas in North Nepal and operating in West Tibet; was aware that tens of thousands of Bhotias and Tibetans were assisting them; was aware that they were getting arms and ammunition from "outside" sources; and was aware of just how dangerous were the guerrilla groups.

It was Nepal, India, and the Western powers who were unaware of the true situation. It would be they who were caught unprepared by their naiveté in the event of any Chinese initiative, just as they had been caught unprepared several times in the past fifteen years. Publicity might not suit present British, American, Nepalese, or Indian policy, but then that policy had hardly proved itself perceptive or satisfactory in the past, and, as far as I personally was concerned, the present policies of these countries in this region were opportunistic, uninformed, weak, despicable, and useless. These policies were based on a chain reaction of fear: Nepal was afraid offending India and China; India was afraid of offending China; Britain and America were afraid of offending India and China. Only China didn't care who was offended by whatever policy.

I finally agreed with the ambassador that we wouldn't publish anything right away, to give time for various governments to discuss possible consequences of our expedition and publicity - say, for three months. It would take that time, at least, for the films to process and schedule the broadcast. In the meantime, the ambassador would approach the Nepal government to report what we had done, but at the same time extend our offer to give an account of our conclusions - and not of our activities! The ambassador reckoned the best opportunity to do this would be on the coming Friday when he was scheduled to have an audience with the king.

After the ambassador had reported to the King of Nepal on Friday, he told me that the King had been annoyed, but had accepted the ambassador's assurances that we were responsible journalists; that we had promised not to publicize the account for three months; and that I had offered to have discussions with Nepal government officials if requested - but only on my conclusions and not any statement admitting to where we might have been. But, apparently, on Saturday morning, the king had called a special Cabinet meeting at which he had demanded from his ministers that if what Patterson had reported was true, why had none of them known of this situation; and, if they had known, why had none of them reported the matter to him?

The ministers were not only confused, they were panicked. The ambassador called me to say that the Foreign Secretary, General Khatry, wanted to see me on Sunday at 2:30 p.m. He had sounded very angry - and he was known to be very tough when he was in this mood!

Adrian, Chris and Hemantha had left Kathmandu for India late on Saturday morning, the jeep loaded with television cameras and equipment. In the afternoon, I had an unannounced visit from Thakur, the Chief of Protocol, with several other officials, including a judge! I assumed that one of the others would be a security official. They had just been out on a drive, Thakur said unctuously, and decided to drop by for a friendly visit. How had I enjoyed my recent trip into the mountains? Did I find Mustang interesting? And what was it like to return to Tibet? All asked with a knowing, jolly, just-between-us laugh.

I was all injured innocence about the suggestions that I would ever visit Mustang when I had no permit. And what did they mean about returning to Tibet? Our permits showed that we had them properly stamped by officials in Setelvass. How was it possible to get into Tibet when the borders were being so closely patrolled? I would learn later that Thakur and the security official were armed, and that they had their hands on their guns throughout their stay (I never noticed that) in the expectation that I would give away some indication that I still had the films, which they would remove forcibly from me. Their problem was that the British Council house in which we were living was considered protected from official search by diplomatic immunity unless they had some demonstrable evidence from me that I had broken their law.

The interview with General Khatry was without any humor. He gave me the full haughty treatment of ignoring my arrival, studying and signing documents, and then glaring at me to demand, "When did you return?"

"A few days ago," I said mildly.

"Where did you go?" he demanded.

I gave him a long look. I did not agree with the British embassy assessment that he was a clever - a deep - man. This, I gathered, was based on the specious evidence that he said little, and occasionally quoted a philosophical observation. Any man who could use a Banskota as his chief operator was, in my view, a political lightweight. If he wanted to play it rough, because he had been publicly rebuked by the King, then I was happy to indulge him.

"General Khatry," I said brusquely, "there are two ways we can conduct this discussion - pleasantly or unpleasantly. I don't care which one you choose, but whichever it is I will reply in kind. Let me put it to you bluntly. You have absolutely no evidence that we have done anything contrary to the laws of this country, so I am at liberty to leave here without saying a word to you or anyone. If you try to stop me, I will call on the British embassy to defend my professional standing. However, I told the ambassador that I would answer any questions regarding my conclusions about the situation on your northern borders based on my recent visit to the territories permitted by your government officials. But I will not be tricked or bullied into some kind of personal confession that will put me in prison by you or any other Nepal politician. Now, we can either talk on these terms, or not at all."

His face was thunderous. "You went to Mustang without permission," he snarled.

I looked at him in surprise. This was even more stupid than I had anticipated. "I did not go to Mustang," I said emphatically.

"You did," he spat out. "And you admitted it in front of witnesses."

Now I was really surprised. Was I going to be framed? I knew it was not beyond them, for the ambassador had said that the King had said all their jobs were at risk unless they could find and destroy the films we had made. But this intimidatory bluster was rubbish.

"Who were the witnesses?" I asked, not expecting a reply.

"Mr. Thakur," he answered confidently. "in front of a Nepali high court judge, among others."

So that was it. Friend Thakur obviously had been given an order to get the films in a frontal attack, and if not the films, get enough information for an arrest; and he had taken along a bunch of cronies to support him. They must all be scared of their jobs and futures.

"Mr. Thakur is a liar," I said calmly, "and so is your high court judge. They probably didn't inform you that my wife was present and listening to what was said, and she is a more credible witness than a frightened Thakur and friends."

He leaned across his desk and pressed a bell, sitting silently until there was a response. When an official came to the door, he instructed him to ask Mr. Thakur to come. A few minutes later Thakur appeared, as urbane and smiling as always.

"Sit down, Mr. Thakur," General Khatry said. nodding to a chair across from me. "Mr. Patterson here denies that he has been to Mustang. You say that he admitted in front of witnesses that he had been there?"

"That is right," Thakur nodded, smiling at me. "Remember, you said that you had a nice time there?"

I shook my head at him, pityingly. "I never said any such thing. I told you quite clearly that I had never been anywhere near Mustang. My wife will confirm what I said, as she was listening to our conversation. But you need not take my word. It can be proved."

"How?" General Khatry jumped at the opening.

"In two ways," I said easily. "First, by checking with the Government liaison officer appointed by your good friend Banskota, who was with us all the time except for one period of about eight days - an impossible time to reach Mustang from where we were near Setelvass. Second, by checking the records of the dates we were in the checkpost at Setelvass."

The silence dragged on, and I let it. If the hook was unpleasant they had only themselves to blame. Eventually, the foreign secretary, after a transparent attempt at shuffling some papers around to make it look as if he had something important, said in a blustering tone, "Another thing. You did not take a permanent government liaison officer with you."

And this was the man on whom foreign governments were depending for intelligent decisions!

"Whatever you have there," I said contemptuously, pointing to the shuffled papers on his desk, "we did have a government liaison officer with us, appointed by your Banskota, with official papers which were stamped together with ours at all official checkpoints. That is our evidence - not yours."

I leaned forward to emphasize my next words. "How many times must I tell you that I need not sit here, I need not stay in Nepal, I need not talk with any of you? It is because I am interested in your people - not in your careers - in the Tibetan people, in the Indian people, that I am here at all."

He gave up on intimidation, but he tried to be politically persuasive "in all our interests", but it added up to personal, and not even national, self-interest.

I told him: "General Khatry, I have heard all that before - and it was all so wrong, so dangerous, so nearly fatal - and could still be totally fatal for Tibet, if not you. Prime Minister Nehru said it in a much more impressive way than you did, or could, and he was proved to be wrong. I want to look back on this time, as I did on the Tibetan revolt situation five years ago, and know that what I did was what my God, my profession and my Asian friends - not career politicians - consider was right."

There was no more to be said. We argued a little more about possible alternatives, with the two of them trying to tempt or trick me into an admission that we had made films in forbidden territory, and that these films were still in my possession in Kathmandu as evidence of illegality, and with me evading any statement incriminating us. The interview lasted an hour and a half, and it ended as it had begun.

I had arranged to give the British ambassador a report on my meeting with General Khatry next day, and I was on my way there when I was stopped by a cable messenger with a cable for me. I read it and put it in my pocket.

When I had finished my report to the ambassador, he told me that he had just heard from General Khatry that he had given orders for Cowell and Menges to be detained and searched at the Nepal-Indian border. The ambassador was annoyed, because he had not been informed by the Nepali authorities of this embarrassing possibility; to the contrary, he had been given to understand by the King that the government was going to handle the matter cautiously and cooperatively. To arbitrarily detain Cowell and Menges at the border meant that either he had been deliberately misled; or the ministers had taken action on their own, without informing the King. General Khatry had said on the telephone to the ambassador that he did not believe Patterson when he said that the films were already out of the country; and that it was his intention to seize the films from Cowell and Menges, who probably had them, and then force Patterson and Cowell to sign statements saying that they had never been to Tibet. That would close the whole issue satisfactorily. The ambassador had asked for an audience with the King to find out what was happening, and he wanted a clear statement from me before committing himself.

I took the cable out of my pocket and silently handed it over to him. He read it:

"BORDER POLICE SEIZED ON INSTRUCTION KATHMANDU SEVEN ROLLS CINOFILM THIRTEEN TAPES THREE STILL FILMS SUNDRY OTHER ITEMS ALL COMPLETELY HARMLESS STOP FULL DETAILS SENT AMBASSADOR PLEASE ASSIST RECOVERY ESPECIALLY TAPES AFTER POLICE LISTENED TO THEM STOP SUGGEST STRONGEST PROTEST ACTION POSSIBLE
    COWELL HOMELINESS   CALCUTTA"

The ambassador looked at me. "Is this genuine?" he asked slowly. "You and Cowell aren't trying to pull another fast one, by any chance?"

I gazed at him in astonishment, then laughed as the meaning behind his question dawned on me. "You mean, is Cowell really in Calcutta, or is this just a fake telegram made to appear to come from Calcutta?" I savored the thought, liking it; and laughed again. "No," I stated firmly. "I like the idea, but it would only make sense if we still had the films - which we haven't."

The ambassador gave me a long steady look. "You are quite sure? This is an extremely serious situation. I have asked for an emergency audience with the king for this afternoon in order to protest against the arrest or detention of Cowell and Menges, and if this cable is correct then I won't pursue the matter other than formal protest at the action."

I assured him: "Before we came to see you, immediately after our arrival in Kathmandu, the films were already out of our possession and out of the country. But, from what I know of the officials of this government, they were probably either frightened, incompetent, or out to blame and get rid of Khatry."

The ambassador thought for a few moments. "I will cancel my request for an emergency audience today. But do you have any objection to my telephoning General Khatry regarding the contents of this cable?"

"None at all," I grinned in approval. "I only wish I were there to see his reaction."

The ambassador put through the call while I was there and, after he had finished, he said drily. "You would gather that he doesn't believe it. He insists that both Cowell and Menges are on their way back to Kathmandu under escort, and are expected at any time."

"There is an easy way to settle the matter," I told the ambassador, pointing to the cable still in his hand. "The address. Send an urgent cable to Cowell to the address

'Homeliness'. If he replies, you will have evidence of his and Menges' presence there to show Khatry or the king."

I drafted the cable in the ambassador's presence:

"PLEASE CONFIRM BOTH IN CALCUTTA STOP OFFICIAL UNDERSTANDING YOU RETURNING KATHMANDU UNDER ESCORT KATHMANDU STOP AM TAKING ALL NECESSARY ACTION STOP ALSO CONFIRM WHETHER MY LETTER TAKEN. PATTERSON"

The last question related to my notes of the whole trip which I had put in a normal letter and addressed to a friend to be kept pending my arrival in Calcutta. If these had been confiscated at the border then I was in trouble, for it was a written confession that could be used against me. It had been a gamble sending it with Adrian and Chris, but it seemed a greater risk keeping it in my possession in Kathmandu.

The reply arrived the following morning:

"CHRIS HEMANTHA MYSELF IN CALCUTTA WITH YOUR LETTER STOP ALL SEIZURES AT FRONTIER TOTALLY HARMLESS STOP PLEASE CONFIRM WHETHER OUR OFFICIALLY EXPECTED RETURN TO KATHMANDU IS TO BE FROM CALCUTTA
COWELL"

I felt a huge surge of relief. I would need these notes if I ever found time to write a book about the experience. When I went to show the ambassador the cable, he shook his head in amused exasperation, and said he would call on the Foreign Secretary for an explanation. He confirmed that it was highly unlikely that the Nepal government would ask India to extradite Cowell and Menges without evidence of illegality. I also told the ambassador that I now considered myself absolved of any responsibility to talk seriously with this Nepal government, and I would leave in a few days to join Adrian and Chris for our next assignment.

In anticipation of having trouble leaving Nepal, I began a planned and cautious round of visits to the various newspaper correspondents in Kathmandu - Nepalese, Indian and Western. I made it appear impromptu, friendly and with no apparent purpose except shop talk because I assumed I was being followed. As I had anticipated, it was inevitable that the journalists would ask about our recent trip to the mountains, and to each one I gave a different piece of true information, but always implying that the government officials suspected us of going to Tibet and had been in touch with Khamba guerrillas, without ever admitting that we had actually done it.

This "planting" of information had the desired effect, for in the next few days Kathmandu became a hotbed of all sorts of rumors. As I came under more and more media and official pressure to say where we had been and what we had done, I suggested to the journalists that they ask the ministers concerned what was happening. I knew this would bring the issue out into the open and force the hands of the officials involved. There was little danger now of the quiet arrest some dark night, but they might well be content to wait until I made a wrong move or they found some evidence of what we had done. But that would be very difficult because the Tibetan porters had been paid and had scattered, and they knew nothing significant of our movements inside Tibet anyway; also, Hemantha was in Calcutta with Adrian and Chris. I just had to get out of Nepal before something important surfaced..

In addition to my excellent relations with the media, I had two other factors working in my favor. My wife had just been asked to stay on in the United Mission Hospital for another month, and everyone naturally supposed that I would be remaining in Kathmandu with her and the children.

And then Chahvan appeared once more! If the fact of my wife's remaining in Nepal gave me the advantage of surprise if I decided to leave suddenly, Chahvan's emergence provided me with the advantage of confusion. He was his usual ebullient self, and acted as if we had never had any differences. So did I. Anyway, I liked the rogue. He congratulated me on getting the films successfully out of the country, and, when I asked him what he knew about it, he grinned and said he had been to Customs and asked. He had more brains than the government officials, which didn't surprise me.

Apparently, he had again landed on his feet, he informed me; he had opened an "International Hostel" for students and others who could not afford hotel rates, and a deputy minister of the government had attended the opening ceremony. Explaining his new venture he said expansively, "In the interests of encouraging good relations between countries of the world, old chap," his eyes mocking and mischievous.

"What's your cut," I asked him with brutal frankness.

"I get my satisfaction out of providing service for all these sincere but poor young men - and women," he added with a suggestive laugh. He stroked his moustache complacently, "Excellent idea for collecting useful information, too, of course. Speaking of information, what's this I hear about you and the others going into Tibet on a raid with the Khambas?"

"What was it you heard?" I asked him with exaggerated interest and innocence.

He gave his shouted laugh. "You are the expert," he conceded with a wave of his hand. "But you still need Chahvan. How are you going to get out of Kathmandu?" he grinned devilishly.

"The same way I came in," I replied. "Who is going to stop me?"

"General Khatry, for one," he said promptly. "The Inspector-General of Police, Palace officials, and the Security boys; they're all out to get you. I tell you, you need my help."

I shrugged my shoulders. "No problem."

"Did you know there are two groups of Intelligence?" Chahvan asked with elaborate unconcern, guessing I would respond.

"Which one are you working for?" I grinned to take the malice out of the question.

It didn't work with Chahvan. "The most important," he retorted. "I can fix you an appointment with Number One if you like?"

"What will it cost me?" I asked ironically.

"Your right arm?" Chahvan grinned.

"Okay," I agreed.

It caught Chahvan unawares, and he looked at me warily. "Do you mean it?"

"Why not?" I demanded innocently. "You know I like meeting important people. And I might want to use him."

"That's better," Chahvan laughed. "I thought you were losing your touch for a minute. When you meet, will you talk about Tibet?"

"Did he send you to meet me with the offer, or did you propose it to him?" I asked.

"Let's say it was a meeting of mutual minds," Chahvan laughed.

I looked at him thoughtfully, working out an idea. "How about this?" I proposed. "I'll talk about a trip some people I know recently made into Tibet, and what they found out - on condition that I get some information in return." I watched him weigh it for what he could get out of it. He nodded slowly, the mocking glint lighting up his eyes again.

"As our American friends say, 'You got yourself a deal' - Boss," he added impenitently. "Tomorrow morning at ten o'clock in the Royal Hotel, okay?"

"Do you keep his time-table as well as his contacts?" I asked him.

"I told him it was an offer you couldn't refuse. See you tomorrow." He saluted smartly in a mock farewell.

It was time to make my final arrangements to leave Kathmandu. I went to the airlines office and made a reservation to leave for Calcutta the next day. Then I spent the rest of the day speaking with several journalists, hinting that they would find some news worth reporting at the airport the following day. I hinted that, because of certain base suspicions of certain highly placed ministers, who wanted to conceal matters of great importance, they might try to stop me leaving the country.

The next day, after I had packed and was ready to leave, I first went to keep my appointment with Chahvan, but saying nothing of my imminent departure to him - or to the top intelligence official he introduced to me, nameless. We sparred around for some time, then I put my prepared proposition to him.

"I will give you a detailed report of conditions on the northern border on the clear stipulation that it is a professional analysis and not a personal confession, if you will give me answers to the following questions: one, was

General Khatry responsible for all the early attempts to head us off: two, for putting Banskota on to us to create problems; and, three, in seeking the arrest of Cowell and Menges recently, was he acting as a front for the palace?"

The intelligence official took time to think about answering, then he said slowly. "General Khatry was the man responsible, acting on his own. He is out of favor with the palace, for other reasons, and he probably thought this would bring him back into favor."

I breathed a sigh of relief inwardly. My next movements depended on the fact that all the officials were desperately seeking the favor of the King after his ultimatum to them, and I needed the goodwill of the palace and the British ambassador. So I gave the intelligence official my personal assessment of the dangers on the northern borders, without divulging anything of the Khambas' strengths and weaknesses, and without admitting that I had ever been there. I was glad when Chahvan stayed behind with the official, because it meant I had a clear trip to the airport without them knowing anything about my impending departure.

The airport was crowded. At first I thought it was because an extra-large tourist party was arriving or departing, but then I was spotted by a number of journalists who said that the Director of United States Aid was due to leave by the same plane as myself, and that the Nepali government officials as well as diplomatic representatives had come to bid him farewell. It could not have been better had I planned it for myself. Now whatever took place would be before every important official and journalist, national and international, in Kathmandu.

But it looked as if there would be no problem, let alone sensation. I checked in at the airline counter, had my luggage weighed, my passport checked and stamped, my currency form cleared, passed customs, and was through into the departure area without trouble. My wife and two sons had come to see me off, and we stood chatting with friends among the various officials, diplomats and journalists.

An announcement over the loudspeakers said that due to low cloud formation and heavy rains the plane departure for Calcutta would be held up for half an hour. The crowds of officials and guests milled and reformed in new groups with refilled glasses of drinks.

A young Nepali in bush-shirt and slacks approached me. "May I see your passport, please?" he asked politely.

I reached for my brief-case, took out my passport - and stopped. There was something not right about the incident. "Why do you want my passport?" I asked, equally politely.

The Nepali hesitated - and I knew. "I, er, want to look at something," he blurted, obviously unprepared for the question.

"Who are you?" I demanded. "Let me see some identification."

The journalists, who had been keeping their eye on me to see what my earlier hints might produce, now approached and one of them asked, "Problems?"

I nodded. "This is it."

The Nepali plain-clothes official looked nonplussed as we were surrounded by journalists with notebooks and cameras, and he signaled to some other officials who were waiting in the rear of the lounge. One of them approached ahead of the others, and said officiously, "I am a police-inspector. Give me your passport."

"No," I said firmly. "First, show me your identification, and then your warrant for this confrontation."

He tried to bluff it out. "I will not show you anything," he stated, his voice rising, while he looked furiously at the scribbling and photographing journalists. "I have orders to stop you going on to the plane."

"You have, do you?" I asked. "Whose orders? Wait there while I phone the embassy."

Before he could move I stepped across to a telephone and dialed the British ambassador, as I had arranged. "I am being detained at the airport," I told him, "by what looks like an unauthorized individual claiming to be a police-inspector, but without identification or warrant. Can you please take some action?"

The ambassador said that he would send the First Secretary right away, and I passed on the news to the now excited journalists, who clamored to know what the crisis was all about. Was I going to be arrested for crossing into Tibet? Had I really been with the Khamba guerrillas? Were we successful in filming an action against the Chinese?

The police were now grouped together across the exits to the departure area. My wife looked pale, the children bewildered and upset. "What is it, Daddy?" Lorne asked. "What do these men want?"

"They want to keep me here in Kathmandu," I told him gently. "But it's all right. Daddy is all right."

I smiled reassurance at my wife. I was really enjoying myself. There could be no real threat; to the contrary, I was convinced that this was another panic reaction - or someone in authority would have signed a warrant. They must still think I had the films in my baggage, and were making a final desperate attempt to get at them by stopping me. I had another idea to put pressure on them.

Just then the loudspeakers called for all passengers to board the plane for Calcutta. I smiled to my family, kissed them, and moved towards the exit. The police inspector stepped in front of me to stop me. With a sudden movement I pretended to stumble, jerked my right arm against him,

Gods and Guerrillas

forcing him to step backwards. "Don't even try without a warrant," I told him.

"You will not get on that plane," he shouted. "I have orders. Your luggage is taken off."

I walked down the steps to the open concourse, ignoring his frantic shouts. He raced ahead of me to the metal barrier guarded by two armed policemen, and he spoke to them, pointing to me. I walked towards them, aware of the shouts of journalists and clicking and flashes of their cameras.

As I drew near the two armed guards, dressed in the Gurkha uniforms of khaki shirts and shorts, with puttees and boots, and carrying the standard razor-sharp curved kukris in addition to their rifles. At the police-officer's command the two guards drew their kukris and closed the gap between them with their crossed kukris, stopping my way through to the plane.

One of them held up his hand, and I knocked it away. There was a shout from the watching journalists. "Can you do it again, George?" one of them shouted. "I missed it."

I did it again, and said to the two stoical guards, and livid police inspector, "Keep your hands off me without a warrant. This officer has no identification and no warrant to detain me, and I have complained officially about him to my ambassador."

With a roar the plane engines started up and all conversation became impossible. So was my departure. But I had accomplished what I had set out to do. Now there was little could be done by the panic-stricken Nepali officials to stop my eventual departure. No official could hide from the King what had happened at the airport today, and there was no way they could argue that I still had the films in my possession and should be detained until they found them.

I walked back to the now jubilant journalists. They had their story, and I explained that I was actually being suspected of having crossed over into Tibet with a television team and filmed Khamba guerrillas attacking a Chinese convoy on one of their military roads. I didn't confirm that it had actually happened.

The British embassy First Secretary, Peter Wild, arrived and, after I explained to him what had happened, he looked around for the police inspector. At first he refused to answer Peter Wild's questions then, under official pressure, he admitted that he had only verbal orders on the telephone to stop me, from an official he refused to name. He departed from the airport a very chastened man.

"What do I do now?" I asked Peter Wild. "These frightened officials are likely to repeat this farce every day - until they're fired. So will I - until they get tired or fired."

"Give me twenty-four hours," Peter said," and you can leave the day after that."

We had only just returned to our house when we had a visitor - Chahvan. He looked at me reproachfully. "Why didn't you tell me you were going to be leaving today" he demanded. "I could have fixed it for you."

"Chahvan," I grinned at him. "Tell me the name of the mystery official who gave orders to the police-inspector to stop me at the airport. Was it your nameless friend in Intelligence?"

"How could he do that?" he asked innocently. "We didn't know you were leaving."

"But you had time to find out while I was going through the usual departure procedures," I reminded him. "It was a hurried and botched job."

Chahvan looked as uncomfortable as he rarely did. "What are you going to do now? Cross the road border like your friends?"

"I leave the day after tomorrow - that is an ultimatum to whoever is interested," I told him.

"Okay," he said agreeably. "I'll fix it for you. This time I'll be there to see you off."

Next morning I received a letter by special messenger:

"Mr. George Patterson,

In connection with your visit to Setelvass His Majesty's Government requires clarification from you and before that you are not permitted to leave Nepal.

Thank you.

Bal Ram Prakural
Magistrate Kathmandu"

Bal Ram Prakural was the "Judge" who had been prepared to support Thakur in saying that I had admitted to them that I had gone to Mustang. Was his letter to me at this late stage just one of those coincidences that occasionally happens? Or was it part of a deeper plot?

I rang Peter Wild to inform him of this latest development, and he said," You won't believe this, but every government official - Foreign Minister, Foreign Secretary, Home Minister, Home Secretary, Inspector General of Police - has denied all knowledge of what took place at the airport yesterday, or of authorizing any police official to take any action.."

I told him that I would believe anything now. He asked how I felt about writing a statement regarding my recent trip, and this would get the officials, and himself, off the petard on which they had impaled themselves. I said I would be happy to write a statement in my own terms. Peter said he would arrange a meeting to get a responsive signed statement from the government agreeing to my leaving the country.

Peter went with me to the office of the Kathmandu Commissioner of Police, a man with a tough reputation. He tried to live up to his reputation in threatening me with "the consequences of my illegal activities." I asked what these were. He said he would bring in the magistrate with "evidence". I told him I would be very interested to meet the lying judge once again The judge had tried bare-faced bluster, and I had told him he was a liar to his face; I would call on my wife to prove this, and he would have to face both of us. I was here to address only what this lying judge had put in writing: to clarify what was I doing in Setelvass.

Finally, the Commissioner of Police produced what he thought was his trump card. After fumbling with papers on his desk, he asked to see my copy of official authorization for the trip. I was about to produce this when I had a sudden thought: could it be that neither he nor any other official had a copy of our authorization? It seemed incompetence beyond belief, but it was worth a challenge. Banskota could have "lost" it for his own reasons.

"Adrian Cowell has all our official papers," I told him. This was true; I only had a photocopy. "They are now in India, as you know."

It was the end - or nearly. After some more face-saving wrangling, the Commissioner handed me a prepared draft of a statement for my approval and signature:

"I wish to tender my apologies to His Majesty's Government of Nepal for having contravened regulations regarding places to be visited as listed in their permit, and for any inconvenience caused thereby. Further, I declare that I have never visited Mustang nor Kodari."

I shook my head in refusal. "No," I stated flatly. "I will not sign this. It is handing you a confession on a plate which you can use to discredit me at any time. I will only deal with what charge you have been prepared to put in writing: that of visiting Setelvass. This visit was authorized in your permit, and it was counter-stamped by your officials there. However, I am prepared to sign this. I deleted his erroneous statement and added my own words

"I wish to tender my apologies to His Majesty's Government of Nepal for having unwittingly contravened their regulations regarding places to be visited, listed in their permit, by having visited Setelvass; and for any inconveniences caused thereby. Further, I have never visited Mustang nor Kodari."

There was no further argument. It was accepted.

The airport was not so crowded the next day, but the journalists were there in expectation of further drama. So was Chahvan. He came towards me, one hand held out in greeting and the other holding a great bunch of flowers. Beside him walked his nameless Intelligence official friend, also smiling.

With a low bow Chahvan handed the bunch of flowers to my wife, declaring, "Lovely flowers for a lovely lady. If you need anything while your husband is away please don't hesitate to ask me to fix it for you." He turned to me, smiling delightedly. "Well, you pulled it off," he said enthusiastically. "I knew you would. I told the officials that unless they let you go they would not only be fired but you would have them in prison before you left the country."

He shouted at a nearby journalist with a camera. "Here, take a picture of my friend and me." He picked up my youngest son, Sean, and standing beside my wife, Lorne and me, smiling broadly, he signaled for the Intelligence official to stand beside me on the other side.

We chatted amiably until the plane departure was announced. When we said goodbye, he added, as I walked away, "Let me know when you come back for another adventure".

"Chahvan", I grinned, "in the words of a famous Irish writer - whom I'm sure you've read - '*You can't go anywhere without meeting clever people. The thing has become an absolute public nuisance. I wish to goodness we had a few fools left.'"*

As I turned away from the laughing Chahvan, he replied. "**'The Importance Of Being Earnest'**, by Oscar Wilde. He also wrote in **The Importance Of Being Earnest**, 'I hope you have not been leading a double life, pretending to be wicked and being good all the time. That would be hypocrisy.'

I was still laughing as I entered the plane and turned to wave good-bye.

EPILOGUE

"The Rest Is History..."

The newspapers had a good time with my story. I had entered Nepal as a controversial figure whose activities were being furiously debated in India's Parliament and media, and I arrived back in India from Nepal with my activities in Nepal and Tibet being widely publicized in international media. India's leading newspaper, **The Statesman**, reported:

"The Nepalese Government has decided on more stringent screening of mountaineering expeditions before granting permits, a high Government source said yesterday.

"The decision follows several incidents in which expeditions have violated permits...

"The British journalist, George Patterson, admitted violating a trekking permit to film a Khamba raid on a Chinese convoy in Tibet..."

The leading Nepali newspaper, **Motherland**, reported:

"George Patterson, a British journalist, who was prevented last week from leaving Kathmandu, left for India yesterday en route to the Far East.

"He was allowed to leave after tendering a written apology for having 'unwittingly' gone into unauthorized areas.

"He was alleged to have crossed the Nepal Tibetan border while journeying to some of the northern districts..."

Well, I suppose it was all the news that was fit to be printed from government sources.

Our film, entitled **Raid Into Tibet**, was shown to great critical acclaim in Britain, one critic declaring:

"The new TV series, 'Rebel' got off to a smashing start last night with a fantastic documentary entitled, 'Raid Into Tibet.' It was a sensational film, full of excitement, daring enterprises, superb photography, crisp commentary - glowing with the virtue of simplicity.

"It was the shatteringly realistic record of a raid by Tibetan Khamba rebels against a Chinese convoy across the Nepalese border in Tibet. 'Raid Into Tibet' was one of the most hair-raising half-hours of television ever seen on television.

"Adrian Cowell, Chris Menges and George Patterson - authority on Asian affairs and the moving spirit behind the film - managed to persuade a band of Tibetan exiles to take them on their mission across rugged country, rope bridges, sheer cliffs and 20,000-feet snow-covered mountain passes..."

Later, the film was awarded television's "Oscar", the **Prix Italia** for the best documentary of the year. It was shown in fifty countries to an estimated well over two hundred million people. Yet it was only of transient importance for Tibet, because the international community of nations continued to pay scant attention to the desperate tragedy of Tibet and the genocidal activities of a China posturing as a 5,000-year-old civilized nation in the United Nations Organization.

China has killed more people in Tibet than did Iraq in Kuwait, or Yugoslavia in Bosnia. China has destroyed more religious institutions in Tibet - and inside China - than Stalin in the old Soviet Union. China has blatantly annexed the two major historical Tibetan provinces of Kham and Amdo - formerly listed on Chinese maps as Sikang and Tsinghai - and arbitrarily truncated Tibet to a minor "autonomous region" of a single province of U-Tsang and a derisory population of 1.2 million. China has "disappeared" between five and ten million ethnic Tibetans - far more than the "disappeared" of Brazil, Argentina, Chile and Peru combined - with this unprotested cartographic and miscegenational absorption. China is ecologically decimating Tibet's forests, lands, crops and livestock in China's own interests. All of this without any legitimacy.

With minimal historical justification the Chinese Communist authorities have raped Tibet militarily, politically, culturally and economically without a single prominent official protest from any major nation. Even when a Chinese Communist leader, Hu Yaobang, belatedly admitted earlier Chinese excesses in Tibet there was no supportive response from any major political or diplomatic representative.

The most despicable political and diplomatic action of the twentieth century is China's rape of Tibet and the related connivance in this of the representatives of the United Nations Organization. History will record and deprecate this deliberate avoidance of responsibility for national genocide by regional and international countries.

Now, as Tibet faces ruthless genocidal extinction within a few years through enforced military occupation, political intimidation, cultural imposition, and religious destruction, there is not a single act of effective protest from either former "protector" Britain or present freedom defender USA.

The Dalai Lama, in his autobiography, *My Land And My People*, has declared categorically:

"One may sum up this brief history by saying that Tibet is a distinct and ancient nation, which for many centuries enjoyed a relationship of mutual respect with China. It is true that there were times when China was strong and Tibet was weak, and China invaded Tibet. Similarly, looking *further back into history, there were times when Tibet invaded China. There is no basis whatever in history for the Chinese claim that Tibet was part of China....This status has been analyzed in the utmost detail in recent years by the International Commission of Jurists in their report, The Question of Tibet and the Rule of Law, submitted to the United Nations in 1959..."*

Meanwhile, the world sycophantically courts a renegade regime in China, while admiring and applauding the Dalai Lama of Tibet, and even rightly honors him with the Nobel Peace Prize - but ignores his passionate appeals for justice, righteousness, love and forgiveness, and for recognition of the fate of his cynically raped and doomed nation.

POST SCRIPT

THE INTERNATIONAL COLLUSION TO SACRIFICE TIBET

(Lecture delivered at the Centre of International Studies, Cambridge University (England) on June 17, 2005)

I went to Tibet as a missionary with one-year medical training in 1946, and after nine months in China I spent the next three years travelling extensively in the two eastern provinces of Tibet, Kham and Amdo, with tribal leaders who were already planning a revolt against the central government of Tibet. Then I lived for the next ten years on the borders of Tibet as a journalist.

Both geographically and physically Tibet was ideal as a "buffer state" – the prize of the 19th century's "Great Game" in Asia, situated between China in the east, Russia in the north and India in the west. Its three-quarters of a million square miles of territory, encircled by 20-30,000-feet mountains on all sides, an average height of 15,000-feet, was inhabited by an estimated population of some five million people, one-third of them living in the western province of U-Tsang under a feudal government of nobles and monks. The other two thirds comprised some sixty tribes descended from Genghis Khan's leftover warriors in the eastern provinces of Kham and Amdo. A rough parallel would be the situation in earlier Britain with Celtic tribes in

Ireland and Scotland, and the Anglo-Saxons in feudal England.

The two Kham and Amdo provinces were arbitrarily annexed by China in a military engagement in 1904, in response to a British Younghusband military expedition from India. Both British and Chinese intrusions were illegal under existing legal agreements between the two east and west neighbouring powers. In 1863, when the Tibetans had defeated an earlier Chinese military engagement in Kham and Amdo, the Chinese Imperial Court had officially confirmed Kham and Amdo as Tibetan territory. In 1904, after the illegal Chinese intrusion by General Chao Erh-feng, China cartographically annexed the territory on their maps by naming it *"Sikang Province"* inside China and without protest by British India.

In 1934 the Kham tribal family of three Pangdatshang brothers unified the Kham tribes in a rebellion against the feudal central Lhasa government. The Pangdatshang family had become the richest trading family in Tibet after their wealthy trader father had helped the 13th Dalai Lama in his two-year exile in India following the 1911 revolution in China. In grateful response the Dalai Lama gave the father Pangdatshang priority trading rights to extend their trade to China, Central Asia, India and the West.

Later, the oldest of the his three sons, Yangpel, became an influential Minister of Trade in Lhasa; so, with the second son, Rapga, (who had translated into Tibetan the ***Three Principles of the People*** by China's former President, Dr Sun Yat Sen, and ***Das Capital*** by Karl Marx), and youngest charismatic son, Topgyay, they were powerfully equipped to foment and accomplish their anti-Lhasa revolution in 1934, and when this was foiled, make plans for a new and more successful revolt.

Gods and Guerrillas

While in exile in India following their aborted rebellion the two Pangdathsang brothers, Rapga and Topgyay, formed a Democratic Party for Tibet, were expelled by the British authorities and went to China, where Rapga sought support from the ruling Nationalists to overthrow the Lhasa regime. Topgyay was made an honorary Colonel of the Nationalist Army by Chiang Kai Shek to help defend China's western frontiers, and Topgyay used this position to obtain weapons and prepare for a post-war revolt against Lhasa. After the Communists took power in Peking in 1949 they contacted the Pangdatshangs with a proposal that their rumoured Khamba plans for another revolution against the Lhasa regime should become a *"Tibetan people's revolt against the feudal reactionaries in Lhasa"*.

The Pangdatshangs proposed that I try to reach India to inform Indian, British, American or the United Nations about the Chinese plans and try to obtain military assistance for the Khambas in their decision to fight the invading Chinese Liberation Army. It involved a thousand-mile journey across unexplored territory in mid-winter.

Miraculously, I survived and was sufficiently convincing for the British High Commission first secretary to arrange a meeting with intelligence officials of India, Britain and the USA, and this led to other meetings with higher officials in Calcutta and New Delhi. Eventually it was decided that nothing could be done to help Tibet. The British said that their intelligence showed the Pangdatshangs were "unreliable"; the Indians were definitely on the side of China, and thought the information from Kham was "unsound"; the Americans were interested, but more concerned with developments in Korea, and considered it unlikely that China would invade Tibet.

In early 1951 the Chinese army launched an attack in Kham Province as the Pangdatshangs had anticipated, and captured its capital, Chamdo, precipitating the flight of the Dalai Lama to Yatung on Tibet's western border with India. Before his departure from Lhasa the newly enthroned 16-year-old Dalai Lama authorized the Ngabu delegation to travel to Peking from Chamdo, under the leadership of the region's governor. But, doubting Ngabu's competence, he sent another delegation to China via India - this time led by Khemey Sonam Wangdi, usually called by his title, "Yapshi Sey", his older sister's husband. The Chamdo delegation arrived in Peking on April 22, 1951, and the delegation from Yatung and Kalimpong arrived a few days later. The instructions to the leaders of both delegations were to hold exploratory talks only; they were not authorized to sign any agreements.

Meanwhile, leading members of the Tibetan government became resident in the Indian border town of Kalimpong, bringing the feudal cabals of religion and politics. This greatly reduced the influence of Shakabpa, the spokesman for Tibet in Kalimpong with the Dalai Lama's brother, Gyalu Thondup, arriving from Taiwan with his Chinese wife seeking for some status.

On 23 May, 1951, to the shocked surprise of the Tibetans in Yatung and India, China announced that the Tibetan delegation had signed an agreement between Tibet and China called the *"May 17th Seventeen Point Agreement"*, stating:

"The Tibetan people shall unite and drive out imperialist and aggressive forces from Tibet and shall return to the big family of the motherland – the people's Republic of China".

When the Yapshi Sey delegation arrived back in India from Peking they claimed they had not signed, but that the Chinese had used a prepared Tibetan seal to stamp their agreement. The Ngabu delegation later denied this, but by that time they were widely condemned in Tibet as Chinese puppets.

In the United Nations, when the issue of the Chinese invasion of Tibet was raised, only a small South American country, El Salvador, was willing to support Tibet, but it was able to get the matter placed on the U.N. agenda. In the discussions which followed the British delegate said Tibet's status was "*ambiguous*", the United States delegate said it was really a matter for India to decide, and the Indian delegate expressed a sanctimonious hope for a peaceful solution. The matter was then supinely dropped without a vote being taken.

While these developments were taking place, in June of 1951 the oldest brother of the Dalai Lama, Taktser Rimpoche, arrived in Kalimpong on a secret mission from the Dalai Lama, and his mother sent for me to meet him. He was carrying two letters from the Dalai Lama: one accrediting him as the Dalai Lama's personal emissary; and the other addressed to the President of the United States requesting help for Tibet and for permission to travel there. He wanted to know if I would help with the arrangements to do this and, when I agreed, we translated the documents so that I could communicate their contents to the American officials in India.

During the negotiations I was in discussions with the CIA agents Bob Lynn in Calcutta and Bill Gibson in New Delhi. When the Dalai Lama returned to Tibet Bob Lynn remained in contact with me regarding developments inside Tibet, but I was aware that Bill Gibson was working with Harrer and his Tibetan contacts Gyalu Thondup and Shakabpa. When Harrer was expelled from India at the request of leading Tibetan officials Gibson continued to liaise with Thondup and Shakabpa.Later, when Thondup took up residence in New Delhi the CIA's John Kenneth

Knaus became a neighbour and collaborator with Thondup. This resulted in two different streams of information for the CIA through Lynn and Knaus. Superficially, this seemed an ideal arrangement for the CIA, except that the Thondup/Shakabpa faction were dismissed contemptuously by the leading Tibetan cabals of Tsarong, Surkhang, and Yuthok, and the religious hierarchy.

The Chinese military occupation of Tibet was precarious, as they soon discovered. They imposed a series of taxes, ostensibly for the "Aid to Korea Fund", on crops, wool and herds of animals, until the people were paying more for the Chinese occupation than they were paying to their feudal nobles and Buddhist monasteries. The increasing intransigence of the Tibetans, especially in Kham, was such that the Chinese "advisory" representative in Lhasa, Chang Ching-wu, refused to meet with the Tibetan cabinet ministers and demanded personal meetings with the Dalai Lama. For the first time a powerful anti-Chinese group calling itself the *Mi-mang Tsong-du* (or "People's Party") began operating in␁Lhasa, denouncing the *17 Point Agreement*, holding demonstrations, and placarding the walls with anti-Chinese posters. In Kham there were sporadic incidents of local rebellion as infuriated groups from within the many tribes attacked the isolated Chinese garrisons.

On 17th November, 1952, a Resolution ending the Korean war drafted by India and the various Arab-Asian delegations. It was approved by China, and India's ambassador Pannikar became the leading diplomatic figure in Peking as a channel of communication for Britain and America as well as the Arab-Asia bloc of representatives. This rise to international prominence for India was further increased with the addition of twelve African nations and became the "*Afro-Asia*" bloc.

On 17th February 1953 in New Delhi Prime Minister Nehru outlined India's new pro-China Asian "third force" policy in international affairs:

"It would be absurd for a number of countries in Asia to come together and call themselves a third force or a third power in a military sense. It may, however, have a meaning in another sense. Instead of calling it a third force or a third bloc, it can be called a third area, an area which – let us put it negatively first – does not want war, works for peace in a positive way and believes in cooperation...Those countries who do not want to align themselves with either of the two powerful blocs (namely the West and the Soviet Union) and who are willing to work for the cause of peace, should by all means come together; and we, on our part, should do all we can to make this possible..."

On 19th April, 1954, India and China signed an agreement in Bandung, Indonesia, entitled *"Five Principles of Peaceful Coexistence"* which were: *(i) mutual respect for each other's territorial integrity and sovereignty; (ii) mutual non-aggression; (iii) mutual non-interference in each other's internal affairs; (iv) equality and mutual benefit; and (v) peaceful coexistence."* In the text of the communiqué which was issued on 29th April 1954 it stated that the question of China's occupation of Tibet was settled between them in the phrase *"the Tibet region of China"*.

Acharya Kripalani, the Leader of the Opposition Party, declared his disagreement:

"Recently we have entered into a treaty with China. This treaty concerns the whole of India. It does not concern a party or a person, it affects us all. We feel that China, after it had gone Communist, committed an act of aggression in Tibet. The plea is that China had the ancient right of suzerainty. That right was out of date, old and antiquated. It was theoretical; it had lapsed by the flux of time...I

consider this as much colonial aggression as that indulged in by Western nations..."

Meanwhile, on the Indian border, the Chinese military build-up inside Tibet began to look ominous to the Indians. Military drill and army exercises were reported to be taking place from dawn to dusk along the Himalayan borders, airfields were being constructed, and there was a constant stream of propaganda to the Chinese troops regarding imminent invasion of Nepal, Sikkim and Bhutan leaked to the media in India. When Nehru raised the matter with the Chinese under pressure from his political opponents he was bluntly informed that China's claims to these border territories were based on the same claim as for their invasion of Tibet.

Nehru visited Viet Nam on 17th October, 1954, and both agreed on the implementation of the Geneva Agreements relating to Indo-China. After the success of India's *"friendship for China"* policy – in Korea, Tibet, and Indo-China particularly – Nehru was invited to Peking and given a mammoth reception. China had also pressured Tibet's two religious leaders, the Dalai Lama and Panchen Lama, to attend. The *pièce de résistance* of the assembly was an arranged meeting between the two Lamas and Prime Minister Nehru, calculated to visually demonstrate that China's annexation of Tibet was officially approved.

During their visit to Peking the Dalai Lama and Panchen Lama were forced to submit to the Chinese proposal for a *"Preparatory Committee for the Autonomous Region of Tibet"* consisting of fifty-one members: fifteen from the Lhasa administration, ten from the '*Panchen Lama's Bureau*', ten from the Chamdo '*People's Liberation Committee*', eleven from monasteries and '*People's Organisations*', and five representing the Chinese Government, with the Dalai Lama as chairman. The members of the Committee were appointed *"with the approval of the Chinese State Council"*, and the three provinces of Tibet were subordinate to it.

Later, the Dalai Lama in exile declared:

"In practice, even this body had little power and decisions in all important matters were taken by the Chinese authorities."

What the Chinese authorities did not know at the time was that the Dalai Lama, on his journey to Peking accompanied by two senior government ministers, had held secret meetings with the Pangdatshang brothers in Kham. After their humiliating treatment in Peking, which also included an insulting scolding of Tibet's Chief Minister Surkhang by Chairman Mao, the Tibetan delegation were convinced that China was committed to total subservience of Tibet to China.

After leaving Peking, on their return journey through Kham and Amdo, the Dalai Lama and his ministers met again with the Pangdatshang brothers and the Amdo leaders, Geshi Sherab Gyaltso and Lobsang Sherab, to give the Lhasa government's official approval to launch their prepared revolt against the Chinese with central government support at an appropriate time.

Shortly after Nehru returned in triumph to India following the critical meeting in Peking I was approached by a high-ranking Indian intelligence official to discuss with me the possibility of arranging a meeting with influential Tibetan leaders to mitigate the damage done to the already sensitive Indian relations with Tibet after the Chinese pre-arranged tableaux in Peking. I informed the agent that there was no such influential Tibetan among the exiled Tibetans in India, or even in Lhasa. However, if the Indian government was prepared to cancel Rapga's order of expulsion and permit him to enter India he was equipped politically to speak for Tibet. I was surprised when the Indian government agreed to my proposal. I sent word to Rapga and he arrived in Kalimpong, on the Indian border, in March, 1955.

His arrival created consternation among the exiled feuding Tibetan officials in India representing various aristocratic and religious interests because of his known radical theories. He created even greater consternation to the Indian officials as he adamantly refused to participate in their proposed long-term subversive propaganda campaign, and insisted that his only interest was in revolt against Chinese military occupation and a subsequent independent and democratic government for Tibet.

Although this alarmed the Indian authorities it was of great interest to the Americans. Rapga wanted supplies of modern weapons for the warring Khambas and he asked me to introduce him to American diplomatic and intelligence people. A CIA official, John Turner, was appointed to meet with Rapga, with me as interpreter (Rapga was fluent in English but wanted me there with him), in typical spy-cover arrangements on a certain seat in the open Mall promenade of Darjeeling's shopping area, over a period of four days.

Rapga then laid out his plan of a Kham bridgehead in south-east Tibet encompassing the Markham region which they controlled. A weapons supply line from Assam to this area (the route down which I had travelled to India seeking help!) would provide a base for the Khambas to attack the Chinese and make it impossible for them to occupy Tibet for any length of time. Rapga envisaged making the Kham region the political and commercial centre for Tibet, with Chamdo as the capital, and making Lhasa a religious centre only. He envisaged a short period of rule to educate former feudal officials and the public in democratic principles, the monasteries would become temporary education centres until a secular administration was formed, hopefully followed by a popularly elected democratic government for Tibet in the future, with the Dalai Lama as religious leader only. The programme would require ten years to implement, five years for the preliminary stages of a revolt, and five years for education and elections. Rapga described Tibet's natural economic resources in return for aid. In addition to its strategic geopolitical advantages there were untapped supplies of known sources of oil, gold and possibly uranium which would adequately pay for any internal development and external trade.

This was not just breath-taking for the CIA official, it was probably too much for the US leaders in Washington because there was no further response. Rapga concluded from the discussions with the CIA and, later, other officials in Calcutta and New Delhi that both America and India were playing a double political game: on the one hand placating China in agreement with India's *"third bloc"* policy on the Bandung Treaty's so-called *"Peaceful Coexistence"*, while at the same time exploring what might be done realistically to aid Tibet to counter Sino-Indian domination in Asia. Whether this might have developed into something positive for Tibet was quickly wiped out.

In Lhasa, the Dalai Lama made a public speech condemning China's ruthless manipulation of the newly introduced *"Preparatory Committee for the Autonomous Region of Tibet"*, of which he was the titular chairman. At the annual, hugely attended public Monlam Festival in Lhasa, the leaders of the "underground" *Mi-man Tsong-du*, with other popular Tibetan officials, also denounced the increasing Chinese political and military actions.

When three of the leaders were arrested and condemned to death they were visited in prison by a Khamba minor tribal chieftain called Andrutshang Gompo Tashi. He was so angered by the decision he returned to Kham, organised a group of rebels in the region of Litang under the banner of *Chu-zhi Kang tru* (a popular local name for Kham meaning "Four rivers, Six mountains"), and launched armed insurrection. He was only one of some sixteen major tribes combining from Batang in Kham to the Amdo northern border with Sinkiang to drive the Chinese out of Tibet. Little of this unrest filtered out to the outside world, except from my reports.

In August 1956 the Chinese official *New China News Agency* finally admitted that a rebellion had taken place *"in some areas in Western Szechuan"*, but that reports in Western media were based on *"distorted and grossly delayed information"*. After denying any widespread unrest in Tibet their propaganda declared *"Indian expansionists and British imperialists have not given up their ambition to invade Tibet and enslave its people"*. The centre of this subversion was said to be *"Kalimpong, the commanding centre of the revolt"*, and went on to describe how I had laid the groundwork of the revolt with my contacts with the Pangdatshangs and concluded:

"In the summer of 1955 Surkhang Wangcheng Galei and Tserijong Lozong-Yeihsi and other rebel elements in Tibet, after following the Dalai Lama to Peking passed through the Szechuan Province on their way back to to Tibet. Surkhang and Tserijong went by separate routes to the Northern and Southern parts of the Kansu Autonomous Chou to instigate and direct rebellion along the way. Data now at hand proves that Surkhang directed the reactionaries in the area...".

In late 1956 the Chinese authorities in Tibet arrested the two top Amdo leader-colleagues of the Pangdatshangs, Geshi Sherab Gyaltso and Lobsang Sherab, and this precipitated a wide uprising against the Chinese in Amdo, led by the Golok tribe. The Goloks captured several hundred Chinese, cut off their noses, and sent them back mutilated. The Chinese replied by sending several thousand troops into the area, but the Goloks were helped by a neighbouring tribe of some 100,000 families in the Dzachuka area, and they slaughtered between seven and eight thousand Chinese and forced their retreat. This led to spontaneous outbreaks in a spreading revolt throughout Kham and Amdo.

The *Mi-mang Tsong-du* leader in Lhasa, Alo Chondze, escaped to Kalimpong and reported that the fighting had spread from Golok, Batang and Litang areas to Nyarong, Taofu, Chatreng and Mili, an area of about 10,000 square miles involving more than a million people. Bridges had been destroyed and roads made impassable, isolating the Chinese soldiers in their garrisons and make them easier to attack.

Deputy Prime Minister Chen Yi went to Lhasa, and in his report he stated that *"Tibet's roads to socialism would be long, and would have to be travelled slowly"*, and that there should be *"guarantees about the political position and living standards of Tibetan nobility and lamas"*, but saying nothing about the Khambas or the causes of their revolt.

One month later, on November 8th the Chinese authorities set up another committee in Lhasa – *"The Chinese People's Political Consultative Committee"* – in an attempt to control the increasingly rebellious country. It consisted of fifteen members and included the tutor of the Dalai Lama, Trichang Rimpoche, Surkhang as Director of the Office, and Puntshok Wangyel, the former Khamba quisling Communist as Vice-Director, but this, too, was ineffective. They persuaded the Dalai Lama to send a delegation to the Khamba leaders to call off the revolt but, instead, the delegation defected to the Khambas and the fighting escalated, to the fury of the Chinese authorities in both Lhasa and Peking.

In India, Gyalu Thondup was working in close collaboration with the CIA's Kenneth Knaus, and it was agreed to take six members of Andrutshang's *Chu-zhi-Kang-tru* to Taiwan and the USA to receive training in the use of radio transmitters, parachute-jumping and modern weapons, to fly back into Tibet secretly to aid the Khamba revolt. It was a ridiculous gesture, owing more to Washington's political guilt over its inability to provide realistic aid to Tibet through Rapga and the Khambas, because of bondage to the Indian and Chinese *"third bloc"* Bandung Agreement of *"Peaceful Coexistence"*.

Meanwhile, the Khamba revolt was sweeping westwards and creating panic among the Chinese military and officials, who were now starving as the single supply road from China was rendered inoperable in the Khamba advance. The Khambas, in turn, were finding extra supplies of weapons from the Lhasa officials who had made the agreement with them during the earlier visit to Peking. By mid-1958 it was estimated by the Tibetans that 20,000 victorious Khambas were approaching Lhasa.

Tibet's geographical and political isolation was further compounded by Prime Minister Nehru's strenuous attempts to suppress all news of the revolt, strongly condemning all media reports – mostly sent by me. I was ordered to attend the office of the local Deputy Commissioner and told that unless I *"discontinued sending misleading and exaggerated reports about Tibet to the Daily Telegraph or other foreign papers, the Indian Government would be constrained to interdict your residence"*.

On March 10th, 1959, the Khamba revolt reached Lhasa. On that day the Dalai Lama had received a curt message from the Chinese authorities to attend a meeting with the

Chinese officials in Lhasa, without his customary escort. It looked ominous to his advisers and they persuaded him to refuse and to consider preparations to leave Lhasa. At the same time the city demonstrations had escalated rapidly with the rumoured arrival of the rampaging Khambas, many already inside Lhasa while the majority were surrounding the city, and thousands of demonstrators remained around the Norbulinka Palace where the Dalai Lama was in residence to prevent the Chinese from forcing an entry.

On March 15th the Dalai Lama secretly left the city disguised as an ordinary armed soldier, with his senior ministers, and escorted by some two hundred armed Khambas. On March 17th the Chinese shelled the Norbulinka Palace assuming that the Dalai Lama was still there. On the same day in the Indian *Lok Sabha*, or Parliament, Prime Minister Nehru was addressing the question of my expulsion, declaring "*Mr Patterson accepted every bazaar rumour as fact*", that what was happening in Tibet "*was a clash of minds rather a clash of arms. There is no violence in Tibet*". There was pandemonium in Parliament when he was forced to announce later that day that "*fighting had broken out in Lhasa and the Indian consulate was damaged in the shelling*".

Even the arrival of the Dalai Lama on the border of India was announced by the Chinese before the Indians, to Nehru's further embarrassment in India's Parliament. The Indian Prime Minister reluctantly agreed to asylum for him and his government ministers, but the Dalai Lama was forbidden to set up a government-in-exile, and no political activities or public recognition other than as religious leader of Tibet. However, the Dalai Lama in his first public address did repudiate the 1951 *May 17th 17-Point Agreement* imposed by the Chinese authorities without his permission.

In November 1959 a three-member delegation went to the UN to request that the question of Tibet be put on the agenda. This was sponsored by Ireland and Malaya, and a mildly worded resolution was passed – but rejected by both India and Britain and the USA abstained. The issue was raised again in 1961 and 1965, but no effective action was taken.

The *International Commission of Jurists* agreed to establish a *Legal Enquiry Committee* and concluded that there was insufficient evidence to demonstrate genocide against China, but there was sufficient proof to show that the Chinese *"had violated the Tibetan right to exist as a religious group...but not the right to exist as a national, ethnical (sic) or racial group"*. They classified this as *"cultural genocide"*.

With the Dalai Lama silenced by the Sino-Indian *"third bloc"* Bandung Agreement stranglehold, except for religious addresses, there was no effective international spokesman or sponsor for Tibet. The Dalai Lama's brother, Gyalu Thondup, was the favoured intermediary, but he was found to be a broken reed, because he was felt by the Khambas to have betrayed their cause over the mishandling of the Dalai Lama's treasure, and his later overt association with the feeble CIA response.

I returned to Tibet twice, in 1964 to secretly film Khamba guerrillas destroying military convoys inside Tibet, and again in 1987 as adviser to a Hollywood film project. I was appalled at the Chinese cultural destruction of Tibet. Monasteries were devastated ruins. The trans-Tibet road was crowded with Chinese military vehicles. The vibrant Tibetans I had known were sullen and without hope. Everywhere there were featureless Chinese buildings, troops, merchants, officials and dress. For the tourists there were Chinese hotels, restaurants, singers, dances, and operas. I found only one small restaurant in Lhasa serving Tibetan food.

I learned that the Pangdatshang brothers had all been executed. Yangpel was abducted from Hong Kong, taken to Peking and, later, to Lhasa where he was paraded through the streets and killed. Topgyay was taken to Peking for *"medical treatment"* and later pronounced dead from some unstated illness. Rapga was shot on the main street of Kalimpong in India and died soon afterwards.

Today, the Dalai Lama is in an impossible situation, even with a Nobel Peace Prize and a declared willingness to remove himself from political leadership in Tibet. Deeply committed to a non-violent solution, yet he knows that any possible solution must include Kham and Amdo, and the warrior Khambas will never agree to Chinese domination. On the other hand, the Chinese, having arbitrarily annexed Kham and Amdo, and only recognising the single central province of U-Tsang as *"the Tibetan autonomous region"*, will never agree to their return to Tibet. Time, millions of Chinese colonisers and international unconcern will confirm their rape of Tibet.

In conclusion, an interesting speculation by hindsight is: if the United States had agreed with Rapga's proposals and supplied Tibet with sufficient weapons instead of radios, they might not have been defeated in Vietnam; and instead might have modified China's current arrogance and threatening expansion in Asia.

George Patterson lived in Asia for thirty years as a missionary, journalist, radio and television broadcaster on "Asian affairs". He has published several books, including **God's Fool, Journey with Loshay, Tibet in Revolt, Patterson of Tibet, Peking versus Delhi**, and **Requiem for Tibet**.

OUR CURRENT LIST OF TITLES

Abernathy, Miles, *Ride the Wind* – the amazing true story of the little Abernathy Boys, who made a series of astonishing journeys in the United States, starting in 1909 when they were aged five and nine!

Beard, John, *Saddles East* – John Beard determined as a child that he wanted to see the Wild West from the back of a horse after a visit to Cody's legendary Wild West show. Yet it was only in 1948 – more than sixty years after seeing the flamboyant American showman – that Beard and his wife Lulu finally set off to follow their dreams.

Beker, Ana, *The Courage to Ride* – Determined to out-do Tschiffely, Beker made a 17,000 mile mounted odyssey across the Americas in the late 1940s that would fix her place in the annals of equestrian travel history.

Bird, Isabella, *Among the Tibetans* – A rousing 1889 adventure, an enchanting travelogue, a forgotten peek at a mountain kingdom swept away by the waves of time.

Bird, Isabella, *On Horseback* in *Hawaii* – The Victorian explorer's first horseback journey, in which she learns to ride astride, in early 1873.

Bird, Isabella, *Journeys in Persia and Kurdistan, Volumes 1 and 2* – The intrepid Englishwoman undertakes another gruelling journey in 1890.

Bird, Isabella, *A Lady's Life in the Rocky Mountains* – The story of Isabella Bird's adventures during the winter of 1873 when she explored the magnificent unspoiled wilderness of Colorado. Truly a classic.

Bird, Isabella, *Unbeaten Tracks in Japan, Volumes One and Two* – A 600-mile solo ride through Japan undertaken by the intrepid British traveller in 1878.

Boniface, Lieutenant Jonathan, *The Cavalry Horse and his Pack* – Quite simply the most important book ever written in the English language by a military man on the subject of equestrian travel.

Bosanquet, Mary, *Saddlebags for Suitcases* – In 1939 Bosanquet set out to ride from Vancouver, Canada, to New York. Along the way she was wooed by love-struck cowboys, chased by a grizzly bear and even suspected of being a Nazi spy, scouting out Canada in preparation for a German invasion. A truly delightful book.

de Bourboulon, Catherine, *Shanghai à Moscou (French)* – the story of how a young Scottish woman and her aristocratic French husband travelled overland from Shanghai to Moscow in the late 19th Century.
Brown, Donald; *Journey from the Arctic* – A truly remarkable account of how Brown, his Danish companion and their two trusty horses attempt the impossible, to cross the silent Arctic plateaus, thread their way through the giant Swedish forests, and finally discover a passage around the treacherous Norwegian marshes.
Bruce, Clarence Dalrymple, *In the Hoofprints of Marco Polo* – The author made a dangerous journey from Srinagar to Peking in 1905, mounted on a trusty 13-hand Kashmiri pony, then wrote this wonderful book.
Burnaby, Frederick; *A Ride to Khiva* – Burnaby fills every page with a memorable cast of characters, including hard-riding Cossacks, nomadic Tartars, vodka-guzzling sleigh-drivers and a legion of peasant ruffians.
Burnaby, Frederick, *On Horseback through Asia Minor* – Armed with a rifle, a small stock of medicines, and a single faithful servant, the equestrian traveler rode through a hotbed of intrigue and high adventure in wild inhospitable country, encountering Kurds, Circassians, Armenians, and Persian pashas.
Carter, General William, *Horses, Saddles and Bridles* – This book covers a wide range of topics including basic training of the horse and care of its equipment. It also provides a fascinating look back into equestrian travel history.
Cayley, George, *Bridle Roads of Spain* – Truly one of the greatest equestrian travel accounts of the 19th Century.
Chase, J. Smeaton, *California Coast Trails* – This classic book describes the author's journey from Mexico to Oregon along the coast of California in the 1890s.
Chase, J. Smeaton, *California Desert Trails* – Famous British naturalist J. Smeaton Chase mounted up and rode into the Mojave Desert to undertake the longest equestrian study of its kind in modern history.
Clark, Leonard, *Marching Wind, The* - The panoramic story of a mounted exploration in the remote and savage heart of Asia, a place where adventure, danger, and intrigue were the daily backdrop to wild tribesman and equestrian exploits.
Cobbett, William, *Rural Rides, Volumes 1 and 2* – In the early 1820s Cobbett set out on horseback to make a series of personal

tours through the English countryside. These books contain what many believe to be the best accounts of rural England ever written, and remain enduring classics.

Codman, John, *Winter Sketches from the Saddle* – This classic book was first published in 1888. It recommends riding for your health and describes the septuagenarian author's many equestrian journeys through New England during the winter of 1887 on his faithful mare, Fanny.

Cunninghame Graham, Jean, *Gaucho Laird* – A superbly readable biography of the author's famous great-uncle, Robert "Don Roberto" Cunninghame Graham.

Cunninghame Graham, Robert, *Horses of the Conquest* – The author uncovered manuscripts which had lain forgotten for centuries, and wrote this book, as he said, out of gratitude to the horses of Columbus and the Conquistadors who shaped history.

Cunninghame Graham, Robert, *Magreb-el-Acksa* – The thrilling tale of how "Don Roberto" was kidnapped in Morocco!

Cunninghame Graham, Robert, *Rodeo* – An omnibus of the finest work of the man they called "the uncrowned King of Scotland," edited by his friend Aimé Tschiffely.

Cunninghame Graham, Robert, *Tales of Horsemen* – Ten of the most beautifully-written equestrian stories ever set to paper.

Cunninghame Graham, Robert, *Vanished Arcadia* – This haunting story about the Jesuit missions in South America from 1550 to 1767 was the inspiration behind the best-selling film *The Mission*.

Daly, H.W., *Manual of Pack Transportation* – This book is the author's masterpiece. It contains a wealth of information on various pack saddles, ropes and equipment, how to secure every type of load imaginable and instructions on how to organize a pack train.

Dixie, Lady Florence, *Riding Across Patagonia* – When asked in 1879 why she wanted to travel to such an outlandish place as Patagonia, the author replied without hesitation that she was taking to the saddle in order to flee from the strict confines of polite Victorian society. This is the story of how the aristocrat successfully traded the perils of a London parlor for the wind-borne freedom of a wild Patagonian bronco.

Dodwell, Christina, *A Traveller on Horseback* – Christina Dodwell rides through Eastern Turkey and Iran in the late 1980s. The Sunday Telegraph wrote of the author's "courage and insatiable wanderlust," and in this book she demonstrates her gift for communicating her zest for adventure.

Dodwell, Christina, *Travels in Papua New Guinea* – The exciting account of the author's two-year solo expedition through this little-known country.

Dodwell, Christina, *Travels with Fortune* – The amazing tale of the author's first adventure, a three-year journey through Africa. This is a truly extraordinary travel book.

Ehlers, Otto, *Im Sattel durch die Fürstenhöfe Indiens* – In June 1890 the young German adventurer, Ehlers, lay very ill. His doctor gave him a choice: either go home to Germany or travel to Kashmir. So of course the Long Rider chose the latter. This is a thrilling yet humorous book about the author's adventures.

Farson, Negley, *Caucasian Journey* – A thrilling account of a dangerous equestrian journey made in 1929, this is an amply illustrated adventure classic.

Fox, Ernest, *Travels in Afghanistan* – The thrilling tale of a 1937 journey through the mountains, valleys, and deserts of this forbidden realm, including visits to such fabled places as the medieval city of Heart, the towering Hindu Kush mountains, and the legendary Khyber Pass.

Galton, Francis, *The Art of Travel* – Originally published in 1855, this book became an instant classic and was used by a host of now-famous explorers, including Sir Richard Francis Burton of Mecca fame. Readers can learn how to ride horses, handle elephants, avoid cobras, pull teeth, find water in a desert, and construct a sleeping bag out of fur.

Glazier, Willard, *Ocean to Ocean on Horseback* – This book about the author's journey from New York to the Pacific in 1875 contains every kind of mounted adventure imaginable. Amply illustrated with pen and ink drawings of the time, the book remains a timeless equestrian adventure classic.

Goodwin, Joseph, *Through Mexico on Horseback* – The author and his companion, Robert Horiguichi, the sophisticated, multi-lingual son of an imperial Japanese diplomat, set out in 1931 to cross Mexico. They were totally unprepared for the deserts, quicksand and brigands they were to encounter during their adventure.

Hanbury-Tenison, Marika, *For Better, For Worse* – The author, an excellent story-teller, writes about her adventures visiting and living among the Indians of Central Brazil.

www.classictravelbooks.com

Hanbury-Tenison, Marika, *A Slice of Spice* – The fresh and vivid account of the author's hazardous journey to the Indonesian Islands with her husband, Robin.

Hanbury-Tenison, Robin, *Chinese Adventure* – The story of a unique journey in which the explorer Robin Hanbury-Tenison and his wife Louella rode on horseback alongside the Great Wall of China in 1986.

Hanbury-Tenison, Robin, *Fragile Eden* – The wonderful story of Robin and Louella Hanbury-Tenison's exploration of New Zealand on horseback in 1988. They rode alone together through what they describe as 'some of the most dramatic and exciting country we have ever seen.'

Hanbury-Tenison, Robin, *Mulu: The Rainforest* – This was the first popular book to bring to the world's attention the significance of the rain forests to our fragile ecosystem. It is a timely reminder of our need to preserve them for the future.

Hanbury-Tenison, Robin, *A Pattern of Peoples* – The author and his wife, Marika, spent three months travelling through Indonesia's outer islands and writes with his usual flair and sensitivity about the tribes he found there.

Hanbury-Tenison, Robin, *A Question of Survival* – This superb book played a hugely significant role in bringing the plight of Brazil's Indians to the world's attention.

Hanbury-Tenison, Robin, *The Rough and the Smooth* – The incredible story of two journeys in South America. Neither had been attempted before, and both were considered impossible!

Hanbury-Tenison, Robin, *Spanish Pilgrimage* – Robin and Louella Hanbury-Tenison went to Santiago de Compostela in a traditional way – riding on white horses over long-forgotten tracks. In the process they discovered more about the people and the country than any conventional traveller would learn. Their adventures are vividly and entertainingly recounted in this delightful and highly readable book.

Hanbury-Tenison, Robin, *White Horses over France* – This enchanting book tells the story of a magical journey and how, in fulfilment of a personal dream, the first Camargue horses set foot on British soil in the late summer of 1984.

Hanbury-Tenison, Robin, *Worlds Apart – an Explorer's Life* – The author's battle to preserve the quality of life under threat from developers and machines infuses this autobiography with a passion and conviction which makes it impossible to put down.

Hanbury-Tenison, Robin, *Worlds Within – Reflections in the Sand* – This book is full of the adventure you would expect from a man of action like Robin Hanbury-Tenison. However, it is also filled with the type of rare knowledge that was revealed to other desert travellers like Lawrence, Doughty and Thesiger.

Haslund, Henning, *Mongolian Adventure* – An epic tale inhabited by a cast of characters no longer present in this lackluster world, shamans who set themselves on fire, rebel leaders who sacked towns, and wild horsemen whose ancestors conquered the world.

Heath, Frank, *Forty Million Hoofbeats* – Heath set out in 1925 to follow his dream of riding to all 48 of the Continental United States. The journey lasted more than two years, during which time Heath and his mare, Gypsy Queen, became inseparable companions.

Holt, William, *Ride a White Horse* – After rescuing a cart horse, Trigger, from slaughter and nursing him back to health, the 67-year-old Holt and his horse set out in 1964 on an incredible 9,000 mile, non-stop journey through western Europe.

Hopkins, Frank T., *Hidalgo and Other Stories* – For the first time in history, here are the collected writings of Frank T. Hopkins, the counterfeit cowboy whose endurance racing claims and Old West fantasies have polarized the equestrian world.

James, Jeremy, *Saddletramp* – The classic story of Jeremy James' journey from Turkey to Wales, on an unplanned route with an inaccurate compass, unreadable map and the unfailing aid of villagers who seemed to have as little sense of direction as he had.

James, Jeremy, *Vagabond* – The wonderful tale of the author's journey from Bulgaria to Berlin offers a refreshing, witty and often surprising view of Eastern Europe and the collapse of communism.

Jebb, Louisa, *By Desert Ways to Baghdad and Damascus* – From the pen of a gifted writer and intrepid traveller, this is one of the greatest equestrian travel books of all time.

Kluckhohn, Clyde, *To the Foot of the Rainbow* – This is not just a exciting true tale of equestrian adventure. It is a moving account of a young man's search for physical perfection in a desert world still untouched by the recently-born twentieth century.

Lambie, Thomas, *Boots and Saddles in Africa* – Lambie's story of his equestrian journeys is told with the grit and realism that marks a true classic.

www.classictravelbooks.com

Landor, Henry Savage, *In the Forbidden Land* – Illustrated with hundreds of photographs and drawings, this blood-chilling account of equestrian adventure makes for page-turning excitement.

Langlet, Valdemar, *Till Häst Genom Ryssland (Swedish)* – Denna reseskildring rymmer många ögonblicksbilder av möten med människor, från morgonbad med Lev Tolstoi till samtal med Tartarer och fotografering av fagra skördeflickor. Rikt illustrerad med foto och teckningar.

Leigh, Margaret, *My Kingdom for a Horse* – In the autumn of 1939 the author rode from Cornwall to Scotland, resulting in one of the most delightful equestrian journeys of the early twentieth century. This book is full of keen observations of a rural England that no longer exists.

Lester, Mary, *A Lady's Ride across Spanish Honduras in 1881* – This is a gem of a book, with a very entertaining account of Mary's vivid, day-to-day life in the saddle.

Maillart, Ella, *Turkestan Solo* – A vivid account of a 1930s journey through this wonderful, mysterious and dangerous portion of the world, complete with its Kirghiz eagle hunters, lurking Soviet secret police, and the timeless nomads that still inhabited the desolate steppes of Central Asia.

Marcy, Randolph, *The Prairie Traveler* – There were a lot of things you packed into your saddlebags or the wagon before setting off to cross the North American wilderness in the 1850s. A gun and an axe were obvious necessities. Yet many pioneers were just as adamant about placing a copy of Captain Randolph Marcy's classic book close at hand.

Marsden, Kate, *Riding through Siberia: A Mounted Medical Mission in 1891* - This immensely readable book is a mixture of adventure, extreme hardship and compassion as the author travels the Great Siberian Post Road.

Marsh, Hippisley Cunliffe, *A Ride Through Islam* – A British officer rides through Persia and Afghanistan to India in 1873. Full of adventures, and with observant remarks on the local Turkoman equestrian traditions.

MacCann, William, *Viaje a Caballo* – Spanish-language edition of the British author's equestrian journey around Argentina in 1848.

Meline, James, *Two Thousand Miles on Horseback: Kansas to Santa Fé in 1866* – A beautifully written, eye witness account of a United States that is no more.
Muir Watson, Sharon, *The Colour of Courage* – The remarkable true story of the epic horse trip made by the first people to travel Australia's then-unmarked Bicentennial National Trail. There are enough adventures here to satisfy even the most jaded reader.
Naysmith, Gordon, *The Will to Win* – This book recounts the only equestrian journey of its kind undertaken during the 20th century - a mounted trip stretching across 16 countries. Gordon Naysmith, a Scottish pentathlete and former military man, set out in 1970 to ride from the tip of the African continent to the 1972 Olympic Games in distant Germany.
O'Reilly, Basha, *Count Pompeii – Stallion of the Steppes* – the story of Basha's journey from Russia with her stallion, Count Pompeii, told for children. This is the first book in the *Little Long Rider* series.
O'Reilly, CuChullaine, (Editor) *The Horse Travel Handbook* – this accumulated knowledge of a million miles in the saddle tells you everything you need to know about travelling with your horse!
O'Reilly, CuChullaine, (Editor) *The Horse Travel Journal* – a unique book to take on your ride and record your experiences. Includes the world's first equestrian travel "pictionary" to help you in foreign countries.
O'Reilly, CuChullaine, *Khyber Knights* – Told with grit and realism by one of the world's foremost equestrian explorers, "Khyber Knights" has been penned the way lives are lived, not how books are written.
O'Reilly, CuChullaine, (Editor) *The Long Riders, Volume One* – The first of five unforgettable volumes of exhilarating travel tales.
Östrup, J, (*Swedish*), *Växlande Horisont* - The thrilling account of the author's journey to Central Asia from 1891 to 1893.
Patterson, George, *Gods and Guerrillas* – The true and gripping story of how the author went secretly into Tibet to film the Chinese invaders of his adopted country. Will make your heart pound with excitement!
Patterson, George, *Journey with Loshay: A Tibetan Odyssey* – This is an amazing book written by a truly remarkable man! Relying both on his companionship with God and on his own

www.classictravelbooks.com

strength, he undertook a life few can have known, and a journey of emergency across the wildest parts of Tibet.

Pocock, Roger, *Following the Frontier* – Pocock was one of the nineteenth century's most influential equestrian travelers. Within the covers of this book is the detailed account of Pocock's horse ride along the infamous Outlaw Trail, a 3,000 mile solo journey that took the adventurer from Canada to Mexico City.

Pocock, Roger, *Horses* – Pocock set out to document the wisdom of the late 19th and early 20th Centuries into a book unique for its time. His concerns for attempting to preserve equestrian knowledge were based on cruel reality. More than 300,000 horses had been destroyed during the recent Boer War. Though Pocock enjoyed a reputation for dangerous living, his observations on horses were praised by the leading thinkers of his day.

Post, Charles Johnson, *Horse Packing* – Originally published in 1914, this book was an instant success, incorporating as it did the very essence of the science of packing horses and mules. It makes fascinating reading for students of the horse or history.

Ray, G. W., *Through Five Republics on Horseback* – In 1889 a British explorer - part-time missionary and full-time adventure junky – set out to find a lost tribe of sun-worshipping natives in the unexplored forests of Paraguay. The journey was so brutal that it defies belief.

Rink, Bjarke, *The Centaur Legacy* - This immensely entertaining and historically important book provides the first ever in-depth study into how man's partnership with his equine companion changed the course of history and accelerated human development.

Ross, Julian, *Travels in an Unknown Country* – A delightful book about modern horseback travel in an enchanting country, which once marked the eastern borders of the Roman Empire – Romania.

Ross, Martin and Somerville, E, *Beggars on Horseback* – The hilarious adventures of two aristocratic Irish cousins on an 1894 riding tour of Wales.

Ruxton, George, *Adventures in Mexico* – The story of a young British army officer who rode from Vera Cruz to Santa Fe, Mexico in 1847. At times the author exhibits a fearlessness which borders on insanity. He ignores dire warnings, rides through deadly deserts, and dares murderers to attack him. It is a delightful and invigorating tale of a time and place now long gone.

von Salzman, Erich, *Im Sattel durch Zentralasien* – The astonishing tale of the author's journey through China, Turkistan and back to his home in Germany – 6000 kilometres in 176 days!

Schwarz, Hans *(German)*, *Vier Pferde, Ein Hund und Drei Soldaten* – In the early 1930s the author and his two companions rode through Liechtenstein, Austria, Romania, Albania, Yugoslavia, to Turkey, then rode back again!

Schwarz, Otto *(German)*, *Reisen mit dem Pferd* – the Swiss Long Rider with more miles in the saddle than anyone else tells his wonderful story, and a long appendix tells the reader how to follow in his footsteps.

Scott, Robert, *Scott's Last Expedition* – Many people are unaware that Scott recruited Yakut ponies from Siberia for his doomed expedition to the South Pole in 1909. Here is the remarkable story of men and horses who all paid the ultimate sacrifice.

Skrede, Wilfred, *Across the Roof of the World* – This epic equestrian travel tale of a wartime journey across Russia, China, Turkestan and India is laced with unforgettable excitement.

Steele, Nick, *Take a Horse to the Wilderness* – Part history book, part adventure story, part equestrian travel textbook and all round great read, this is a timeless classic written by the foremost equestrian expert of his time, famed mounted game ranger Nick Steele.

Stevens, Thomas, *Through Russia on a Mustang* – Mounted on his faithful horse, Texas, Stevens crossed the Steppes in search of adventure. Cantering across the pages of this classic tale is a cast of nineteenth century Russian misfits, peasants, aristocrats—and even famed Cossack Long Rider Dmitri Peshkov.

Stevenson, Robert L., *Travels with a Donkey* – In 1878, the author set out to explore the remote Cevennes mountains of France. He travelled alone, unless you count his stubborn and manipulative pack-donkey, Modestine. This book is a true classic.

Strong, Anna Louise, *Road to the Grey Pamir* – With Stalin's encouragement, Strong rode into the seldom-seen Pamir mountains of faraway Tadjikistan. The political renegade turned equestrian explorer soon discovered more adventure than she had anticipated.

Sykes, Ella, *Through Persia on a Sidesaddle* – Ella Sykes rode side-saddle 2,000 miles across Persia, a country few European woman had ever visited. Mind you, she traveled in style, accompanied by her Swiss maid and 50 camels loaded with china, crystal, linens and fine wine.

Trinkler, Emile, *Through the Heart of Afghanistan* – In the early 1920s the author made a legendary trip across a country now recalled only in legends.

Tschiffely, Aimé, *Bohemia Junction* – "Forty years of adventurous living condensed into one book."

Tschiffely, Aimé, *Bridle Paths* – a final poetic look at a now-vanished Britain.

Tschiffely, Aimé, *Mancha y Gato Cuentan sus Aventuras* – The Spanish-language version of *The Tale of Two Horses* – the story of the author's famous journey as told by the horses.

Tschiffely, Aimé, *The Tale of Two Horses* – The story of Tschiffely's famous journey from Buenos Aires to Washington, DC, narrated by his two equine heroes, Mancha and Gato. Their unique point of view is guaranteed to delight children and adults alike.

Tschiffely, Aimé, *This Way Southward* – the most famous equestrian explorer of the twentieth century decides to make a perilous journey across the U-boat infested Atlantic.

Tschiffely, Aimé, *Tschiffely's Ride* – The true story of the most famous equestrian journey of the twentieth century – 10,000 miles with two Criollo geldings from Argentina to Washington, DC. A new edition is coming soon with a Foreword by his literary heir!

Tschiffely, Aimé, *Tschiffely's Ritt* – The German-language translation of *Tschiffely's Ride* – the most famous equestrian journey of its day.

Ure, John, *Cucumber Sandwiches in the Andes* – No-one who wasn't mad as a hatter would try to take a horse across the Andes by one of the highest passes between Chile and the Argentine. That was what John Ure was told on his way to the British Embassy in Santiago-so he set out to find a few certifiable kindred spirits. Fans of equestrian travel and of Latin America will be enchanted by this delightful book.

Warner, Charles Dudley, *On Horseback in Virginia* – A prolific author, and a great friend of Mark Twain, Warner made witty and perceptive contributions to the world of nineteenth century American literature. This book about the author's equestrian adventures is full of fascinating descriptions of nineteenth century America.

Weale, Magdalene, *Through the Highlands of Shropshire* – It was 1933 and Magdalene Weale was faced with a dilemma: how to best explore her beloved English countryside? By horse, of course! This enchanting book invokes a gentle, softer world inhabited by gracious country lairds, wise farmers, and jolly inn keepers.

Weeks, Edwin Lord, *Artist Explorer* – A young American artist and superb writer travels through Persia to India in 1892.

Wentworth Day, J., *Wartime Ride* – In 1939 the author decided the time was right for an extended horseback ride through England! While parts of his country were being ravaged by war, Wentworth Day discovered an inland oasis of mellow harvest fields, moated Tudor farmhouses, peaceful country halls, and fishing villages.

Von Westarp, Eberhard, *Unter Halbmond und Sonne* – (German) – Im Sattel durch die asiatische Türkei und Persien.

Wilkins, Messanie, *Last of the Saddle Tramps* – Told she had little time left to live, the author decided to ride from her native Maine to the Pacific. Accompanied by her faithful horse, Tarzan, Wilkins suffered through any number of obstacles, including blistering deserts and freezing snow storms – and defied the doctors by living for another 20 years!.

Wilson, Andrew, *The Abode of Snow* – One of the best accounts of overland equestrian travel ever written about the wild lands that lie between Tibet and Afghanistan.

de Windt, Harry, *A Ride to India* – Part science, all adventure, this book takes the reader for a thrilling canter across the Persian Empire of the 1890s.

Winthrop, Theodore, *Saddle and Canoe* – This book paints a vibrant picture of 1850s life in the Pacific Northwest and covers the author's travels along the Straits of Juan De Fuca. This is truly an historic travel account.

Younghusband, George, *Eighteen Hundred Miles on a Burmese Pony* – One of the funniest and most enchanting books about equestrian travel of the nineteenth century, featuring "Joe" the naughty Burmese pony!

We are constantly adding new titles to our collection, so please check our websites:

horsetravelbooks.com and classictravelbooks.com

Lightning Source UK Ltd.
Milton Keynes UK
UKOW052025080213

206040UK00001B/42/A